THE BELCOURT THEATRE

NASHVILLE'S OLDEST NEIGHBORHOOD CINEMA

T. Minton

VANDERBILT UNIVERSITY PRESS
NASHVILLE, TENNESSEE

Published 2026 by Vanderbilt University Press

Library of Congress Cataloging in Publication Data

Names: Minton, T. (Teddy) author
Title: The Belcourt Theatre : Nashville's oldest neighborhood cinema / T. Minton.
Description: Nashville, Tennessee : Vanderbilt University Press, 2026. | Includes bibliographical references and index.
Identifiers: LCCN 2026024127 (print) | LCCN 2026024128 (ebook) | ISBN 9780826500649 paperback | ISBN 9780826500656 epub | ISBN 9780826500663 pdf
Subjects: LCSH: Belcourt Theatre (Nashville, Tenn.)--History | Motion picture theaters--Tennessee--Nashville--History | Historic theaters--Social aspects--Tennessee--Nashville | Arts facilities--Tennessee--Nashville--History
Classification: LCC NA6846.U62 N376 2026 (print) | LCC NA6846.U62 (ebook)
LC record available at https://lccn.loc.gov/2026024127
LC ebook record available at https://lccn.loc.gov/2026024128

Front cover image: The front of the Belcourt Theatre, September 2025. Photograph by Angelina Castillo.

CONTENTS

ACKNOWLEDGMENTS

THIS BOOK BEGAN as a research project about a theater, but it became something larger: a record of a community, an institution, and a century of people who believed that film, performance, and public gathering matter. Like the Belcourt itself, this book was made possible by many hands. It is the product of archivists, librarians, historians, colleagues, narrators, donors, editors, friends, family members, film lovers, and audiences who helped preserve the materials, memories, and stories that made this history possible.

I am especially grateful to the archivists, librarians, curators, and research staff whose work allowed this project to move across collections, institutions, and geographies. Much of the Belcourt's institutional knowledge has been lost over time, interrupted by organizational transitions, changes in ownership, and the ordinary fragility of memory. What survives is scattered across repositories throughout the United States. This book depended on the people and institutions that preserved those fragments, made them accessible, and helped me bring them back into conversation with one another.

The wider research for this book depended on the generosity and expertise of historian Brenda Colladay; Shannon Walker and Harold Housley at Arizona State University; Nancy Heathman and Michael Trebing at Cage Free Visual; Robert Spinelli at Cheekwood Estate and Gardens; Tara Craig and Jocelyn K. Wilk at Columbia University Rare Book and Manuscript Library; Kevin Fleming, Kathleen Campbell, Ashley Mooney, April Conner, and Brianne Wright at the Country Music Hall of Fame and Museum; the Folger Shakespeare Library; Drew Cuthbertson and Kim Reis at Imagn Images; Amy Smotherman at the Junior League of Nashville; Patrick Kerwin and Josie Walters-Johnston at the Library of Congress; Grace Wright Hulme at Metropolitan Nashville/Davidson County Archives; Amy York at Middle Tennessee State University's Walker Library; Rachel Morris and Olivia Beaudry at the Middle Tennessee State University Center for Popular Music; Jeffrey Lawson at Missouri State University's Duane G. Meyer Library Special Collections and Archives; Dr. Marti Cantrell at Nashville Children's Theatre; Kathleen Feduccia at Nashville Public Library; John Calhoun and Nailah Holmes at the New York Public Library for the Performing Arts, Billy Rose Theatre Division; Rebecca Jewett at Ohio State University's Thompson Library Special Collections; Jen Larson and Tim Davis at the Opry Archives; Bonnie M. Seymour at the Parthenon Museum; Veronica Sales, Lindsay Hager, Rebecca Howard, the Digital Services Team, and Trent Hanner at the Tennessee State Library and Archives; Tranae Chatman and Debbie Shaw at the Tennessee State Museum; Kara Molitor at UCLA Film & Television Archive; Steve Hersh at the University of Florida's George A. Smathers Libraries; Dannie Marsella at the University of Rochester River Campus Libraries; Benjamin Singleton at the University of South Carolina Moving Image Research Collections; Mary Somerville McSparran, Brynna Farris-McManus, and Sarah Calise at Vanderbilt University's Jean and Alexander Heard Libraries, Special Collections and University Archives; and Tom Cahill at Yale University's Beinecke Library.

I also owe a particular debt to the Internet Archive and Newspapers.com. The Internet Archive's commitment to preserving millions of sources as digital historical records, making those collections accessible to remote researchers, enabling text searching, and supporting access for users across platforms and devices, including screen readers, was indispensable to this project. As a researcher and writer with print disabilities, I know that accessibility is not an abstract value. It determines what histories can be found, read, interpreted, and preserved. Without that work, much of this institutional history would have been harder to recover and synthesize and some of it might have remained lost to time.

This research was also strengthened by the support of local and state history organizations whose work continues to deepen Nashville's understanding of itself. My thanks to Myers Brown at Belmont Mansion; the Intermuseum Council of Nashville; the Nashville Historical Foundation; Mary Ellen Pethel, Jessica Fitzpatrick, at Nashville Sites, and Demetria Kalodimos and Amelie Andalle, whose assistance there was crucial; Sarah Calise at Nashville Queer History; Linda T. Wynn at the Tennessee Historical Commission; and Jennifer C. Core at the Tennessee Historical Society.

At the Belcourt, this book grew out of a broader centennial effort to gather, preserve, and interpret the theater's history. I am grateful to the organization's staff, board members, and community supporting organizers past and present, whose labor, memory, and belief in this project helped make the work possible. Stephanie Silverman and Cindy Wall offered essential review, perspective, and guidance, helping me think not only about the facts of the theater's history, but about the responsibility of telling it well. Lisa Ellen Williams provided mentorship, insight, and support that shaped the project in ways both visible and unseen.

The Belcourt Stories oral history project became one of the foundations of this book. To every narrator who participated: thank you for trusting us with your memories, experiences, and reflections. Oral history asks people to give more than information. It asks them to revisit places, relationships, ambitions, failures, griefs, and joys that shaped their lives. Your stories helped restore texture to the record and made clear that Belcourt's history—and the story of Nashville's place in the wider ecosystem of cinema history and film culture—cannot be told only through buildings, programs, films, or institutions. It must also be told through the people who sat in its seats, stood on its stage, worked its box office, threaded its projectors, raised money for its survival, and carried its meaning forward through human relationships and adjacent, supporting labor.

I am equally grateful to those who donated personal items and archival materials to the Belcourt 100 archival collection. These objects and fragments of memory helped build a fuller record of the theater's past and ensured that future researchers will have that many fewer scattered traces from which to work.

Several professional collaborators helped turn this research into a durable public record. My thanks to Zack Ellis at Theirstory for creating a service that supported the oral history work, and to Angelina Castillo for photography that helped document the project with a careful, artful eye. I am also grateful to Vanderbilt University Press staff Steven P. Rodriguez, Patrick Samuel, Betsy Phillips, Joell Smith-Borne, Alissa Faden, Jenna Phillips, and Gianna Mosser, for their editorial, production, marketing, and publishing support. Their work helped bring this manuscript from a local history project into book form.

On a personal level, I thank my family and friends for their encouragement, patience, and support throughout the long process of researching and writing this book. Projects like this require more than time at a desk or in an archive. They require people willing to listen, reassure, ask questions, make space, and believe that the work matters even when it is difficult to see its final shape.

Finally, I am grateful to the wider Belcourt community: the film fans, loyal audiences, members, Belcourt 100 Donor Circle, and generous supporters who made both this book and the centennial project possible. For one hundred years, people have kept returning to this place. They have booked events, bought tickets, volunteered time, shared stories, donated money, saved ephemera and personal items, attended plays, concerts, and screenings, introduced new audiences by bringing friends and family, asked questions that reframed the meaning of place and community, and insisted that a neighborhood theater could still matter. The Belcourt has endured because countless people kept choosing it. This book is for all of you.

INTRODUCTION

IN 1925, A NEW THEATER opened in Nashville's Hillsboro Village neighborhood. The Hillsboro Theatre, as it was first called, promised audiences the marvel of silent cinema, the thrill of vaudeville performance, and the comfort of a modern neighborhood venue. One hundred years later, that same building—now renamed the Belcourt Theatre—stands as the longest-operating movie theater and one of its oldest continuously used entertainment sites in Nashville. More than a nostalgic landmark, the Belcourt is a living record of the city's complex relationship with theater and film—and by privilege of being around for so long—it is also a lens through which to view broader currents in American cinema culture.

Over the years, the Belcourt has been home to vaudeville performers and Grand Ole Opry broadcasts, community theater productions and student showcases, classic film retrospectives and global arthouse premieres (see Appendix 1). It was never simply a theater; it was a stage, a platform, a gathering space. In that sense, it has always been more than a commercial theater—it has been a civic institution made up of the people who built it, the artists who performed there, the films screened, the plays staged, and the communities it has served. Drawing from more than two thousand primary and secondary sources (not all of them used, but all of them surveyed)—including photographs, theater records, press clippings, ephemera, and oral history interviews—this book offers a comprehensive account of how the Belcourt endured while more than ninety other Nashville movie houses vanished (see Appendix 2). Through a century marked by war, economic upheaval, desegregation, urban transformation, and radical shifts in media technology, the Belcourt persisted. And in its persistence, it reshaped what a neighborhood cinema could mean to its city.

Its founding was rooted in the vision of Joseph "Papa Joe" Lightman, a Hungarian Jewish immigrant and local builder, and his son, M. A. Lightman, a Vanderbilt graduate, vaudeville performer, and entrepreneurial showman. Their backgrounds in construction and entertainment coalesced in the building of the Hillsboro Theatre. Located in a rapidly developing neighborhood shaped by streetcar expansion and postwar suburban growth, the theater brought modern film exhibition to the doorsteps of Nashville's professional and academic classes. The Lightmans later expanded their exhibition empire, with M. A. founding Malco Theatres, a major regional chain.

The Belcourt would go on to play a central role in housing Nashville Little Theatre Guild, Experimental Theatre, Children's Theatre, Community Playhouse, and New Theatre Nashville, anchoring the city's civic theater tradition. From the 1920s through the 1960s, it hosted classical, modernist, and realist plays, staged by volunteer ensembles and professional actors alike, serving as a hub for artistic experimentation and a training ground for talented locals—many of whom emerged to find success on a national scale. Its commitment to community performance connected it to the national Little Theatre Movement and made it a vital cultural institution.

Even during segregation, the Belcourt stood at the intersection of racial dynamics—placed strategically in a white-only neighborhood at a time when Black spaces were being systemically marginalized and erased. While Black patrons were often excluded or segregated in mainstream theaters, a parallel Black film culture flourished in Nashville's Lincoln, Bijou, and Fred Douglass Theatres. Visionaries like W. G. Hynes and F. E. Miller helped build an alternative cinema culture that affirmed Black dignity, resisted caricature, and cultivated independent film spaces within a Jim Crow South. Though the Belcourt was not initially part of that world, its later organizational efforts to support antilynching in the 1930s, desegregate in the 1960s, and collaborate with Black institutions since then have marked important moments of cultural convergence and repair.

The Belcourt's evolution into a film house was further solidified during the 1960s under Fred Massey, who introduced a slate of foreign and independent films. Screenings like *Purple Noon* (René Clément, dir., 1960) and *A Taste of Honey* (Tony Richardson, dir., 1961) marked a new era of sophisticated programming that drew students, cinephiles, and culturally curious audiences.

Yet even as it found new relevance, the theater struggled against the rise of multiplexes and the decline of neighborhood cinemas.

By the 1980s and 1990s, the Belcourt had deteriorated into near obsolescence. Physical disrepair, outdated equipment, and changing media habits left it on the brink of closure. Only through a grassroots campaign—galvanized by local organizers and sparked by a call to action in the *Nashville Scene*—was the Belcourt saved from redevelopment. The formation of the nonprofit Belcourt YES! in 1999 marked the beginning of the theater's transformation into Nashville's nonprofit film center.

From that rescue effort emerged a reimagined institution. Under new leadership of figures like Stephanie Silverman and Toby Leonard, the Belcourt deepened its programming mission, embraced educational initiatives, and joined the national arthouse theater network. It became a top-grossing venue for independent cinema, expanded access to classic and international films, and positioned itself as a national model for community-based film exhibition.

Belcourt Stories, the oral history project that helped spark this research and preservation initiative, captures the theater's evolving legacy through first-person testimony and archival documentation. With the rare distinction of having remained open for a full century, the Belcourt now has the opportunity to reflect on its past while documenting the broader cultural ecosystem it has shaped. The oral histories do more than recount the theater's transformation into a nonprofit arthouse; they offer a cross section of the city itself—featuring the voices of film lovers, artists, educators, and civic leaders whose lives and work intersect with Belcourt's mission. Today, the Belcourt is more than a movie theater. It is a historical touchstone, a platform for cultural exchange, and a living laboratory for Nashville's film culture and history.

This book is structured to follow both a chronological and thematic arc. Early chapters trace Nashville's theatrical roots, its embrace of pre-cinematic visual culture, and the founding of the Belcourt within the shifting urban landscape of the 1920s. Mid-century chapters explore the Belcourt's dual identity as a playhouse and movie house, its entanglement with desegregation and modernism, and its engagement with both mainstream and avant-garde cultural currents. Later chapters chart its decline in the 1980s, its near loss in the 1990s, and its rebirth in the 2000s as a film center connected to local, regional, and national networks.

This book does not aim to catalog every film shown or every detail of Nashville's broader exhibition history—though, thanks in part to the work of institutional historians and Belcourt staff such as Jon Keller and Bob Roberts, who made contributions to this project through their own independent research, a comprehensive record now exists of every film screened, every play performed, and every actor who appeared on its stage. Rather, this book tells the story of a single institution as a microcosm of larger forces: the evolution of American cinema, the shifting fabric of urban life, and the role of cultural memory in shaping how communities understand themselves.

The author's two-year research effort, beginning with newspaper searches and evolving into a substantial history project and institutional collection, brings together local oral histories and national archival repositories to weave this comprehensive narrative.

This book is for the Belcourt community—its staff, supporters, and audience—but also for general readers of film history, Southern history, and cultural preservation. It is for those who believe in the power of local storytelling and the value of sustaining spaces where culture and community intersect.

Ultimately, the Belcourt Theatre endures not through nostalgia, but through continuous reinvention and civic investment. As it begins its second century, it offers a case study in how film and cinema can foster public life, inspire creativity, and connect generations through a shared cultural experience.

1

HOW CINEMA CAME TO NASHVILLE

NASHVILLE BEFORE FILM

WHEN PEOPLE THINK OF NASHVILLE, "Music City" is the phrase most often used to describe the city's relationship to culture—a music industry ecosystem stratified by artists, their business representatives, and fans; venues and festivals; record labels and publishing companies; radio stations; educational institutions; and all the various organizations that support professional development.

While true, long before the city's identity became synonymous with music, Nashville was already a place where many forms of storytelling and entertainment flourished—and it still is. By the time cinemas began to open in the early twentieth century, this rich history created fertile ground for them to take root. These houses for film weren't an anomaly but the natural continuation of a deep-seated cultural tradition. To understand how a nonprofit film center like the Belcourt could flourish in Nashville, we first have to understand what came before: a century-long evolution of exhibition, performance, and technological wonder that built the city's appetite for moving pictures.

Cinema didn't arrive in Nashville in a vacuum. From the city's establishment in 1806, when Nashville had a population of about five hundred, the city's earliest residents—including Indigenous people, white settlers of European descent, enslaved laborers, and a modest community of free African Americans—envisioned it as a commercial and creative center for education,

FIGURE 1.1. Nashville's Public Square, c. 1884. Posters advertising a theatrical performance hang on the building at right. Ralph G. Morrissey photography collection. Courtesy of the Tennessee Historical Society Collection, Tennessee State Library and Archives.

culture, and the arts.[1] Long before film reels and projection booths, the city was already exploring visual spectacle in its many analog forms.

Theatrical and visual entertainment grew quickly in the city. Theaters and exhibition spaces became vital to the economy, attracting visitors and creating jobs. This demand caused Nashville's first city leaders to recognize the need for regulation. To maintain order and ensure that exhibitions met the city's cultural standards, local officials began enforcing laws that shaped the entertainment industry.

In 1806, Mayor Joseph Coleman introduced Nashville's first licensing law for theater performances, requiring exhibitors to pay a $22 fee to stage their productions.[2] By 1837, Mayor William Nichol expanded these regulations, dictating how long performances could run, what types of exhibitions were allowed, and even the kinds of goods that could be sold inside theaters.[3]

While these regulations were meant to keep order, they also reflected the city's recognition of entertainment as a serious business—one that would only grow in economic and cultural importance.

In 1818, Ralph Eleaser Earl founded the Nashville Museum of Natural and Artificial Curiosities on Public Square—where it remained until 1827.[4] A portrait artist and intellectual by training, Earl was deeply informed by the idea that art and education should be intertwined. Earl was inspired by Charles Willson Peale's Philadelphia museum of oddities, and Earl's version offered Nashvillians access to a world beyond the Cumberland River—taxidermy animals, fossils, minerals, and mechanical novelties. One particular machine that Earl incorporated into his exhibitions was the magic lantern, using it to bring history and nature to life in ways that static displays could not. Earl's embrace of moving-image technology is what truly set the museum apart.

These were not just artifacts but immersive, narrative-driven exhibits that sparked wonder. Earl's museum was a microcosm of Nashville's early desire to become a cultural epicenter, much like Philadelphia or New York, and developing cultural identity as a locus for entertainment, education, and showmanship. Earl believed that the Nashville Museum, and interdisciplinary institutions for exhibitions like it, could drive societal progress, both practically and artistically, locally and nationally. He gave a statement to the *Nashville Republican* newspaper in 1820 boosting his cause, proclaiming, "An institution of this nature is of importance to the public in various points of view. It is ever useful, not simply to the sciences, but equally to the arts. . . . Is it not useful to the artisan, who by the observation of nature in her primitive form is better instructed in the art of its manufacture?"[5]

At the same time, theaters began cropping up. The Nashville Theatre, built in 1817 on Market Street in a remodeled salt house, became a magnet for live performance—a proving ground for traveling actors, musicians, and spectacle showmen who passed through Tennessee on their way to larger cities—functioning as the site of five subsequent theatrical businesses for the city.[6] Traveling troupes performed Shakespeare, marionettes entertained crowds, and panoramic backdrops transformed stages into imagined worlds. This was Nashville's first exposure to immersive storytelling. By the 1830s, the theater had staged more than seven hundred performances of nearly three hundred plays, from Shakespearean dramas to lighthearted comedies and variety shows.[7]

While stage performances remained the dominant form of entertainment, Nashvillians were increasingly drawn to pre-film technologies that offered a more immersive visual experience. Magic lantern shows were among the most popular, dazzling audiences with their ability to create illusions of motion and depth. A skilled exhibitor could manipulate the slides to make figures appear to move, and by layering images, they could create rudimentary special effects—flickering candlelight, shifting shadows, or ghostly apparitions.

By the 1840s, panoramas—enormous paintings, sometimes stretching over a thousand feet—had emerged as one of the more popular forms of moving image. Panoramas were designed to be unrolled in front of audiences to simulate a moving landscape. One notable exhibition in 1847 was The Great Moving Picture of the Hudson River, likely the twelve-foot canvas created the year before by New York cartographers Wade & Croomes, presented at the Masonic Hall, a leading venue for these pre-film exhibitions.[8] Spanning every major town and landing along the Hudson River, this spectacle transported audiences to another world, making them feel as if they were floating down the river themselves, on a journey of American progress.

Another variation on this theme was the diorama. Unlike panoramas, which were only able to convey grandeur and scope, dioramas added fuller dimension to the moving image by using layered paintings and three-dimensional set

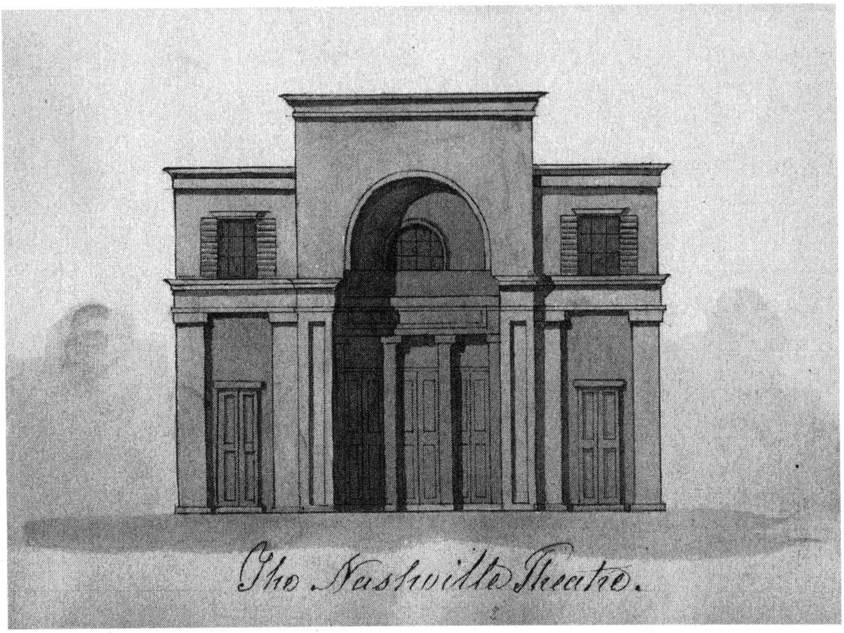

FIGURE 1.2. William A. Eichbaum, Nashville Theatre, c. 1850. Pen-and-ink wash drawing. Courtesy of the Special Collections Division, Nashville Public Library, Nashville, Tennessee.

pieces to create the illusion of perspective and movement, depth and realism, and best of all, action. These immersive tableaux were animated using simple yet ingenious mechanisms, such as pulleys, levers, and lighting effects, which simulated movement and brought static scenes to life.

Often enhanced with lighting effects, such as oil lamps, candles, and later Edison-era light bulbs, these exhibits were enhanced with drama and could easily give the impression of a sunrise, a storm, or a distant city glowing on the horizon. At one notable diorama exhibition in 1841, spectators in Nashville witnessed a grand depiction of Napoleon Bonaparte's funeral procession, complete with miniature human figures, creating a hauntingly lifelike effect, adding to the somber grandeur of the event.[9]

Marionette shows, staged plays, magic lantern lectures, and large-scale moving paintings and sets demonstrated that Nashville's audience was not only ready to be entertained—they were hungry for visual immersion. Even in these early years, the seeds of cinema culture were present. not in film, but in format. Mechanical illusions, lantern slides, dioramas, and traveling panoramas brought distant lands and historic events to life in ways that mimicked later cinematic forms, many still used, even in the second decade of the twenty-first century.

These early experiences with the moving image weren't just novelties; they helped Nashvillians develop visual literacy—an understanding of how images could tell stories, evoke emotions, and transport audiences to new realities. When movies would finally arrive at the end of the nineteenth century, Nashvillians were already primed to embrace them, having spent decades rooted in the landscape of cinema culture.

On February 25, 1862, Nashville fell to federal forces. As the first major Confederate capital to be captured during the Civil War, the city's occupation marked a critical turning point, not only in military strategy but in civic identity. From that moment forward, the city became enmeshed in the mythology of the "Lost Cause," its historical memory tethered to both defeat and reinvention.

When Union forces took control of Nashville, the city became a key military hub, filled with soldiers, supply depots, and makeshift hospitals. Theaters and exhibition spaces were among the first buildings to be repurposed. The Masonic Hall, which had once hosted grand exhibitions of panoramas and magic lantern shows, became Union Army Hospital No. 8. The iconic venue was stripped of its theatrical character and filled with some four hundred hospital beds, becoming a cultural nexus for the dramas of war.[10] The city's once-thriving entertainment economy nearly ground to a halt as the realities of war consumed every aspect of daily life.

While traditional theaters had been mostly shuttered or were recovering, open-air spectacles became the dominant form of entertainment. These grand public events were part exhibition, part morale booster, and part business opportunity—an attempt to offer citizens a distraction from the war while reinforcing patriotic narratives.

The Civil War carved deep scars into Nashville's social and physical landscape. But even during Reconstruction, the city's cultural momentum didn't stall, it evolved. The devastation of war left Nashvillians eager for relief, and spectacle once again became a civic salve. In 1866, showman A. J. Flynn, manager of Nashville's Old Theatre, staged hot air balloon ascensions. Flynn used the public performance of aerial flight as an opportunity to promote the theater and the war-demolished city as a business venture by encouraging wealthy onlookers and capitalists who paid to ascend in the balloon to consider the view from above as a glimpse of the city's postwar potential.[11]

These weren't just stunts. They were narratives of rebirth and possibility. From the sky, Nashville's scars were visible, but so too was its future.

In a city struggling to define itself, outdoor spectacles surged in popularity. Pageants like 1867's *The Crusader's Triumph* turned downtown streets into stages filled with knights, chariots, and unchained lions.[12] Public Square became a platform for panoramic exhibitions and visual recreations of faraway places and historical events. By the late nineteenth century, spectacles like *A Night in Pekin* brought thousands of viewers to the streets and amphitheaters, blending storytelling with pyrotechnics and sound, elaborate stage sets, costumed performers, and projected images.[13]

Marketed as "the biggest exhibition Nashville ever witnessed," *The Last Days of Pompeii* drew thousands and stunned audiences into silence with its sheer scale.[14] Among the cast was ten-year-old John Lark Taylor, whose later career in theater and early film would eventually lead to him helping establish Nashville's first theatrical guild inside the Belcourt.

This period marked a crucial transformation: entertainment became collective, immersive, and increasingly visual. These were no longer just shows, they were communal experiences built around shared awe. They were the soil in the city's entertainment landscape, the places where the roots of Nashville's cinema culture were not just planted, but established for what grew next: film.

NASHVILLE AT THE BEGINNING OF FILM

BY THE LATE NINETEENTH CENTURY, Nashville's appetite for immersive storytelling was evolving alongside new technologies, leading directly into the earliest moving images on film. By the 1890s, film had entered the city less as a disruption than as an extension of an existing culture already predisposed to visual narrative. The first motion picture screenings in Nashville took place before dedicated movie theaters existed, appearing instead in makeshift exhibition spaces, crowded offices, and grand exposition halls. As the city's entertainment entrepreneurs scrambled to bring this new technology to eager audiences, they set in motion a transformation that would define Nashville's cultural landscape for the next century.

The first real spark came with Edison's kinetoscope in February 1895, installed in the Wilcox Building, a four-story office and retail space on the corner of Church Street and High Street.[15] Patrons dropped a coin into the slot of these single-viewer machines, small, wooden cabinets with a peephole at the top. Leaning in, they watched as brief, looping films played before their eyes: an acrobat flipping through the air, a boxer throwing punches, a woman twirling her parasol. Kinetoscopes offered a tantalizing preview of what film could be, but their solitary nature limited their reach. That changed with the Vitascope. On June 12, 1896, Nashville hosted its first public film projection inside the Jackson Building on North Cherry Street.[16] For the first time, images projected onto a screen moved while a crowd watched together.

Live music accompanied the projections, and this pairing was crucial. The young pianist, aforementioned local child actor Lark Taylor, who played alongside these early film reels, described the emotional context and immersive effect of this new cinematic experience: "A screen in the back, a projection booth in the front, black curtains over the windows, [they] installed a piano, a number of folding chairs, [they] engaged me to play the piano, and were ready for business . . . a beautiful hand colored film of a pretty young dancer in diaphanous, waving skirts, floated about gracefully on her toes."[17] Based on Taylor's description, the theater's first screening was likely the Edison film *Serpentine Dance by Annabelle* (1896). Nashville's entertainment professionals—pianists, vocalists, and projectionists—quickly adapted to this new art form, showing that cinema was less a departure from tradition and more a modern extension of it.

By 1897, the Tennessee Centennial Exposition, modeled after Chicago's World's Fair, further cemented Nashville's position as a visual culture hub. Marking the state's one hundredth birthday, a grand celebration unfolded over six months, transforming two hundred acres of what is now Centennial Park into an expansive showcase of art, technology, and entertainment. The event featured exhibitions, pavilions, and amusement rides, commemorating the centennial of statehood with remarkable flair.[18] Attractions like Edison's Mirage and the Gettysburg Cyclorama blended projection, painted illusion, and theatrical staging—all elements of what would eventually become movies.

Edison's Mirage, located in the Vanity Fair section of the park at the intersection of Broadway and Cairo Street, was an innovative exhibition hall dedicated to groundbreaking electrical inventions, particularly motion pictures.

FIGURE 1.3. View of Edison's Mirage cinema in the Vanity Fair section of the Tennessee Centennial Exhibition, 1897. Courtesy of the Parthenon Museum.

Visitors enjoyed a fully immersive experience within a remarkable 360-degree rotating theater, described as the "first of its kind in the world."[19] The theater's unique, carousel-like structure featured an octagonal revolving stand. At its center stood a stationary platform housing seven projectors. The first section served as the entrance and exit, facilitating audience movement, while the remaining seven sections each held seventy raked seats facing a surrounding panoramic screen. Every two minutes, the theater automatically rotated, shifting each seated audience segment to face a new portion of the screen, where a different silent kinetoscope film was projected.[20] This design, revolutionary for its time, offered an unprecedented cinematic experience, setting Edison's Mirage apart from the first theaters inside office buildings like the Wilcox and Jackson Buildings.

Central to the Mirage were films, many produced and distributed by the Edison Manufacturing Company, curated by exhibitor Henry Roltair, a showman famous for crafting elaborate amusement park installations.[21] Prominent among Roltair's 1897 programming were *The Corbett-Fitzsimmons Fight* (1897), *Black Diamond Express* (1897), and the provocative and groundbreaking *May Irwin Kiss* (1896). May Irwin, a celebrated stage actress, played a significant

FIGURE 1.4. Entrance to the Cyclorama of the Battle of Gettysburg at the Tennessee Centennial Exposition, 1897. The circular structure displayed Civil War relics and was popular with both Union and Confederate veterans. Webb-Wrenne Family Papers. Courtesy of the Tennessee State Library and Archives.

role in bridging theater and film. In this short film, Irwin reenacted a playful moment from her musical-comedy *The Widow Jones* (1895). Her on-screen kiss, the first ever captured on film, marked a pivotal cultural milestone, solidifying movie-making as a legitimate artistic medium distinct from, and yet related to, traditional theater.[22]

Also located in the Vanity Fair section, on Broadway, across from the Haunted Swing, was the Gettysburg Cyclorama, an enormous circular panoramic painting vividly portraying the critical moment of General Pickett's charge during the 1863 Civil War battle. Although not a motion picture, the cyclorama anticipated cinema's immersive storytelling capabilities, encircling viewers with a seamless 360-degree depiction of the historic scene.[23] The cyclorama was essentially the nineteenth-century equivalent of the twentieth century's IMAX 3D, an immersive film format that combines a massive, high-resolution screen, powerful surround sound, and stereoscopic 3D projection to make images feel larger, deeper, and more physically enveloping.

This striking artwork was created by French artist Paul Philippoteaux and a dedicated team of assistants over a painstaking sixteen-month period. They used seven tons of paint, working with a substantial budget of $80,000, an extraordinary sum at the time.[24] Perfectly staged military debris lined the floor, seamlessly blending into the painted battlefield. From a single vantage point, spectators could almost hear the cannon fire, smell the gunpowder, and feel the weight of history pressing in around them. This stunning illusion of movement and depth was a precursor to cinema's ability to transport audiences into another time and place. The cyclorama was hailed as a masterpiece, drawing both Union and Confederate veterans, who stood shoulder to shoulder, reliving the battle that had once divided them.

Visitors to the Centennial Exhibitions in Vanity Fair weren't just watching—they were entering entire visual worlds. For many, it was their first brush with cinema, but it felt familiar. Nashville's exhibitors had been preparing them for this kind of experience for decades.

NASHVILLE'S FIRST CINEMAS

THE INTRODUCTION OF FILM INTO traditional theater spaces marked a turning point for entertainment in Nashville. Moving pictures were no longer a mere novelty confined to the cramped viewing booths of the kinetoscope parlors, they were now part of the city's mainstream cultural experience. With theaters like the Grand Opera House and the Vendome Theatre integrating film screenings into their programming, a new industry was taking shape.

But where there was opportunity, there was also competition. Business owners, eager to capitalize on the public's fascination with cinema, raced to secure film reels, projectors, and the best exhibition spaces. In 1898, the Grand Opera House began showing Biograph films between vaudeville acts.[25] A year later, after the Grand became the first brick-and-mortar theater to adapt film programming, and the market for making and distributing had grown enough to present exhibitors more options, the Vendome Theatre followed suit, bringing Vitagraph films to local audiences in October 1899.[26]

The fight for Nashville's first film audiences was intense, and it set the stage for a rapidly evolving entertainment economy—one that would shape the city's cultural landscape well into the twentieth century.

In response to Nashville's new love of cinema, a new class of businessmen emerged in Nashville: the film exhibitors. Unlike traditional theater owners, who were focused on all forms of live performance and exhibition, film exhibitors were navigating an entirely different business model, one that was still being invented.

There was no standard film rental system in the late 1890s. Theater owners either purchased reels outright or made special arrangements with traveling exhibitors who brought films from other cities. The cost of a film projector was prohibitively expensive for most small business owners, meaning that only well-established venues could afford them. And what about marketing the experience? Because motion pictures were still new, exhibitors had to educate the public on why films were worth seeing and persuade them to try something new. Newspaper ads emphasized the realism and spectacle of the moving image, promising audiences that they would witness something they had never seen before, mixing hyperbole with fact, a precedent that continues into the twenty-first century.

The changeover from the nineteenth to the twentieth century was also a period marked by changes to and upgrades in infrastructure. Theaters installed projection booths, blackout curtains, and dedicated sound systems. Pianists and vocalists provided live accompaniment, bringing emotional resonance to silent film reels. Projectionists worked with volatile nitrate film, mastering a dangerous craft that demanded precision, while juggling multiple tasks. They had to crank the projector, the phonograph, or music box, talk to the audience, and try to put out fires—sometimes literally.

The Dixie Theatre's opening on April 11, 1907, marked a turning point.[27] For the first time in Nashville, film had a dedicated, permanent venue. It wasn't an add-on to vaudeville or a temporary exhibit in a storefront. Located on 5th Avenue North, the Dixie featured 170 seats, a permanent screen, and a schedule of curated film programming.[28] Its opening night combined film, music, and live vocals in a multi-sensory event.

Local musicians William B. Scott and Margaret Dwyer provided the music for the first night's films. They opened the screening with a performance of "The Town at the End of the Line," a Tin Pan Alley melody composed by

FIGURE 1.5. Tile inlay for the Rex Theatre, 5th Avenue North, c. 1950, advertising five-cent movies. Opened in 1912 and later operated by the Crescent Amusement Co., the theater closed in 1957. The site became the Fifth Third Center in 1986. Ralph G. Morrissey Collection. Courtesy of the Tennessee Historical Society Collection, Tennessee State Library and Archives.

Arthur J. Lamb and John W. Bratton.[29] The lyrics, rich with imagery, set the scene for a journey—a train steaming down the tracks.

Scott was a vocalist of local renown, while Dwyer had once studied under Franz Joseph Strahm, the world-renowned conductor and pianist who had left the grand stages of Europe to bring his music to Nashville's Vendome Theatre.[30]

What made this moment even more significant was the team behind it. The Sudekums, son Tony and father Henry, were first-generation German Americans. They weren't traditional theater impresarios. They came from a background in baking and confectionery. But like many early cinema entrepreneurs, they, along with their partners Wiley J. Williams, J. M. Currey, and Paul W. Hoggins, saw opportunity in a rapidly changing entertainment landscape.[31] What began as a gamble, as they bet that Nashville was ready for a movie-first experience, became a dynasty. They were right. The nickelodeon era had begun, and the Dixie was only the start for them.

Their success gave rise to the Crescent Amusement Company, which over the next few decades would grow into a regional powerhouse, operating a network of theaters across the southeastern United States. The Sudekums understood something fundamental: the movies weren't a passing fad. Cinema was an evolution in how people engaged with narrative, technology, and community.

But more importantly, they understood that film needed infrastructure. Not just projectors and screens, but buildings, ticket booths, ushers, and curated programming. As the Crescent Amusement Company expanded, they began building larger, more ornate venues, places that blended the allure of Hollywood with the accessibility of neighborhood movie houses.

This period in Nashville was also marked by a convergence of technological advancement and civic growth. Electricity was becoming more common. Public transportation connected neighborhoods to downtown. Middle-class leisure time was expanding. These weren't small shifts. They were structural, creating the conditions necessary for cinema to become a habit in people's lives.

By 1910, films had moved from novelty to necessity. They became a weekly ritual for families, workers, and students. Programming expanded to include serialized dramas, historical epics, and newsreels. Theaters added musical scores, live narration, and better seating. And critically, going to the movies became affordable. Nickelodeons had five-cent admission (hence the "nickel" in nickelodeon), so patrons didn't need great wealth to experience them. The narratives of silent films were largely defined by pantomime and intertitles, so viewers didn't necessarily even need a shared language to understand them or see the world on screen. In the beginning, films were democratic in nature, which had specific appeal for working-class people and immigrants.

THE LEGACY OF THE NINETEENTH CENTURY

BY THE TURN OF THE twentieth century, Nashville had already developed a robust infrastructure for visual performance. Long before cinema arrived, the city's residents were well-acquainted with shared visual experiences, an early civic language that shaped the city's cultural identity. From gas-lit panoramas and traveling dioramas to magic lantern shows and Edison's projected images, visual media was embraced by Nashville audiences as more than entertainment. It was a tool for interpreting their world.

The city's appetite for engaging, communal experience was evident in puppet shows, vaudeville acts, open-air productions, and even hot air balloon ascensions. These events reflected a local culture that valued performance, narrative complexity, and the innovation of new technologies. In Nashville, visual storytelling had long been central to public life.

What defines a city's cultural identity is not only the art it produces, but the art it chooses to sustain. Well before the Belcourt Theatre opened its doors, Nashville had maintained a culture of spectacle for over a century, one that fostered audiences eager for innovation and collective storytelling. Whether delivered through painted scrolls, shadow puppets, or reels of nitrate film, the objective remained the same: to move people, expand their perspectives, and offer a space—often a darkened room—where imagination could take root.

So when cinema arrived, it didn't exactly revolutionize the status quo. It was part of an existing tradition. The city was already primed to build spaces where film culture could thrive, not only as mass entertainment but as part of a broader, evolving tradition of public performance and innovation. Nashville didn't simply adopt film, it was ready to champion it.

One of those spaces, the Hillsboro Theatre, would later become the Belcourt Theatre. When it first opened in the 1920s under a different name, it was more than a new movie house, it was a culmination of decades of local engagement with visual culture and performance technologies. But its creation wasn't inevitable. Like all institutions, it was the result of deliberate choices by individuals and communities. Yet the Belcourt was no anomaly either. It extended a lineage already deeply embedded in the city's cultural framework.

Its later transformation into a nonprofit institution dedicated to education, access, and community-driven programming may appear exceptional. But it was rooted in the city's historical tendency to treat cinema not merely as entertainment, but as a vital cultural form, one capable of carrying intellectual, artistic, and civic significance.

Before it was officially Music City, Nashville was also a city of images. And because early cinema, especially during the silent era, relied so heavily on music, film culture in Nashville didn't challenge tradition, it advanced it. Cinema became the logical next step in the city's self-definition as a creative and intellectual hub.

It's tempting to frame Nashville's early cinema culture as unique. In many ways it was, at least in the sense that the city was at the vanguard compared with many other cities in the state and region. But it also reflected national trends in compelling ways.

During the turnover of the nineteenth to the next century, cities across the United States were grappling with modernity. Urbanization, industrialization, and immigration were rapidly reshaping American life. Film emerged as a powerful medium through which people processed these shifts. It became a language of new aspirations, anxieties, and social change.

What distinguished Nashville was its position at the intersection of Southern cultural revival and Northern-style infrastructure. The city's universities provided intellectual capital. Its central location made it a transportation and communication hub. Its Civil War legacy gave it symbolic resonance. And its appetite for performance, driven by both religious and secular traditions, made it particularly receptive to spectacle-driven art forms.

Nashville wasn't New York or Chicago, but it wasn't a cultural backwater either. It had enough density, diversity, and institutional muscle to sustain ambitious and experimental film culture, and that crossed the racial divide still evident under Reconstruction and Jim Crow segregation. The city wasn't just consuming national trends, it was helping shape a regional, and in some cases national, cinematic identity.

This historical scaffolding explains why Nashville, two centuries after the founding of the Nashville Museum of Natural and Artificial Curiosities, and a century after the opening of the Hillsboro Theatre, continues to support an institution like the Belcourt Theatre. The city and its people laid the groundwork through decades of public exhibition and engagement, educational investment, and creative and civic imagination. The Belcourt didn't appear in a vacuum. It emerged from a city with a long-standing desire and commitment to creativity, entrepreneurship, storytelling, innovation, and shared experience.

2

BECOMING NASHVILLE'S NEIGHBORHOOD THEATER

IN THE BROADER NARRATIVE OF American cinema exhibition, the emergence of neighborhood theaters marked a distinct shift in how film was consumed, experienced, and integrated into everyday life. The Belcourt's historic theater exemplifies this broader transformation, not just in its architectural design and cultural role, but as an early model of the entrepreneurial and community-driven shifts that defined the 1920s. Its founding anticipated key characteristics of today's nonprofit and independent cinema models. In many ways, the Belcourt at the beginning is a prototype for what many neighborhood cinemas would later become across the United States: locally rooted, mission-driven, and responsive to both artistic and civic needs.

HILLSBORO VILLAGE

THE HILLSBORO THEATRE'S HISTORY IS rooted in Hillsboro Village, a once-rural district transformed by urban expansion. By the early twentieth century, Hillsboro Village was on Nashville's suburban edge, steadily evolving from farmland into a lively residential and commercial neighborhood driven by streetcar accessibility. This transition mirrored national trends wherein transportation advancements reshaped suburban landscapes.

Before it was Hillsboro Pike—established in 1848 as a toll road that became the main artery of Hillsboro Village, also called 21st Avenue—the artery originated as a pre-Columbian Indigenous pathway, evolved into an early

American frontier trail, and was later utilized as a critical route during the Civil War.[1] Specifically, during the Battle of Nashville in December 1864, Hillsboro Pike was strategically important, witnessing intense fighting as Union forces maneuvered to outflank Confederate positions at Shy's Hill.[2] The route gained prominence in nineteenth-century Nashville, serving as a key connection between the city and neighboring Williamson County. Farmers, traders, and travelers passed through the area, which remained largely rural even as Nashville itself grew into a major Southern city.[3]

Following the Civil War, the area remained pastoral, but by 1910, developers recognized its potential. The Belmont Land Company secured the rights to install a streetcar line along 21st Avenue South, catalyzing suburban development. This transportation advancement drew middle-class white families, eager to balance proximity to downtown Nashville's conveniences with suburban tranquility. Hillsboro Village soon blossomed into a bustling enclave boasting academic institutions like Ward-Belmont College (now Belmont University) and Peabody College (now integrated into Vanderbilt University), which served as cultural and educational anchors.[4]

By the 1920s, Hillsboro Village had fully transitioned from a rural byway into a self-sustaining urban neighborhood. Shops, cafés, and businesses cropped up along 21st Avenue South, serving the growing population of professors, students, professionals, and families who now called the area home. By 1925, the neighborhood touted a plethora of options, well over twenty, like Miss Leila Stinson's Oriole Tea Room (1303 21st Ave. S.), H. G. Hill's Grocery (1813 21st Ave. S.), an American National Bank branch (1806 21st Ave. S.), Peabody Pharmacy and Mrs. Mildred Land Brown's Little Flower Beauty Shoppe (1809 21st Ave. S.), and Zeh's Bakery & Pastry (1808 21st Ave. S.).

In this bustling environment, a first-generation American named M. A. Lightman, with an instinct for showmanship and entrepreneurship, saw his opportunity: a neighborhood theater that would bring cinema right to the doorsteps of Hillsboro Village's growing population. It was in this environment, where the complexities of modernity met community, that the Belcourt's original theater would find its first audiences.

But the story of the theater is bigger than one man. M. A. Lightman's story begins with his father.

THE LIGHTMANS

LONG BEFORE THE LIGHTMAN NAME became synonymous with cinema in the South, Joseph "Papa Joe" Lightman was just another immigrant chasing the American dream. He arrived in the United States via Ellis Island with little more than ambition and an entrepreneurial instinct. If family lore is to be believed, a spectacularly bad stroke of luck cost him his entire life savings before he even had a chance to spend it. Whether he lost his money in a card game or left it behind in a violin case at a train station, the story serves as a fitting metaphor for Joe's life—a man who stumbled, adapted, and always found a way forward.[5]

Born on Christmas Day 1864 in Pátroha, a small Hungarian village, Joe came of age in a time of unrest. The Austro-Hungarian Empire loomed large over daily life, offering little in the way of upward mobility, especially for Jewish families facing increasing restrictions and social hostility. The promise of America, however distant, was clear: freedom, opportunity, and the chance to build something that belonged to him.

Between 1870 and 1920, more than 26 million immigrants arrived in the United States.[6] Among them were an estimated 1.5 million Hungarians, including Joseph, his brother Morris, and Joe's future wife, Fannie Neuworth, whom he married in 1887.[7] Joe arrived in the New York Harbor in 1882, but he didn't linger in the City of Dreams. He stayed one year then made his way to Nashville to begin again.[8]

Joe was part of a wave of Jewish immigrants who bypassed the traditional enclaves of the Northeast, heading instead for smaller but rapidly growing cities where competition was thinner and opportunity was, in theory, easier to grasp. Nashville, with its thriving postwar economy, bustling riverfront, and growing immigrant population, was exactly the kind of place where a sharp-minded entrepreneur could carve out a niche.

And carve he did. Like many first-generation immigrants, Joe was a serial entrepreneur, dipping into produce and dry goods, catering, and tavern management.[9] If there was money to be made, Joe found a way to be in the room. His ventures weren't always glamorous, but they gave him the foothold he needed to build his family's future, business by business, storefront by storefront, and building by building.

FIGURE 2.1. Portrait of Joseph "Papa Joe" Lightman, c. 1917. Photograph by unknown.

FIGURE 2.2. Portrait of Maurice Abraham "M. A." Lightman, c. 1917. Photograph by unknown.

But Joe wasn't just a businessman; he was a personality. With his thick European accent and a shrewd but affable presence, he quickly embedded himself into Nashville's social and political landscape. When he landed a position on the county court, his fellow Nashvillians dubbed him "Squire Lightman," a nod to both his official title and the air of Old World authority he carried with him.[10] His political ambitions extended beyond the courthouse, including an unsuccessful but memorable run for Commissioner of Streets and Sidewalks, a campaign that cemented him as a recognizable figure in local circles, even if he never held the title.[11]

The Lightmans were chasing a dream; they were also building it—literally. For over thirty years, the family ran one of Nashville's premier contracting firms, leaving behind a legacy of craftsmanship that still stands today. Their work was never just about constructing buildings; it was about shaping the city's identity, brick by brick, foundation by foundation.

Some of Nashville's most recognizable structures bear the Lightman imprint. Their family home, the Gilbert Mansion on West End Avenue, built in 1908, became a landmark in its own right, a reflection of the era's grand residential architecture. Davidson County's first public high school, Hume-Fogg, completed in 1911, still stands as a cornerstone of the city's educational history. Their contributions also extended to federal projects, including additions to the US Customs House, incrementally completed between 1905 and 1919, blending Gothic Revival design with Nashville's growing urban sophistication.[12]

Beyond institutional landmarks, the Lightmans were also behind essential residential and medical projects. Sterling Court Apartments, built in 1915, provided modern urban housing, while Vanderbilt Hospital, completed in 1923, served as a beacon of advanced medical care in the region.[13] Whether through grand civic structures or everyday residences, the Lightman family didn't just build buildings, they built Nashville's future.

Papa Joe's success wasn't just about money; it was about creating a foundation for future generations. His son, Maurice Abraham, or M. A., Lightman inherited not just his business sense but his relentless drive, using it to catapult the family from tavern proprietors to cinema pioneers. The opening of the Hillsboro Theatre in 1925 wasn't just a new venture, it was the realization of a multigenerational pursuit of prosperity.

For all of his business acumen, Joe likely never imagined that his family's name would become synonymous with film exhibition across the South. But his legacy, one of ambition, reinvention, and perseverance, lives on in the theaters his family built and in the city that he helped shape with each venture, each risk, and each roll of the dice.

By the early twentieth century, Joe had put down firm roots in Nashville's business community, and his son M. A. was watching, learning, and eventually participating in his father's ventures.

M. A. took that inherited entrepreneurial instinct and ran with it. He enrolled at Vanderbilt University, where he studied engineering, but books weren't enough to hold his attention.[14] Instead, he gravitated toward a more kinetic world, first as a vaudeville performer, then as a wrestler, and even as a top-ranking competitive Bridge player.[15] He had charisma, a knack for entertainment, and, most importantly, a deep love for showmanship. But it wasn't until he saw a long line of people wrapped around a silent movie house in small-town Alabama that he had his real epiphany: Cinema was growing, and it was the vanguard of entertainment.[16]

In the transition from the 1910s to 1920s, a new model of exhibition was emerging across the country: the neighborhood theater. Unlike the massive, gilded movie palaces, which were also emerging across the country in urban cores, these smaller cinemas catered to smaller communities, offering a more

New Hillsboro Theater Opening This Week.

FIGURE 2.3. Patrons stand outside the original entrance to the Hillsboro Theatre on 21st Avenue on opening night. *The Tennessean* (Nashville, TN), evening edition, May 20, 1925. Courtesy of Tennessee State Library and Archives.

intimate and convenient experience for people who had made their homes outside of downtowns, or lived in more rural towns, and didn't want to or couldn't travel into the city center.

With that in mind, M. A. Lightman took a gamble. In 1915, Lightman left his engineering job and opened his first movie theater in Sheffield, Alabama.[17] It was a modest start, but it proved one thing: He had an eye for what people wanted. Lightman wasn't one to sit still. He had watched how the movie business was evolving, and he knew that if he wanted to stay ahead of the curve, he had to think bigger.

When the Hillsboro Theatre opened in 1925, it was not the beginning for Lightman, who had already been accumulating theaters under his company Malco Amusement. The first theaters Lightman opened in this chain grew out of that 1915 purchase in Sheffield and soon after, in nearby Florence, Alabama. Lightman spent the decade expanding his footprint and growing his theater operations, where he built and acquired other neighborhood and downtown cinemas throughout the southeastern United States.

Lightman recognized that suburban audiences craved entertainment just as much as those in the city's downtown movie palaces, and he remained committed to being an exhibitor that promised his customers affordable, independent entertainment in their communities. By 1925, Malco owned the Majestic theater in Eldorado, Colorado, the Rialto in Camden, Arkansas, and the Princess and the Strand in Little Rock, Arkansas, as well as his first Alabama theaters. The Hillsboro was just another link in the chain.

He brought that lesson back to Nashville, where a new neighborhood called Hillsboro Village was rising along the streetcar lines, and in that neighborhood, he saw an opportunity. In 1925, M. A. Lightman would play one of the biggest hands of his life, and soon after face an adversary who would challenge his win.

From the moment it was conceived, the Hillsboro Theatre was more than just a movie house—it was a statement of progress. In April 1924, the *Nashville Banner* reported a major commercial development in Hillsboro Village: a new theater project led by M. A. Lightman, a rising force in the Southern cinema industry. The article announced Lightman's purchase of a vacant lot at the corner of Carlton, later renamed Belcourt, and 21st Avenues for $9,000, a prime piece of real estate previously owned by Chris Contos, a well-known restaurateur whose business acumen had helped shape the commercial future of the area.[18]

Contos, already a pioneer in Hillsboro Village area with the expansion of his Little Pappas Restaurant (the first location at 212 Fourth Ave. N. since 1899, and the newest at 1307 21st Ave. S.) had recognized the neighborhood's untapped potential, but it was Lightman who saw a different kind of future for the space, one illuminated by the flickering light of the silver screen.[19]

For Lightman, the Hillsboro Theatre wasn't just another expansion in his growing chain, it was a flagship, a model for what neighborhood cinemas could become. He took full advantage of the *Banner*'s coverage to unveil early details of his ambitious plans: a $50,000 structure with an attractive storefront and moving picture house behind it.[20] Lightman's vision was grander than a nickelodeon, but not as opulent as a movie palace, yet the execution was still critical. To bring the project to life, Lightman turned to his most trusted partner, his father, Joseph "Papa Joe" Lightman, and the family's well-established Lightman Construction Company.

At the time, the Lightman Construction Company was at the peak of its influence, busy and moving from one project to the next, like the Standard Golf and Country Club freshly completed just months earlier in December 1924.[21] The Hillsboro Theatre, however, was different. Unlike the grand public buildings and commercial structures that the Lightmans had built before, this project was personal. It wasn't just about construction, it was about crafting a cultural anchor for a growing neighborhood, a place where the community could gather, escape, and be transported through film.

By spring of 1925, the theater was nearly ready to open its doors. Originally slated for a May 4 debut, the project hit minor delays, though exactly what caused them remains unclear.[22] Finally, on Monday, May 18, 1925, the Hillsboro Theatre opened to the public, an event that would mark the beginning of its more than century-long presence in the city's entertainment history.[23]

The Hillsboro Theatre was born into a Nashville in motion, a city where suburban expansion, streetcar connectivity, and the developing golden age of cinema were colliding in real time. Its story, like the films it would soon project, would be one of transformation, reinvention, and enduring cultural impact.

IMAGINING THE HILLSBORO

STEPPING UP TO THE HILLSBORO Theatre in its earliest days was a different experience than at most other times in the building's history. First, the original entrance faced 21st Avenue, not Belcourt Avenue, its facade a striking mix of contemporary 1920s design principles, blending modernism with the ornate flourishes of Italian Liberty style. The building's brick work was crafted by the Liberty Brick and Tile Company and frames an elegant cornice, adorned with an ornamental finial bearing the theater's name inlaid in stone above the entrance, a feature that continues to be visible. A dazzling electric sign, installed by the Mullen Electric Company, captured the attention of passersby. The bold sans-serif marquee stood out against the storefronts, announcing the evening's film lineup in bright, geometric lettering, transforming the block into an unmistakable landmark, its glow beckoning moviegoers from across the city.

Beyond the entrance, patrons walked into a carefully designed interior, a lobby featuring immaculate tilework, and walls lined with poster displays showcasing upcoming features and performances. A corridor led patrons into the grand auditorium, where they were met with one of the only original architectural features to endure: an ornate proscenium arch designed by master image-maker and plaster craftsman Raffaello Mattei of Gromignana, Italy, for the G. Mattei Ornamental Plaster Company of Nashville. Behind

FIGURE 2.4. Portrait of plaster artist Raffaelo Mattei at his homestead in Gromignana, Italy. Date and photographer unknown. Courtesy of Loretta Mattei.

it was a retractable silver screen, a cutting-edge feature designed specifically for optimal film projection.

The theater came with a fully equipped stage, dressing rooms, and a thirty-foot flyloft. Electronically controlled velvet curtains added a level of sophistication, allowing for dramatic reveals that heightened the anticipation of both films and live performances inside the proscenium. The eight hundred Spanish-leather seats that lined the main auditorium were refined, offering both comfort and luxury. There was even a balcony that sat roughly three hundred, bringing the total capacity to near eleven hundred.

Before the era of synchronized sound, movie theaters relied on live music to bring silent films to life. The Hillsboro Theatre installed a custom-built Kimball organ in 1925, an instrument that, though modest in size, was praised (though likely hyperbolically) as among the best in the city. It was a two-manual, five-rank organ placed near a small orchestra pit in front of the stage apron.

M. A. Lightman anticipated the growing importance of automobiles and incorporated a private parking lot with valet service into the theater's design.

By the 1920s, car ownership had skyrocketed, and theaters across the country were forced to adapt to a new reality. Consumers no longer needed to rely on public transit to reach entertainment hubs. Hillsboro's parking lot was a deliberate acknowledgment of this cultural shift, a move that placed it ahead of many of its contemporaries.

From its inception, the Hillsboro was more than just a place to catch a movie; it was an entertainment hub. Designed to showcase all aspects of the theater arts, it offered silent films, vaudeville acts, live musical performances, and community events. For its debut, the Hillsboro Theatre bet on what they thought was a winning horse. The opening week's marquee featured D. W. Griffith's *America* (1924), a sweeping silent epic that romanticized the American Revolution, followed by *The Thief of Bagdad* (Raoul Walsh, dir., 1924), a big-budget fantasy adventure that dazzled audiences with its lavish production design. These were not just any films—they were blockbusters of the silent era, carefully selected to set the tone for the theater's reputation and the spectacle of the grand opening. Promotional coverage for *America* made that ambition explicit, describing the film as "the outstanding masterpiece of the entire moving picture field."[24]

A savvy businessman on many fronts, M. A. Lightman was surely aware of the film's local ties and how those could be used to promote the opening week's program. One such tie was Lucille La Verne, a Nashville native and one of the film's co-stars. Although La Verne's local reputation at the time is somewhat unclear, press coverage surrounding the film's opening night noted her Nashville connection.[25] La Verne later appeared in other Griffith-directed films before moving into voice acting in the 1930s, when she played what became her most famous role—actually a dual role—as both the Evil Queen and the Witch in Walt Disney's *Snow White and the Seven Dwarfs* (1937).

The film also had other interesting cultural links, grounding it in the local cinema community. In the lead-up to opening night, the film was heavily boosted by Nashville's Campbell chapter of the Daughters of the American Revolution (DAR) a lineage-based women's organization whose members trace their ancestry to participants in the American Revolution. Though the DAR presents itself as a civic group devoted to patriotism, historic preservation, and education, it has also long been criticized by as a site of white privilege and exclusion.

The national chapter of the DAR had petitioned the Motion Picture Producers and Distributors of America (MPPDA) president, Will H. Hays, for a "complete, accurate and dramatic version of America's greatest of all stories, the Revolutionary War, told with a true mastery upon the screen."[26] Hays obliged, enlisting Griffith to craft a film that functioned as both art and propaganda. Since then, however, *America* has been criticized for its racist elements and for falling short of the formal mastery associated with Griffith's strongest filmmaking. The result is a work whose cultural significance exceeds its artistic achievement.

Hays continued on as a propagandist, building an entire career around it. The MPPDA was the predecessor to the more modern Motion Picture Association (MPA), the organization that shapes industry standards by rating films and protecting copyrights. As chair, Hays oversaw the Motion Picture Production Code, better known as the "Hays Code," a set of moral guidelines that governed Hollywood's self-censorship from the 1930s through the 1960s.

Although *America*—and the cultural and political work surrounding it—has largely receded from twenty-first-century discussions of Griffith's legacy and influence, its selection as the first film shown at the Hillsboro offers a revealing glimpse into the cultural milieu of both the surrounding neighborhood and Nashville in 1925, where whiteness remained centered and privileged.

THE HILLSBORO'S PROGRAMMING

BEFORE OPENING THE HILLSBORO, M. A. LIGHTMAN had spent the years from 1918 to 1920 in the independent distribution arm of the silent film industry as the president of Criterion Film service, a company based out of Atlanta, Georgia. Criterion got its start working the Southern territories of the United States with films produced by the Arrow Film Corporation such as *Huns Within Our Gates* (1918), and *The Deemster* (Howell Hansel, dir., 1917), and the Keystone Film Company which helped produced the early careers of silent stars like Charlie Chaplin and Harold Lloyd.[27]

This experience gained Lightman valuable industry connections and insight into the booking and promotion of silent films. As a result, he marketed the Hillsboro to young, white families and college students from the surrounding suburbs, appealing very directly to the demographics of the neighborhood.

The Hillsboro Theatre's film selection showcased both high-profile films from major studios and smaller productions from independent or regional outfits, ensuring there was always something new on the screen, or a second chance to see something a customer might have missed the last time it had played a screen in Nashville. The blending of large studio productions with independent films reflects the competitive structure of the 1920s film industry, when major studios like Paramount, MGM, and Universal began to control major urban theaters through vertical integration, under what has been coined the "star system"—a business strategy that involved creating personas for actors, paying them large salaries, and controlling their own branded movie theaters—while independent exhibitors like the Hillsboro Theatre had to book films from various distributors and operated without direct contact with major studios.

FIGURE 2.5. Advertisement promoting the Hillsboro Theatre's opening-day programming, with support from local businesses. *The Tennessean* (Nashville, TN), May 17, 1925, 39.

Some of the big-budget epics and prestige films that played the Hillsboro included the films *The Mark of Zorro* (Fred Niblo, dir., 1920), and *The General* (Buster Keaton and Clyde Bruckman, dirs., 1926). These films reflect the era's penchant for action and adventure films featuring swashbuckling heroes, and historical epics that dramatized the nation's past with revisionist narratives about the nation's role in colonialism and slavery.

Lesser-known films today, but compelling in their prime, that played the Hillsboro include films such as *Her Own Free Will* (Paul Scardon, dir., 1925), *The Dangerous Flirt* (Tod Browning, dir., 1925), and *Gambling Wives* (Dell Henderson, dir., 1924), all of which are now presumed lost. These films highlight the transitory and ephemeral nature of many silent films. Smaller productions had shorter theatrical runs and the physical media were often discarded after their initial release, either by distributors who failed to return them to their studio or studios that sometimes destroyed prints and negatives of silent films after they stopped being commercially viable. The Library of Congress estimates that about 70 percent of all silent films have been lost, though many continue to be rediscovered in private collections and other archives all time.[28] Of the 178 silent films that screened at the Hillsboro Theatre, 56 are presumed to be lost.

The Hillsboro's programming from this era represents the final, transitory years of silent film dominance just before sound, or "talkies," revolutionized cinema in the decades following.

Unlike downtown's grand movie palaces, which catered to massive crowds, neighborhood theaters like the Hillsboro were intimate, community-driven spaces that operated under a mixed programming model, making them all-purpose venues for entertainment. The Hillsboro Theatre's programming was focused on booking local talent, as opposed to larger, national touring acts which came through Nashville's Theater Owners Booking Association–controlled Bijou Theatre, or the Crescent Amusement Company–controlled Loews Vendome and Princess theaters.

From its inception, the stage regularly welcomed vaudeville acts and other live musicians, like future Grand Ole Opry star Fiddling Sid Harkreader and his Arkansas Charleston Dancers; recitals featuring dancers like Margaret Ward Winkler; theatrical guilds from local schools like St. Bernard Academy and the Peabody College Dramatic Club; and minstrel shows, such as the Wallace Minstrels and the Capital City All-Star Minstrels.

This blend of cinema and live performance wasn't just a novelty, it was a survival strategy. With the arrival of radio and new entertainment options, theaters had to offer more than just movies. The Hillsboro Theatre understood this early on, positioning itself not just as a film exhibition space, but as a true cultural center for Hillsboro Village and a destination for Nashvillians across the city.

But the movie industry was changing fast, and if Hillsboro was going to last, it would need to evolve with the times.

THE ORGANISTS

BEFORE THE FLICKER OF a silent film could come to life on screen, it needed music, and the Hillsboro had two important organists—Clara Butts and Edward Benedict—one a local legend and the other a nationally recognized guest star.

By the time Edward Bowman Benedict arrived in Nashville for the grand opening of the Hillsboro Theatre, he was already a celebrity in the world of theater organists. Billed as the "World Famous Organist," Benedict's performance on the newly installed Kimball organ was as much a musical demonstration as it was a celebrity sighting.

Born in Lincoln, Nebraska, in 1883, Benedict's journey to musical stardom took him from church choirs to the opulent movie palaces of the silent era, where he perfected the art of live film accompaniment. A trained tenor, his career evolved beyond voice into directing, teaching, and, most notably, mastering the theater organ. By the early 1910s, Benedict had positioned himself at the forefront of the industry, playing in major venues across the Midwest and West Coast, commanding impressive salaries that reflected his unmatched ability to translate moving images into sound.[29]

In May 1925, his national tour with the W.W. Kimball Organ Company brought him to Nashville's newest cinema landmark, where he joined local star organist Clara Butts (Mrs. E. T. Sheetz) for an unforgettable day of performances.

Clara Butts was the staff organist who gave those first moving images at the Hillsboro their soul. Born in Portland, Tennessee, in 1899, Mrs. E. T. Sheetz was a musician of rare talent, weaving her way through the golden

FIGURE 2.7. Portrait of organist Edward Benedict. *Melody* 3, no. 12 (1919). Courtesy of the Silent Film Music Archive.

FIGURE 2.6. Advertisement for future Opry star Sid Harkreader's family-friendly performance at the Hillsboro Theatre. *Nashville Banner*, April 8, 1926, 12.

age of theater organs, live radio, and silent film accompaniment. By the mid-1920s, Clara had already built an impressive career, playing wedding halls, church sanctuaries, and grand theaters alike.[30] But it was in Nashville's Vendome Theatre that she left her most profound mark, sitting at the console of the house organ.

Her marriage to E. T. Sheetz, whose family had been deeply embedded in Nashville's theater scene for decades, only further tied her to the city's artistic pulse. E. T. was the son of seasoned theater manager W. A. Sheetz Sr., who had begun his career at the Masonic Hall before landing at the Vendome Theatre where he worked for thirty-five years.[31] And when radio took its place as the next great entertainment revolution, Clara was there, too, broadcasting live performances on WSM Radio, ensuring that her music reached far beyond the walls of any single venue.[32]

Though time has faded much of her story, Clara Butts's music is an echo of Nashville's early cinematic and broadcasting eras, an important part of Nashville's soundtrack.

THE BELMONT THEATRE

FOR TWO YEARS, THE HILLSBORO Theatre had been the cinematic heart of Hillsboro Village. But by 1927, the M. A. Lightman's company was gaining competitors, and so was Hillsboro, by proxy. Synchronized sound was on the horizon, but it wasn't yet the giant turning the cogs of the industry. Lightman was up against another titan of the industry, a Nashville exhibitor named Tony Sudekum and his chain of movie theaters, the Crescent Amusement Company.

On August 31, 1925, Hillsboro Village got a new theater named the Belmont Theatre. It was a statement of power, wealth, and Hollywood's tightening grip on the industry. Built for an astonishing $2 million, the Belmont was a true movie palace, a place where audiences weren't just entertained, they were transported. Inside, ornate fountains, imported Cuban tile, wrought iron railings, and a sweeping promenade created an atmosphere of sheer escapist grandeur. With seating for 1,350 patrons, fully furnished dressing rooms, and opulent decor, the Belmont wasn't just a bigger theater—it was a different kind of experience entirely, one that made Hillsboro's more modest, community-driven atmosphere feel small in comparison.[33]

The Belmont's architectural pedigree was undeniable. Designed by Marr & Holman, the same firm behind the Tennessee Supreme Court building and United States Post Office, it was part of a grander vision orchestrated by Tony Sudekum, the city's dominant theater mogul.[34] By 1925, Sudekum's Crescent Amusement Company controlled dozens of theaters across the South, and, more importantly, he had the exclusive contracts for first-run films from Hollywood's biggest studios. That single advantage spelled disaster for independent operators like M. A. Lightman, who now found himself locked out of major studio deals, relegated to second-run films, dwindling audiences, and an uncertain future.

Lightman wasn't blind to the shift; he saw the writing on the wall almost immediately. With Belmont dominating first-run programming and Hillsboro's seat count paling in comparison, he knew that the silent film business

FIGURE 2.8. Advertisement for the opening of the Belmont Theatre, located at the corner of 21st Avenue and Blakemore Avenue. *Nashville Banner*, August 30, 1925, 35.

in Hillsboro Village and Nashville—possibly even the South—was no longer sustainable. But rather than shutting the theater down completely, he did what smart business owners do: he adapted.

THE HILLSBORO THEATRE CLOSES

ON SEPTEMBER 14, 1927, just two short years after opening, the Hillsboro screened its final silent film and faded to black as a movie house. That film was a big-budget historical drama starring John Barrymore, *The Beloved Rogue* (Alan Crosland, dir., 1927).

But rather than a closing act, this was a pivot, one that would ensure the building's survival long after other silent-era cinemas had disappeared.

Rather than shuttering Hillsboro completely, he sold off the original entrance and lobby space on 21st Avenue, which was converted into retail space. In an effort to architecturally rebrand the building, the theater's entrance was moved to Carlton Avenue. On October 14, 1927, he signed a lease with the Nashville Little Theatre Guild, a community theater group that had already begun staging performances inside the venue.[35] In doing so, Hillsboro Theatre was reborn, not as a silent movie house, but as a new site for live theater.

While many other small, independent theaters folded in the wake of Hollywood's consolidation, Hillsboro Theatre evolved, embracing a new cultural wave: the "little theatre" movement. Across the country, intimate, community-driven playhouses were emerging as alternatives to the increasingly commercialized world of film exhibition. Hillsboro, now a hub for local playwrights, performers, and directors, was at the forefront of this shift in Nashville.

As for Lightman, his time in Nashville had come to an end, but his influence in the exhibition space was still respected and in some ways, had only just begun. After his father's death eight months later, he relocated to Memphis, where he built what would become one of the South's most successful regional theater chains: Malco Theatres.[36] What started as a small network of neighborhood cinemas would grow into a multigenerational empire, with thirty-seven theaters still in operation today.

Though he left Hillsboro Theatre behind, Lightman's business philosophy endured. He understood that a theater was never just a building: It was an experience, a reflection of its community, and a place that had to evolve to survive. His instincts had helped launch a legacy that outlived the silent film era, the rise and fall of vaudeville, and the challenges of corporate consolidation.

Hillsboro Theatre may have closed its doors to silent film in 1927, but it had already found its next chapter. In the decades that followed, it would become a cornerstone of Nashville's theater scene, giving rise to new talent and shaping the city's cultural identity. It had once been Lightman's vision, but now, it belonged to the artists and audiences who would keep it alive for generations to come.

THE LEGACY OF THE HILLSBORO THEATRE

BY THE TIME THE HILLSBORO Theatre opened its doors in 1925, Nashville had already been primed for a deeper, more civic-minded relationship with film. This wasn't simply a city of consumers; it was a city of students, educators, and storytellers. Alongside its musical heritage, Nashville fostered a self-image rooted in enlightenment and public engagement. The presence of higher education institutions like Vanderbilt University, Fisk University, and Peabody College had long cultivated a public inclined to see culture, film included, not only as entertainment, but as education, information, and even moral inquiry.

That duality—a place where amusement meets inquiry—forms the cultural DNA of what would later become the Belcourt Theatre. Long before it adopted the nonprofit model or became an institution for independent and foreign film, the seeds of its purpose were already sown. The city's early encounters with visual media, ranging from nineteenth-century lantern lectures to panoramic spectacles at the 1897 Tennessee Centennial Exposition, embedded the idea that visual storytelling could function as a tool of civic instruction. Audiences weren't just looking to escape; they were also looking to understand, to explore, and to think.

This approach intensified in the early twentieth century as moving pictures gained traction as both mass entertainment and public pedagogy. Edison's Mirage and the Gettysburg Cyclorama, attractions at the Centennial Exposition, left a deep imprint. They weren't just spectacles, they were narratives told through imagery, designed to teach and persuade. Nashvillians learned early that image and ideology could be fused in compelling ways, a sensibility that would inform the next generation of exhibition spaces, including Hillsboro.

By the 1910s, movie theaters had moved beyond mere novelty. They were becoming indispensable community anchors. Downtown cinemas drew diverse urban crowds, while smaller neighborhood venues like Hillsboro allowed local audiences to make cinema a part of their routine. Matinees, double features, and short reels didn't just fill time, they created shared experiences. Couples went on dates. Children came for serials. Families turned it into a ritual. The physical space of the theater became a microcosm of civic life, one where strangers sat in collective awe, reacting in tandem to laughter, shock, and grief on screen.

But these theaters did more than entertain. They played a subtle, ongoing role in shaping public values. As cinema matured, so too did its audience, and with it, an awareness grew that film could both reflect and challenge social norms. In Nashville, film offered a mix of progressive promise and retrograde tropes. Audiences saw glimpses of modern gender roles, technological dreams, racial caricatures, and historical mythologies, often within the same feature. It was messy, contradictory, and very real. These tensions laid the groundwork for later conversations about inclusion, equity, and representation in cultural spaces.

By the 1920s, Nashville had fully adopted cinema as part of its identity. Theaters were as much landmarks as courthouses or libraries. Exhibition had become a local industry, and films were more than passing diversions, they were how the city processed its past, projected its ambitions, and mediated its place in a rapidly changing world. It was in this evolving landscape that the Hillsboro Theatre found its footing, not just as another venue, but as something quietly different.

The difference wasn't only aesthetic, though its Spanish Revival architecture and interior design did stand out. The difference was philosophical. The Hillsboro Theatre was strategically located near two universities and a growing educated middle class. Its surrounding neighborhood had been shaped by intellectual curiosity, artistic inclination, and civic aspiration. In such an environment, a theater could be more than a business. It could be a platform. A forum. A vessel for both imagination and dialogue.

That's what the Hillsboro eventually became. Over time, and through various organizational hands, the venue transcended the commercial exhibition model. It began to host not only studio films, but also local performances, public lectures, and community events. Its programming expanded to reflect Nashville's layered history of exhibition, one that blended highbrow and popular, independent and mainstream, introspective and spectacular. In doing so, it echoed the city's long-standing embrace of film as both show and statement.

Crucially, the Hillsboro Theatre also benefited from its independence. Not owned by a major studio or embedded in a corporate chain, it maintained a level of autonomy that allowed for curation over commercialism. While other venues pursued box office trends, Hillsboro had the capacity to chase meaning. It could take risks and highlight films that challenged rather than reassured. This ethos, carried forward into its nonprofit incarnation as the Belcourt Theatre, would prove essential in the decades to come.

In truth, the Hillsboro wasn't an outlier in Nashville's entertainment history, it was the next logical step. The city had been preparing for such a place for over a century. From itinerant projectionists with kinetoscopes to entrepreneurs with nickelodeons, from Civil War panoramas to organ-scored silents, the public had developed a taste not just for watching, but for learning. Film had become infrastructure—not just part of commerce, but part of community.

By the early twentieth century, that infrastructure expanded into every part of civic life. Schools screened educational reels. Churches hosted morality films. Political campaigns used moving images for persuasion. Newsreels collapsed the distance between Nashville and the wider world, turning global conflicts and national events into local experiences. Cinema became a conduit, connecting residents to history, current events, and cultural currents. It was this civic integration of film that made space for institutions like the Belcourt to thrive.

One of the most important but underappreciated elements of this history is the role of the exhibitor, not just as a businessperson, but as a curator of public experience. In Nashville, figures like M. A. Lightman and Tony Sudekum shaped not only the physical landscape of entertainment, but also its emotional and intellectual tone. They made decisions about which stories were told, how they were presented, and to whom they were accessible. In that sense, exhibition was never neutral. It was always a cultural act.

The Belcourt's roots in its original Hillsboro Theatre reflect this history of intentional curation and community integration. From its earliest days, it was not just a place to show films, it was a space to think, to feel, and to gather. Its story is one of adaptation, yes, but also of continuity. The Belcourt didn't appear from nowhere. It emerged from a city already steeped in cinematic possibility, already primed for a theater that could educate, challenge, and serve.

In a time when commercial pressures continue to reshape the cinematic landscape of the twenty-first century, the Belcourt's nonprofit model and community-centered programming remain a reminder of what exhibition can be: not just profitable, but purposeful. Not just popular, but profound.

3

NASHVILLE'S SILENCED CINEMA HISTORY

BLACK CINEMA CULTURE AS RESISTANCE

IN EARLY TWENTIETH-CENTURY NASHVILLE, when Jim Crow laws dictated every aspect of public life, Black audiences created their own cinematic culture in defiance of exclusion. W. G. Hynes, a pioneering Black filmmaker and exhibitor born June 16, 1864, the same year as the Civil War Battle of Nashville, became one of the first to nurture this parallel film world.[1] Hynes transformed a childhood fascination with magic lanterns into a professional enterprise. By 1907, Hynes was touring major cities like Louisville, Chicago, and New Orleans, presenting silent films like Edwin S. Porter's *Uncle Tom's Cabin* (1903).[2] His entrepreneurial spirit led him to establish Nashville's Leroy Theatre in 1912 and the Royal Palace Theodome in 1914.[3] Hynes also founded the National Lecture Bureau, dedicated to producing films and lecture series about Black cultural and religious life, ensuring that cinema preserved Black heritage as well as entertained.[4]

Parallel to these individual successes, Nashville's Black neighborhoods and business districts, both disparagingly and favorably labeled as part of the city's "Black Bottom" or the "Brown Block," became critical sites of cinematic innovation. Theaters such as the Bijou, Majestic (later the Lincoln Theatre), and Fred Douglass Skydome thrived as community hubs that challenged Hollywood's degrading portrayals of Black life. These theaters screened "race films," independent productions crafted by Black filmmakers to authentically depict their communities' experiences. Films like director

FIGURE 3.1. A postcard depicting the Bijou Theatre located at 423 4th Avenue North. Built in 1904, it became one of the South's leading African American theaters in 1916, hosting vaudeville and motion pictures made by African American filmmakers. Nashville Room Postcard Collection. Courtesy of Nashville Public Library Special Collections and Archives.

FIGURE 3.2. The Bijou Theater (423 Fourth Ave. North), c. 1953. Visible at the foot of the Tennessee State Capitol building. Both it and the Masonic Lodge to its left were razed for the construction of Municipal Auditorium and James Robertson Parkway, part of the city's Capitol Hill Redevelopment project. Metropolitan Development and Housing Photograph Collection. Courtesy of Metropolitan Government Archives of Nashville and Davidson County.

William Robert Daly's *Uncle Tom's Cabin* (1914), starring Sam Lucas, the first African American actor to portray the titular character, or Noble Johnson's *The Law of Nature* (1916) and *Trooper of Company K* (1917) celebrated Black dignity and valor, offering rare affirmations against Hollywood's racialized caricatures.[5]

Notably, the Fred Douglass Skydome, managed by influential entrepreneur A. N. Johnson Jr., was renowned for its "non–Jim Crow" films. It became a venue where audiences could engage deeply with culturally affirming cinema. The Skydome also hosted amateur nights, providing critical opportunities for local performers to gain visibility and professional experience.[6]

This flourishing cinematic ecosystem was always under siege by racism and white supremacy, creating tensions and inequities that profoundly shaped Nashville's cinematic landscape. In 1918, D. W. Griffith's racist epic *The Birth*

FIGURE 3.3. Original cast of *Shuffle Along*, 1920s. Group portrait photograph. F. E. Miller (seat 5) and Aubrey Lyles (seat 6) are pictured in the center of the second row from the bottom. Eubie Blake Photograph Collection. Courtesy of the H. Furlong Baldwin Library, Maryland Center for History and Culture.

of a Nation (1915) screened at the white-owned Vendome Theatre, sparking fierce opposition from Nashville's Black community. Activists, clergy, and Black-owned newspaper *The Nashville Globe* helped mobilize vigorous protests, highlighting the broader struggle against Hollywood's harmful racial narratives.[7]

Cinema was not only a cultural issue but also an economic battleground. Black entrepreneurs like J. C. Napier and A. N. Johnson Jr. emphasized property ownership and economic independence through businesses centered around film.[8] Their theaters symbolized resistance against systemic racism, proving that economic self-determination and cultural pride could coexist and reinforce each other.

Even as Black Nashvillians built a robust cinematic culture, many artists and entrepreneurs moved north during the Great Migration in search of opportunities beyond Jim Crow's constraints. Among them were brothers Irvin C. Miller and F. E. Miller, sons of W. L. Miller, the influential editor of *The Nashville Globe*. Educated at Fisk University, Irvin and F. E. Miller went on to shape American entertainment in significant ways. Along with their father, they were connected to the legacy of *Shuffle Along* (1921), the groundbreaking Broadway production created with fellow Fisk alumnus Aubrey

Lyles. F. E. Miller and Lyles also became associated with early Black film culture, appearing in works such as Oscar Micheaux's *A Son of Satan* (1924).

F. E. appeared in seventeen films and wrote four, starring in a string of groundbreaking all-Black Westerns, including *Harlem on the Prairie* (Sam Newfield, dir., 1937), *Harlem Rides the Range* (Richard C. Kahn, dir., 1939), and *The Bronze Buckaroo* (Richard C. Kahn, dir., 1939). Although the contributions of the Millers and Lyles shaped early Black cinema nationally, they have often been overlooked in mainstream histories about Nashville's cinematic legacy.

SEGREGATION AT THE CINEMA

MEANWHILE, SEGREGATION STRUCTURED the city's physical theaters as starkly as its neighborhoods. At the dawn of the twentieth century, Nashville, steeped in Jim Crow segregation, clearly demarcated cultural spaces along racial lines. "De jure" segregation, separation enforced by law, and "de facto" segregation, separation in practice, without legal mandates, often stemming from social or economic factors, dictated every aspect of public life. This included movie theaters.

For white audiences, opulent theaters like the Vendome and Parthenon offered luxurious escapes into cinematic worlds. Meanwhile, Black Nashvillians were subjected to severe restrictions. When allowed entry, they entered through back doors, were denied access to amenities like restrooms and concessions, and were relegated to cramped, uncomfortable balconies mockingly called the "crow's nest," a reference to blackface minstrel culture and grim reminder of the era's pervasive racism.

The Hillsboro Theatre did not stand apart from the racial order of early twentieth-century Nashville. It was one of its products: a new theater in a new white neighborhood, built on land marked by Black institutional loss and surrounded by the restrictions that shaped who could live, move, and gather there.

THE LEGACY OF RACISM AND SEGREGATION

THE RACIAL EXCLUSION THAT SHAPED Nashville's cinematic landscape also defined the physical geography of its theaters, including the Hillsboro Theatre. The Hillsboro represented the Roaring Twenties' ideals of progress and modernity, yet epitomized this exclusion by explicitly catering to white audiences, with no evidence there was balcony seating or a rear entrance available for Black audience members. History suggests they were never invited or allowed, with the unique exception of Opry performer DeFord Bailey during the 1930s.

Hillsboro Village's development occurred on land historically associated with racial dispossession. Roger Williams University, founded in 1866 as a prominent Black educational institution, occupied land overlooking Hillsboro Village that stretched all the way to the edge of the future site of the Hillsboro Theatre.[9] After suspicious fires in 1905 destroyed critical buildings, including Centennial Hall, the land was quickly appropriated by white developers intent on creating segregated neighborhoods. These developers incorporated restrictive covenants explicitly barring Black individuals from property ownership, further entrenching racial segregation.[10]

These segregationist policies extended to public transportation, with streetcar suburbs like Hillsboro Village deliberately structured to exclude Black residents from full participation. In 1905, Tennessee's legislature mandated racial segregation on streetcars, severely restricting Black mobility and reinforcing social hierarchies. Not surprisingly, the Hillsboro itself operated under these same Jim Crow policies, of either complete exclusion or the less likely scenario, segregation by inferior seating.[11]

As Nashville continued to expand over generations, the Hillsboro thrived in this racialized geography, serving white prosperity while Black Nashvillians endured systemic limitations on where they could live, work, and participate in civic life.

Similar to the loss of Roger Williams, the fate of Black theaters was shaped by racism and dispossession as urban renewal projects took hold in the 1950s. The Bijou Theatre, once a cornerstone of Black entertainment in Nashville, was demolished in 1957 as part of the Capitol Hill Redevelopment Project and later replaced by the Nashville Municipal Auditorium. Efforts to preserve the theater, along with a neighboring Masonic lodge, reached the US Supreme Court but failed.

Initiated under the American Housing Act of 1949, the Capitol Hill project established a 112-acre district around the Tennessee State Capitol. Designed with a mid-century modern aesthetic and oriented toward automobile travel, the plan centered on James Robertson Parkway. It became the first federally funded urban renewal effort in the nation, setting a precedent for similar projects between 1958 and 1968 that displaced African American communities across the country.

The redevelopment erased nearly all traces of Nashville's North Capitol neighborhood, once known as the Black Business District and home to a thriving industrial and commercial community.

Racial segregation officially ended in Nashville with the enactment of the Civil Rights Act of 1964 on July 2, which outlawed segregation in public spaces, including theaters, and prohibited employment discrimination based on race, color, religion, sex, or national origin nationwide. Shortly thereafter, in August 1964, the Belcourt Theatre marked a significant organizational turning point by hosting an inclusive casting call for New Theatre Nashville's production of the musical *Show Boat*.[12] For the first time since DeFord Bailey's performances at the Opry thirty years prior, the Belcourt stage welcomed Black performers—this time as equals—notably Dr. Lloyd Lusk and Sandra Dixon, who portrayed Joe and Queenie, marking a turning point in the theater's story.[13]

ENVISIONING A MORE INCLUSIVE FUTURE FOR CINEMA

AT ITS CENTENNIAL, the contemporary Belcourt Theatre emerges from this complex history as both a beacon of independent cinema and a symbol of racial privilege. One way that the Belcourt recognizes its relationship to the past is by acknowledging and centering the contributions of Nashville's early Black filmmakers, exhibitors, audiences, and performers who crafted a parallel cinematic world, vibrant and resilient, against oppressive odds.

This history compels a reconsideration of how Nashville's cinematic legacy is framed and remembered. It challenges the selective memory that marginalizes the profound influence of Black contributions. Acknowledging these contributions is essential not just for historical accuracy but as a necessary step toward cultural inclusivity and restorative justice.

Another way to fully honor Nashville's cinematic heritage is to amplify the voices of those who have been historically pushed to the margins. After the Belcourt Theatre reopened at the beginning of the twenty-first century, the theater has had an opportunity, and a responsibility, to help lead that work. Since becoming Nashville's nonprofit film center, the organization

FIGURE 3.4. Bijou Theater construction in front of the theater, July 17, 1957. African American patrons look on as demolition begins. Record Group 412, Photographs Collection. Courtesy of Metropolitan Government Archives of Nashville and Davidson County.

that is Belcourt has worked to recognize silenced histories and celebrate the contributions of those once excluded. In doing so, the theater has helped Nashville shape a film culture that is more equitable, more accurate, and more complete.

The Belcourt's suite of programming and engagement practices are grounded in both cultural awareness and strategic curation. In 2024 alone, the theater presented 3,847 screenings, featuring 356 unique film titles, 114 new or first-run releases and 242 repertory or classic films. Of these, the Belcourt showcased 80 foreign-language films from 46 different countries, presented across 26 languages, underscoring the theater's commitment to maintaining a globally oriented curatorial lens.

Efforts to further broaden representation in the theater's programming on the eve of their centennial is also reflected in Belcourt's inclusion. In 2024, of these thousands of total film screenings, the theater presented forty-two new films by women directors (alongside fifteen repertory titles directed by women), and nineteen by filmmakers of color. This deliberate programming strategy not only reflects the theater's ongoing commitment to equity in screen storytelling but demonstrates a savvy understanding of both audience development and the shifting historical canon. By continuing to screen films on 35mm and offering twenty-one curated series, including retrospectives and thematic programs, the Belcourt actively bridges film history with contemporary voices, positioning itself as a dynamic, accessible platform for diverse perspectives within cinema.

Beyond the screen, the Belcourt's outreach model deepens this inclusive vision. Through its robust education and engagement programs, the organization reaches thousands annually with initiatives such as free public events, in-school workshops, post-screening discussions, and professional development for educators. These programs are designed not merely to supplement filmgoing, but to foster cinematic literacy and civic dialogue. Strategic partnerships with local schools, community organizations, and artists ensure that the theater's resources are redistributed across demographic and economic lines.

This approach is rooted in the Belcourt's mission to engage, enrich, and educate through the power of film, not as passive entertainment, but as a participatory cultural force. The success of this model is evident in the theater's dual role as a bastion of independent cinema and as a civic space where underrepresented stories are not only welcomed, but centered. By sustaining that role, the Belcourt helps foster a more inclusive cinematic future, one that learns from the past without being bound by it.

As Nashville's film community looks ahead, it must grapple with persistent questions about whose stories have been preserved, and whose have been excluded. The Belcourt Theatre's narrative, influential as it is, represents only part of a broader, richer tapestry. To fully honor Nashville's cinematic heritage, it is crucial to amplify and celebrate the stories that have historically been silenced and find new ways to let them be heard from the past and in the present, a work that is ongoing.[14]

In recognizing these parallel histories, the Belcourt and Nashville at large have the opportunity—and responsibility—to illuminate and rectify past erasures, fostering a future where cinema truly reflects and respects all voices.

4

BEING NASHVILLE'S PLAYHOUSE

DURING THE CULTURAL, POLITICAL, and economic transformations that marked the transition from the nineteenth to the twentieth century, the Belcourt's stage emerged as a vital civic forum. It became a space for actor training, public dialogue, and community formation. Though each company that occupied the theater left its own legacy, all relied on the same foundational elements: a flexible performance space, committed volunteer labor, and an engaged audience eager to see their values, questions, and identities reflected on stage.

The Belcourt served as a proving ground for new voices and dramatic forms. It supported both modernist and realist experimentation, introduced Nashville audiences to international playwrights, and nurtured generations of local talent. Over time, the venue expanded its role to become a multi-use civic institution, hosting programs for schools, churches, charities, and cultural organizations across the city.

Its impact was foundational. The Belcourt helped establish Nashville not just as a place where community theater was performed, but as a city where community theater held civic and cultural significance. Its programming, operations, and physical infrastructure all reflected a shared belief: that live performance could—and should—serve the public good.

The Belcourt was never just a building. It was, and continues to be, an engine of civic culture. Its early decades offer a case study in how regional theaters, when supported by civic infrastructure and collective imagination, can shape a city's artistic identity and forge lasting connections between performance, politics, and public life.

NASHVILLE LITTLE THEATRE GUILD (1926–1932)

BY THE EARLY TWENTIETH CENTURY, Tennessee's theater scene, especially in Nashville, had matured into a robust and increasingly professionalized industry. Prominent national performers, including celebrated Shakespearean actress Julia Marlowe, made regular appearances in the city. At the same time, Nashville began to export its own talent.[1] Among the first to achieve national recognition was John Lark Taylor.

Taylor's trajectory mirrored that of many turn-of-the-century actors. In 1898, he joined New York's Augustin Daly Stock Company, making his Broadway debut in *The Taming of the Shrew* (1891) opposite Tyrone Power Sr. After touring with companies in California and Nashville, Taylor returned to New York and joined the Sothern-Marlowe Company in 1906, performing alongside E. H. Sothern and Julia Marlowe for nearly a decade. In 1922 and '23, he appeared in Arthur Hopkins's production of *Hamlet*, starring John Barrymore. By 1925, Taylor had sold his New York residence and returned to Nashville with the goal of continuing to perform, an ambition that ultimately led to the founding of the city's first formal little theater company.[2]

In the 1910s and 1920s, a quiet revolution reshaped American theater. Known as the Little Theatre Movement, this national wave of civic idealism and artistic experimentation offered a nonprofit, ensemble-driven alternative to the commercial dominance of Broadway. Drawing inspiration from European models, little theaters emphasized local talent, literary merit, and intimate venues. From Provincetown to Chicago to San Francisco, collectives emerged nationwide.[3] Nashville's contribution began in 1926 with the founding of the Nashville Little Theatre Guild (NLTG)—the city's first sustained effort aligned with this national movement.

By this time, the national Little Theatre Movement was already well established. Rising costs for travel, royalties, and licensing had pushed many actors away from Broadway and into smaller regional communities, where they formed nonprofit ensembles.[4] These groups emphasized local participation, artistic experimentation, and civic purpose, and frequently staged

FIGURE 4.1. Lark Taylor as the Prince of Arragon in the Sothern & Marlowe production of *The Merchant of Venice*, c. 1915. Studio portrait photograph, inscribed "Sincerely yours." Taken at Hall's Studio, 1456 Broadway, New York. Courtesy of the Folger Shakespeare Library, Washington, DC.

performances in modest, intimate venues.[5] Tennessee's earliest little theater organizations included the Johnson City Little Theatre Players in 1920, Memphis Little Theatre in 1921, and Chattanooga's company in 1923, with the Memphis group being the first in the state to secure a dedicated, professionally equipped performance venue.[6] The second was Nashville's, a vision materialized inside the Hillsboro Theatre by Lark Taylor.

Operating for seven seasons, until its dissolution in 1932, the Guild mounted more than sixty plays and served not merely as an entertainment outlet, but as a civic institution. It advanced progressive ideals through regional adaptations of national trends and introduced modernist experimentation to local audiences. Its legacy lies in the integration of artistic ambition, community participation, and educational outreach, a model for what civic theater could become.

FIGURE 4.2. Stagecrafters theater group picnic at Montgomery Bell Academy, Nashville, Tennessee, c. 1918. Group portrait photograph. Future Nashville Little Theatre Guild and Community Playhouse members pictured include: top row (standing), Joe Hill (position 1) and John Lark Taylor (position 5); middle row (standing), Catharine Winnia (position 1), Ellen Wallace (position 4), Madge West Joseph (position 6), and Jane Douglas Crawford (position 7); bottom row (sitting), Dr. H. B. Schermerhorn (position 4) and Charles S. Mitchell (position 5). Madge West Joseph Scrapbooks. Courtesy of the Special Collections Division, Nashville Public Library.

FOUNDATIONS AND EARLY LEADERSHIP

Two semi-private troupes, the Stagecrafters and the Nashville branch of the Drama League of America, founded by members of the Centennial Club, established the groundwork for organized civic theater in the city.[7] Their productions of classical works, along with play readings, lectures, and touring ensembles in schools and club auditoriums, fostered ties with local actors, educators, and institutions such as Ward-Belmont and the Orpheum. This network of cultural support would prove essential in shaping Nashville's theater community.[8]

The Stagecrafters and the Drama League provided much of the personnel, talent, and leadership needed to launch the Nashville Little Theatre Guild. Many of their members went on to serve as the Guild's early organizers, performers, and patrons. From this foundation, the Guild emerged in 1926, co-founded by John Lark Taylor, Jane Douglas Crawford, and Dr. H. B. Schermerhorn, with support from the Drama League, the Stagecrafters, and Hillsboro Theatre founder M. A. Lightman.[9]

Lightman leased the Hillsboro Theatre to the Guild after closing it as a silent movie house, giving Nashville its first permanent home for community theater. The Guild soon matured, connecting local talent and civic enthusiasm to the broader national movement for volunteer-led, semi-professional theater. In doing so, it established a pathway for theatrical development in the city and laid the groundwork for future theater-style entertainment.[10]

Early leadership came from Taylor himself and was followed by a succession of Yale drama school graduates: Ramon Savich (1927–1929), Rufus S. Phillips (1930–1931), and Julian Rochelle (1931–1932).[11] The Guild's structure merged civic governance with artistic leadership, with board members frequently taking active roles onstage or behind the scenes. Figures such as Sam Tarpley, Dr. H. B. Schermerhorn, and Mrs. B. Kirk Rankin Jr. blended public service with creative investment, features that defined the Guild's ethos and carried across each chapter of the Belcourt's theater to follow.

PROGRAMMING AND REPERTOIRE

Though the first staged production at the Hillsboro Theatre was a three-act play, *The Intimate Strangers* (1921) by Booth Tarkington, performed by Vanderbilt's Dramatic Club, it was the Nashville Little Theatre Guild that formalized the space as its home and set the tone for what would follow. With

FIGURE 4.3. Cast of the Little Theatre Guild's first production, *The Imaginary Invalid*, May 15, 1926. Group portrait photograph. Madge West Joseph Scrapbooks Collection. Courtesy of the Special Collections Division, Nashville Public Library.

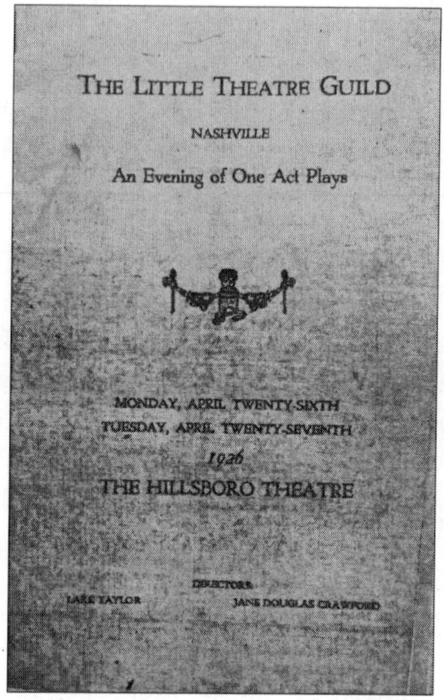

FIGURE 4.4. Playbill cover for the Nashville Little Theatre Guild's second production, April 26–27, 1926. Printed playbill of four one-act plays. Nashville Community Playhouse and Theatre Nashville Records. Courtesy of the Special Collections Division, Nashville Public Library.

its inaugural production of Molière's *The Imaginary Invalid* (1673), the Guild firmly established its commitment to European literary drama and ensemble-driven performance. Its early seasons featured short comedies and one-act plays, some written by Guild members, before gradually evolving into full-length works of greater emotional and intellectual depth.

The Guild's programming strategy embraced a curated eclecticism, blending classical European texts with American realism and experimental forms. Its repertoire included domestic realism and moral dramas, such as George Kelly's Pulitzer Prize–winning *Craig's Wife* (1925) and Martin Flavin's *Children of the Moon* (1924), which examined social conformity and familial repression; symbolic and modernist works like Henrik Ibsen's *Ghosts* (1881) and *The Wild Duck* (1884), and Anton Chekhov's *The Sea Gull* (1896), which introduced Nashville audiences to the psychological depth of nineteenth-century European drama; and sharp social satires such as Ben Hecht and Charles MacArthur's *The Front Page* (1928) and George Abbott and Philip Dunning's *Broadway* (1926), which critiqued industrialism, journalism, and urban decay. The Guild also staged comedies of manners like Noël Coward's

Hay Fever (1924) and *The Vortex* (1924), which lampooned bourgeois pretension, social taboos, and generational vanity.

Often pairing new American plays with established literary standards, the Guild curated a diverse cultural repertoire that included both canonical figures and rising voices. Productions ranged from George Bernard Shaw's socialist political comedy *Candida* (1894) to George S. Kaufman and Marc Connelly's populist satire *The Butter and Egg Man* (1925), a juxtaposition that reflected the Guild's commitment to both intellectual rigor and cultural relevance.

The Guild also featured playwrights from inside, which became a cornerstone of the Guild's artistic strategy. One-act programs like *Long, Long Ago* written by co-founder Lark Taylor and *Poor Columbine*, a pantomime play written by associate Guild director Jane Douglas Crawford, were featured alongside the works of A. A. Milne and Grand Guignol.[12] These pairings served multiple functions: they allowed for the testing of bold or unfamiliar content, gave actors opportunities to rotate through diverse roles, and encouraged experimental staging suited to the Belcourt's intimate proscenium. These programs reflected the Little Theatre Movement's laboratory ethos, privileging risk, flexibility, and ensemble growth over polish and perfection.

REGIONAL WRITERS AND LOCAL VOICES

Regional writers also found recognition on the Guild's stage, including Southern playwright Lula Vollmer, whose Broadway hit *Sun-Up* (1923) was staged in May of the Guild's fourth season (1928–1929). Produced in collaboration with the Stagecrafters, *Sun-Up* was already well known to Nashville audiences; the role of Widow Cagle had been originated by Nashville native Lucille La Verne in both the original Broadway production and its 1924 silent film adaptation. In the Guild's version, the part was taken up by longtime Ward-Belmont dramatics instructor Catharine Winnia, marking her first appearance in what would become a long and influential career on Nashville's stages.[13]

Set in the rural Appalachian Mountains during World War I, *Sun-Up* is a stark realist tragedy that examines the human cost of war, the transformation of family and gender roles, and the isolating effects of cultural insularity. Its use of vernacular language, ethnographic detail, and moral urgency made it a natural fit for the Little Theatre Movement's socially conscious aims.

For Nashville audiences negotiating the cultural shift from rural to urban life, the play reflected back their lived experience with poignant clarity.

COMMUNITY AND CIVIC ENGAGEMENT

The Guild cultivated a loyal audience through subscription tiers and social programming. Lobby receptions, fashionable ushers, and frequent mentions in the society pages helped transform its performances into major cultural events. Among its most notable patrons was Tennessee governor Benton McMillin, who served from January 16, 1899, to January 19, 1903; his attendance signaled the Guild's reputation among civic elites. His wife, Lucille Foster McMillin, was a prominent women's suffragist and president of the Tennessee Federation of Women's Clubs.[14] Between her service as Tennessee's delegate to the 1924 Democratic National Convention and her 1933 appointment by President Franklin D. Roosevelt to the United States Civil Service Commission, she played an active role in the Guild, both behind the scenes on committee chairs and onstage in multiple lead roles, credited as "Mrs. Benton McMillin."[15]

While the Guild's core audience was white, middle- to upper-class patrons, it made several efforts to democratize access and outreach, despite its location in the racially segregated suburb surrounding the theater. Partnerships with the Junior League and local colleges promoted education and civic engagement, while benefit performances supported charitable causes and disaster relief efforts.

The Guild's second season coincided with its continued use of the Hillsboro Theatre, then still operating as a silent-era movie house. To accommodate rehearsals and performances, the theater suspended film exhibitions from October through December 1926. That season's final production, *The Star Sapphire* by playwright Robert Housum, opened on December 27, 1926. Cast members included Guild and theater founder M. A. Lightman, who played a butler named Blunt.[16]

However, Nashville was reeling from a catastrophic flood caused by five days of rain that began on Christmas Day. On December 28, 1926, the Cumberland River crested nearly 56 feet above normal, leaving ten thousand residents homeless, many of them African Americans living in the city's "Black Bottom" neighborhood, later rebranded "SoBro" in the 1990s.[17]

FINANCIAL STRUGGLES AND DISSOLUTION

Despite the flood, the Guild managed to stage opening night of *The Star Sapphire*, though the remainder of the week's performances were canceled. In a remarkable show of resilience, the Guild mounted an encore on January 1, 1927, followed by a benefit performance on January 5, raising $250, over $4,000 in 2025 currency, for flood relief.[18] According to the program's foreword, the benefit was a joint effort between members of the Nashville Little Theatre Guild, the Nashville Symphony, and the Chamber of Commerce.

The January 5th benefit, titled "Benefit for Flood Sufferers," was held at the Orpheum Theatre (208 7th Avenue N.) and featured a live musical score by members of the Nashville Symphony Orchestra. The performance included a vocal solo by Mrs. Thomas H. Malone Jr., a renowned soprano, Belle Meade resident, and vocal instructor at Ward-Belmont College. A frequent performer at civic events, weddings, and fundraisers, Malone had toured nationally for twenty-five years and was considered the premiere soloist for the Nashville Symphony in the early 1920s.[19]

In addition to the performances, the Guild hosted a New Year's Eve "backstage party" on December 31, 1926, for members of the Junior League and other community supporters. Held on the 1925 Hall stage, the space was transformed into a ballroom where guests danced, mingled, and enjoyed refreshments.[20] This festive gathering, resembling the theater's future red-carpet-style receptions, was likely the first gala hosted in the historic hall, beginning a tradition of celebratory events on the stage that continued into the twenty-first century with the Belcourt's annual *A Red Carpet Evening*.

Though short-lived, the Guild played a formative role in Nashville's arts infrastructure. It developed a trained volunteer corps, produced actors who would later define other institutions, and normalized collaborations between theater and civic groups. Its artistic standards, audience strategies, and democratic governance served as a blueprint for successor organizations.

Despite its cultural success, the Guild struggled financially and weathered many changes in leadership. The Great Depression, rising interest in radio and films with sound—talkies—and the rising costs of renting the Hillsboro from Lightman, while attendance and theater subscriptions slipped, all contributed to their financial strain.[21] In 1932, the organization dissolved, leaving a void filled in part by the Nashville Experimental Theatre and, later, the

FIGURE 4.5. Portrait of Madge West Joseph, 1930s. Studio portrait photograph. Director of the WSM Players and actress with the Nashville Little Theatre Guild and Playhouse. Courtesy of the Grand Ole Opry Archives.

Nashville Community Playhouse. On Friday, April 29, 1932, the Nashville Little Theatre Guild staged their final play, a performance of Victorien Sardou's *Diplomacy* (1877).

LEGACY OF THE GUILD

Although the Little Theatre itself eventually closed, the Guild's influence endured through its alumni. Among the most notable was Madge West Joseph, who built a successful career on stage, screen, and television while remaining active in Nashville's theater community.

Born Margaret West Joseph in New York City on May 18, 1892, she began acting at the age of five, playing Cupid in the 1907 silent film adaptation of *Ben Hur* with William S. Hart. During her childhood, she performed under the direction of David Belasco, the celebrated American theatrical producer, and by 1917 had become one of Broadway's youngest leading ladies.

In 1920, West moved to Nashville as the bride of investment banker John Barthell Joseph, who died in 1947. A founder of the Little Theatre Guild, she credited the Guild with reviving her interest in acting, which she had set aside before relocating. Joseph went on to sustain a lifelong career, appearing in feature films such as *The Miracle Worker* (Arthur Penn, dir., 1962), *Butterfield 8* (Daniel Mann, dir., 1960), and *For the Love of Ivy* (Daniel Mann, dir., 1968), alongside Elizabeth Taylor, Sidney Poitier, Anne Bancroft, and Patty

Duke. She also became a familiar face in television commercials, representing companies including beverage company Welch's and toilet paper company White Cloud.

Joseph's contributions extended beyond performance. She served as director of the Junior League Children's Theatre, co-founded and sat on the board of the Nashville Community Playhouse, and was a member of the Stagecrafters and the Centennial Club. In addition, she directed and produced radio plays and commercials through the WSM Players, securing her place as a vital figure in Nashville's cultural life.

By 1933, Guild founder John Lark Taylor had moved to WSM radio, announcing broadcasts and performing in radio dramas, a job he held until his retirement in 1942.[22] Other Guild principles—ensemble performance, literary excellence, civic service—continued to shape theatrical institutions based at the Belcourt for decades to come.

The Nashville Little Theatre Guild's seven seasons represent a landmark in Southern theater history. Its productions bridged elite and popular tastes, introduced modernist aesthetics to a regional audience, and affirmed that meaningful, transformative theater could emerge from local initiative. In the context of the national Little Theatre Movement, the Guild stands out as a rare Southern exemplar: a civic-minded company that expanded Nashville's cultural vocabulary and modeled the potential of democratic, community-driven art.

NASHVILLE EXPERIMENTAL THEATRE (1934)

DURING THE DEPTHS OF the Great Depression, a short-lived but influential theatrical initiative took shape at Nashville's Belcourt Theatre. Founded in 1934 with funding from the Works Progress Administration, the Nashville Experimental Theatre (NET) was established to employ local artists and theater workers, offering both economic relief and cultural enrichment.

NEW DEAL ORIGINS

Under the direction of Rufus S. Phillips, previously affiliated director of the Nashville Little Theatre Guild, NET had ambitious civic and artistic goals. Phillips outlined the group's purpose clearly: to stage accessible modern and classical plays at affordable prices under a pay-as-you-go subscription model, cultivate local talent in acting, writing, and stagecraft, and provide meaningful employment aligned with President Roosevelt's broader New Deal recovery initiatives.

The Experimental Theatre emerged in Nashville at a moment when ideas about socially engaged, community-based theater were gaining force but had not yet been formalized through federal programs like the Federal Theatre Project, which began in 1935. In practice, the company was already doing much of what those later initiatives would promote, encouraging attendance by working-class people through discounted tickets and radio broadcasts and framing theater as a public, accessible art form that promoted inclusive community participation. Had it survived longer, it might have been recognized as part of that broader shift. Instead, it dissolved before the federal framework fully emerged in the mid-thirties, emphasizing how forward-thinking its socially relevant and politically engaged theater was in its time.

AMBITIOUS PRODUCTIONS

Thanks to the Guild's success in cultivating a core group of amateur performers, more than a dozen members transitioned into the city's new experimental theater project. The company's flagship production, *Alice Sit-by-the-Fire* (1905), a comedy by Sir James M. Barrie, premiered on February 7, 1934. Its story, centered on parental expectations, youthful rebellion, and imaginative freedom, offered a gentle critique of prevailing social conservatism while remaining accessible to mainstream audiences. The company quickly followed with *Once in a Lifetime* (1930) by George S. Kaufman and Moss Hart, staged the following month. This ambitious production featured an ensemble cast of over sixty amateur performers and five full set changes.[23]

By this time, the NET had expanded its influence beyond the stage, becoming regular performers on WLAC radio. This exposure broadened the Guild's reach and strengthened its role in the city's civic arts scene.[24] WLAC, an AM radio station, carried a powerful nighttime signal that reached audiences across the central and eastern United States. As the golden age of Radio began, families gathered around radios for dramas, comedies, and news, making high-powered stations like WLAC a vital and affordable source of entertainment during the Great Depression.

Although WSM was Nashville's first major station to reach 50,000 watts of "clear-channel air," which boasted a stronger signal, WLAC was one of a select group of US stations authorized to broadcast at higher power and occupy exclusive nighttime frequencies. This allowed the NET's performers to reach listeners well beyond the city, placing them within a national audience.

RADIO AND AVANT-GARDE EXPERIMENTS

As its name implied, NET embraced avant-garde forms, staging both adaptations and original works inspired by modernist innovators. Among its most ambitious efforts was the Kaufman-Hart production of *Once in a Lifetime*, a satire of Hollywood that included a play-within-a-play and demanded complex staging.[25] NET also presented *About Chickie's Daughter*, an original radio serial adapted by Rufus S. Phillips and Leslie Sterne from Elenore Meherin's popular broadcast drama *Chickie*.[26] Further expanding its experimental reach, the group staged a radio adaptation of the "World's Oldest Passion Play" from Freiburg, Germany, first staged in the 1200s and later brought to US audiences as a touring production in 1928. These avant-garde productions, many broadcast live on Nashville's WLAC radio, were an innovative approach to the changing landscape of community theater and marked NET as a bold, if brief, outlier in Nashville's theater history.

SHORT LIFE, LASTING LEGACY

Despite its creative ambition, NET's existence was short-lived; folding by the end of 1934, it re-formed the following year under a newly established institution, the Nashville Community Playhouse, also under the leadership of Rufus S. Phillips. Nevertheless, NET's legacy was substantial and enduring. Its alumni significantly influenced Nashville's subsequent cultural institutions.

Fred Coe, who performed in NET productions, later became one of American television's most respected figures, producing groundbreaking dramatic works through the Goodyear and Philco Television Playhouse shows while remaining committed to civic theater ideals. Performers like Charles Mitchell, Dr. Robert Morehead, Frances Wilson, and La Una Gay Parkes transitioned to prominent roles at the Community Playhouse, carrying forward NET's ensemble-driven and socially engaged philosophy. Actors such as Betsy

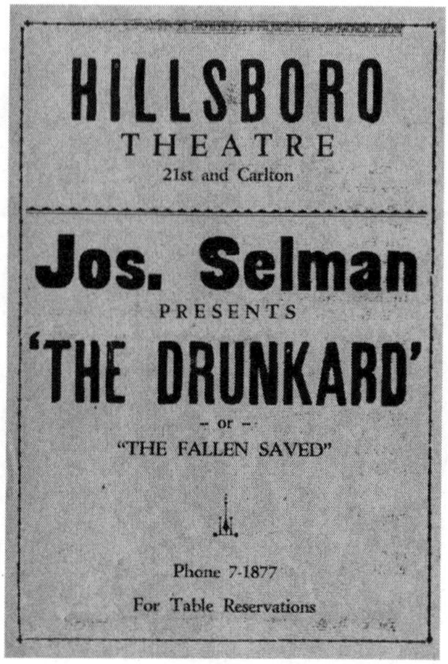

FIGURE 4.6. Playbill for the Avon Players production of *The Drunkard*, November 1934. Presented at the Hillsboro Theatre. Courtesy of the Metropolitan Government Archives of Nashville and Davidson County.

Howe, John Thompson, and Leslie Sterne moved into influential roles at Nashville Children's Theatre, helping solidify the city's reputation for quality youth theater and educational programming. Technical staff and collaborators, including notable figures like Edwin Keeble, Frank Melfi, and Casper Kuhn Jr., also remained active in Nashville's evolving cultural scene, shaping community theater through ongoing artistic and institutional contributions.

In addition to the Nashville Experimental Theatre, the Hillsboro Theatre briefly hosted another residency: the Avon Players, a repertory company led by Joseph Selman. Their productions were modest in scale, ranging from Shakespearean works to more contemporary fare such as the 1844 American temperance parody *The Drunkard* by William Henry Smith.

The Avon Players staged *The Drunkard* for one week, from November 29 to December 5, 1934, with midnight performances followed by informal after-parties. The production then moved to the Orpheum Theatre for an "indefinite run," reimagined as an audience-participation event "stripped of formality." Patrons, supplied with free food and beer—a novelty during the Depression—were encouraged to smoke, eat, drink, jeer the villain, cheer the hero, and do anything but "crack peanuts during the performance." Despite this inventive format, the show closed by the week of December 24.

Selman had announced that the Avon Players, previously based in Atlanta, would alternate between Nashville engagements and road tours throughout the South. The small nine-member company, including Selman himself, did conduct regional tours, though their Nashville residency proved short-lived.[27]

Although Nashville Experimental Theatre existed only briefly, its role as an incubator for progressive artistic experimentation left a lasting impact. It demonstrated that even short-lived artistic endeavors could meaningfully influence cultural development and civic engagement. NET's single season at the Belcourt was not merely a historical footnote, but rather an essential prologue, highlighting theater's potential as a dynamic, inclusive, and transformative civic institution.

NASHVILLE CHILDREN'S THEATRE (1931–1958)

THE NASHVILLE CHILDREN'S THEATRE (NCT), founded in 1931 by the Junior League of Nashville, began as a volunteer-led initiative aimed at introducing local children to theater, and remains the city's oldest existing performing arts organization.[28] NCT's inaugural production, *Aladdin and the Wonderful Lamp* (eighteenth century), premiered on the Belcourt stage in partnership with the Nashville Little Theatre Guild, which remained the venue's primary tenant at the time. Volunteers from the Junior League managed every aspect of the production, from acting and directing to costume design and set construction. Guild director Julian Rochelle was placed in charge of executing the production, while other members such as Mrs. B. Kirk Rankin and Barbour Howe played lead roles, signaling the new company's professional aspirations from the outset.[29] This early collaboration demonstrated a high level of artistic ambition and underscored the Children's Theatre's commitment to quality and civic partnership from the very beginning.

FOUNDING AND FIRST PRODUCTIONS

In its earliest years, NCT's performances primarily reached children from schools, orphanages, and hospitals through special matinee events. Productions such as Henry Savile Clarke and Walter Slaughter's 1886 musical *Alice*

FIGURE 4.7. Third annual Nashville Children's Theatre Ice Cream Carnival, May 13, 1941. Photograph taken in the parking lot of the Community Playhouse. In the left foreground, actors Frank Sutton (pointing cane) and Tom Tichenor are pictured socializing with local children. *Nashville Banner* Archives Collection. Courtesy of the Special Collections Division, Nashville Public Library.

in Wonderland in 1932 (based on Lewis Carroll's *Alice's Adventures in Wonderland* and *Through the Looking-Glass*), featuring elaborate, handmade masks based on John Tenniel's iconic illustrations from Carrol's novels, quickly elevated the theater's artistic reputation.[30] These early shows set a standard for innovation and visual imagination, blending educational content with high-quality entertainment.

GROWTH AND MARIONETTE ERA

After the Little Theatre Guild folded, shortly following the Nashville Children's Theatre's successful *Alice in Wonderland* production, NCT regrouped and shifted its focus to marionette plays, which it primarily staged at the nearby Belmont Theatre. Meanwhile, M. A. Lightman worked to keep the Hillsboro Theatre from closing entirely. It ultimately took him a year to fully lease the space, but by July 1933, he had reached an agreement with Lawrence Neal, managing director of a new stock company project called the Broadway Players. A merger of the Orpheum Players and the Civic Repertoire Players, directed by Eugert Yarian, the Broadway Players aimed to bring professional actors from outside the city to perform alongside Nashvillians and reestablish the Hillsboro stage as a permanent venue for live theater. Plans included redecoration and modest renovations.[31]

As part of this effort, Neal invited Judith Clayton's Marionette Company—Clayton being a strong supporter of NCT—to use the theater for free, offering daytime shows to children during school hours. The Broadway Players' first and only production, Noël Coward's *Private Lives* (1930) ran from September 4 to 8, 1933.[32] A second planned production, *The First Mrs. Frazier* (1929) by Irish playwright St. John Ervine, was announced for the following week but never materialized for reasons unreported.[33] The project was soon replaced by the Nashville Experimental Theatre, likely a reflection of the financial strain of maintaining touring stock companies during the Depression.

By May 1933, NCT had resumed performances at the Hillsboro Theatre, though it continued to stage shows at other venues as well. During this time, while Nashville Experimental Theatre operated out of the Hillsboro, NCT continued to grow. By 1935, the Hillsboro's stage was revived again, with the dovetailing of NET into the Nashville Community Playhouse, which shared the space with the Children's Theatre.

FORMALIZATION AND EDUCATIONAL PARTNERSHIPS

By 1936, NCT had grown significantly, prompting its formal incorporation as an independent organization.[34] The theater adopted a structured governance model with a dedicated board of directors and advisory board, membership tiers, and specialized volunteer committees. Professional artistic standards were emphasized through collaborations with directors from the Nashville Community Playhouse and local academic institutions, establishing a disciplined approach to children's theater rarely seen elsewhere at the time.[35]

In 1937, the organization achieved a landmark institutional partnership by securing a state exemption allowing direct ticket sales through Nashville's public schools.[36] This groundbreaking agreement integrated theater into the local education system, dramatically increasing attendance and embedding cultural enrichment within Nashville's school curriculum.

FIGURE 4.8. Tom Tichenor, promotional portrait, c. 1947. Studio photograph by Schofield Studios. Courtesy of the Grand Ole Opry Archives.

FIGURE 4.10. Portrait of actress, producer, and director Marjorie Cooney. Courtesy of the Grand Ole Opry Archives.

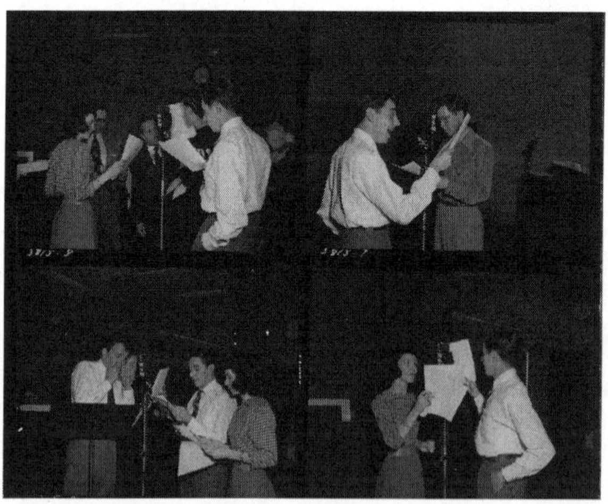

FIGURE 4.9. Tom Tichenor and cast of *Wormwood Forest* performing inside WSM studios, January 22, 1949. Contact sheet photographs. Special guests include Walt Disney (as Mickey Mouse and as himself) and Clarence Nash (as Donald Duck). Also pictured are John Culley, Christine Tibbott, and Jane Dabney Hopkins. Courtesy of the Grand Ole Opry Archives.

INNOVATION IN AUDIENCE PROGRAMS

Innovative audience-engagement initiatives further strengthened NCT's civic impact. One example, the "Ice Cream Carnival" launched in 1938, rewarded loyal attendance by offering an annual festival for children who attended every production in a season.[37] The carnivals regularly took place in the parking lot next to the theater, drawing hundreds of children each year. Such events fostered audience loyalty, deepened community engagement, and underscored NCT's unique blend of theater, education, and civic responsibility.

Despite a brief setback during Season 8 (1942/1943), the only year in its history without a production, due to the United States' entry into World War II, the Nashville Children's Theatre experienced steady growth and success throughout the 1930s alongside its host, the Nashville Community Playhouse. As both companies expanded, they found themselves increasingly competing for access to the stage and rehearsal time at the Playhouse. The needs of the Community Playhouse, as the managing entity of the venue, generally dominated the available calendar slots.[38]

PROFESSIONALIZATION UNDER TOM TICHENOR

This growth was in no small part due to the ever-increasing professionalization of the plays under the artistic direction of figures such as visionary puppeteer and dramatist Tom Tichenor, who greatly enhanced NCT's national profile. Tichenor's original scripts, inventive puppet designs, and educational workshops drew national acclaim, and theaters across the country frequently sought permission to use his materials.

Like many alumni of the Theatre Guild, Playhouse, and Children's Theatre before him, Tichenor also found success in broadcasting. From 1947 to 1951, he staged the children's radio serial *Wormwood Forest* on WSM, which was later picked up for a year-long national run on NBC and attracted guest stars like Walt Disney. Created and written by Tichenor, with music first by Owen Bradley, and later by Elmer Alley, the show also featured other Playhouse and Children's Theatre alum, such as *Wormwood*'s producer and director, Marjorie Cooney, and actresses Christine Tibbott and Jane Dabney Hopkins.

Similarly, actor-directors like Inez Alder and Wyman Kane established rigorous rehearsal practices and production standards, solidifying NCT's reputation as one of America's leading children's theaters. By the end of the 1940s, NCT had sold over 5,500 season memberships annually, regularly filling the Belcourt to capacity.[39]

OUTGROWING THE BELCOURT

By the mid-1950s, the Nashville Children's Theatre had outgrown the Belcourt and officially become a 501(c)3 nonprofit organization. Its popularity and expanded programming led to space limitations so severe that as many as two thousand children were turned away annually due to scheduling and capacity constraints. In response, civic leaders, most notably Ann Stahlman Hill, led a campaign for a dedicated children's theater facility. In 1959, the Nashville Board of Park Commissioners approved $250,000 in public funds to construct the Hill Theatre, making NCT the first children's theater in the United States to be housed in a purpose-built, publicly funded venue.[40] NCT officially opened the doors to their new facility in 1960, a milestone that not only ensured NCT's continued growth but also solidified its role as a cornerstone of Nashville's cultural and educational life.

The Nashville Children's Theatre's twenty-seven-season residency at the Belcourt (1931–1958) established a lasting blueprint for community-based, professional-quality children's theater, not only in Nashville, but nationwide. Its success proved that youth-centered theater could function as a vital cultural and educational institution, grounded in civic life and fueled by volunteer dedication, artistic excellence, and forward-thinking pedagogical values. Crucially, it was the community's support and reliable access to the Hillsboro Theatre stage that enabled NCT to evolve into the enduring organization it is today.

LASTING LEGACY

In retrospect, the Belcourt era was the crucible of NCT's national legacy. It was on this stage that future talents like 1940s film star Claude Jarman Jr., songwriter and record producer Buzz Cason, and filmmaker Gene Nash made their first appearances. It was here that Nashville's children discovered theater not as a distant spectacle, but as a reflection of their own lives and imaginations. And it was during these years that the foundation was laid for what would become one of the nation's longest continuously operating children's theaters.

NASHVILLE COMMUNITY PLAYHOUSE (1935–1958)

ESTABLISHED IN 1935, THE NASHVILLE Community Playhouse (NCP) became the city's longest-running civic theater institution of the twentieth century during its time at the Belcourt Theatre. Formed from the remnants of several dissolved groups, including the Orpheum Players, Civic Repertoire Players, Stagecrafters, and members of the Nashville Little Theatre Guild and Experimental Theatre, NCP quickly emerged on Belcourt's stage as Nashville's leading community theater organization. It set new standards for artistic excellence and civic engagement in a time of economic hardship and cultural transition.

FOUNDING AND EARLY SEASONS

Six months after the dissolution of the Experimental Theatre, the producers of the Grand Ole Opry began renting the Hillsboro Theatre for live broadcast, and the newly formed Nashville Community Playhouse staged its first production, Gertrude Tonkonogy's *Three Cornered Moon* (1933).[41] Season 1 (1935/1936) at the Playhouse, under Rufus S. Phillips's direction, was a major cultural turning point and an institutional signifier, as it was the first time in Nashville's history that a local theater organization produced an entire season of American playwrights.[42] By Season 1's end, the books were balanced, and their profit was $6.95.[43]

This led successfully to a second season, under the leadership of Yale drama school graduate Fred "Fritz" Kleibacker, kicked off by S. N. Behram's 1932 work *Biography*, which was so popular its final show was oversold, leading to a delayed opening and the producer having to add fifty additional seats for the performance.[44] Verne Phelps's set design for the February 1937 production of Maxwell Anderson's *Winterset* (1935) attracted national attention, appearing in a summer issue of *Theatre Arts Monthly* magazine, and later in the book *Curtains Going Up*, a retrospective history of the first decade of the Little Theater movement in America.[45]

PROFESSIONALIZATION AND TRAINING

Kleibacker further professionalized the Playhouse's operations, introducing a comprehensive training model of offering workshops in acting, scenic design, theater management, marketing, and playwriting.[46] These initiatives attracted even more students than before from Vanderbilt University, Ward-Belmont College, and local high schools, none of which had the same level of professional offering or a stage of equal size and quality, significantly enriching Nashville's theatrical landscape. Ward-Belmont would eventually gain more educational programming, offering students classes like stage craft and production by the early 1940s, but still cooperated with the NCP to offer students observational visits backstage and allow them attend rehearsals and performances.[47]

FACILITIES AND ARTISTIC EXPANSION

By 1937, the theater had weathered much of the financial uncertainties of the Great Depression, enough for Community Playhouse's second season to begin by making small improvements and customizations to the building, like enlarging the lobby and moving the box office away from the door facing Carlton Avenue.[48]

By 1938, Kleibacker was actively expanding the artistic scope of the Nashville Community Playhouse. Season 4 (1938/1939) opened with Robert E. Sherwood's *Idiot's Delight* (1935), a bold choice given its then recent controversy. The 1936 Pulitzer Prize–winning play, about a group of diverse guests, including an arms dealer, a scientist, and an American couple, stranded in a Swiss hotel during a looming European war, had previously been staged by the Memphis Little Theatre, where it drew protests for allegedly promoting anti-Italian sentiment, a criticism that was echoed by the Italian government in response to MGM's film adaptation.[49]

For the Nashville production, Kleibacker commissioned an original score from Hank Fort, a frequent contributor to both the Playhouse and Nashville Children's Theatre during the 1940s and 1950s.[50] A graduate of the Peabody Demonstration School and Ward-Belmont College, Fort was also a prolific songwriter, credited with more than four hundred compositions, including minor hits recorded by Petula Clark and the Andrews Sisters.

Another highlight of Season 4 was the musical revue *By Request – 1940*, written by Sarah Jeter and Louise Smith and presented April 24 through 27, 1940. The parody show featured original songs and skits by Playhouse members, and included notable locals like Marjorie Cooney on piano and a cameo by famed Ryman Auditorium manager Lula C. Naff.

FIGURE 4.11. Portrait of Mrs. Eleanor Hankins ("Hank") Fort, c. 1940s. Popularly known by the stage name Hank Fort, she composed songs including "Put Your Shoes on Lucy" and "Nashville's Such a Friendly Place." Nashville Room Historic Photographs Collection. Courtesy of the Special Collections Division, Nashville Public Library.

FIGURE 4.12. Featured cast of the Nashville Community Playhouse production of *By Request*, 1940. Pictured clockwise from top: Edith Davis, unidentified, Joanne Hampton, Delbert Mann, Dolly Dearman, and Bill Davidson. Delbert Mann Collection. Courtesy of Vanderbilt University Special Collections.

The season concluded with the Playhouse's first series of professional summer workshops. In August 1939, students staged a production of Shakespeare's *Julius Caesar*, directed by Fred Coe with Delbert Mann as assistant director. Inspired by Orson Welles's recent version, the production was simple and highly stylized, with actors appearing in modern dress.

Fred Coe was born in 1914 and moved to Nashville in 1924, where he enrolled at Peabody Demonstration School. By the age of fourteen, he was writing and directing his first plays. As a teenager living on 18th Avenue South, he staged marionette shows for his landlord's son. He later became active at Hillsboro Presbyterian Church, where he formed the Hillsboro Players in 1931, performing with Rebecca Rice, who would later join the Playhouse, alongside friends Donald Phillips and Morrell Fisher.

Coe entered Peabody College for Teachers in 1933, where he met his future wife, Alice Griggs. Through his involvement with the New Deal's National Youth Administration, established in 1935 to provide work and vocational training during the Great Depression, and its sister program, the Nashville Experimental Theatre, Coe met Delbert Mann, then head of the Hume-Fogg Dramatic Club. The club produced many future Theatre Guild, Playhouse, and Children's Theatre alumni. By the late 1930s, the Hillsboro Players had merged into the Community Playhouse, where Coe, Griggs, and Mann appeared together in *Winterset* (1935), directed by Fritz Kleibacker in February 1937.

That same year, the Community Playhouse's work began to reach beyond Nashville. As the Playhouse drew national attention as a serious civic theater, its workshop branch also entered one of the South's most urgent reform conversations. Members of the Playhouse Workshop traveled to Atlanta as guests of the Association of Southern Women for the Prevention of Lynching, where they performed Walter Spearman's *Country Sunday*, a one-act drama written for the Association's campaign against mob violence. The play centered on the machinery of false accusation, racial fear, and inherited prejudice, showing how private white panic could become public racial terror. Its appearance in the Playhouse's orbit did not undo the exclusions built into Nashville's segregated theater culture, nor did it make the Hillsboro Theatre an interracial space. But it did mark a moment when a white civic theater based in that building became connected, however briefly, to a regional reform movement that used performance as a tool of public conscience.[51]

Kleibacker went on to encourage both Coe and Mann to attend his alma mater, Yale. Coe enrolled in 1938. Just as Hume-Fogg had been a training ground for the Playhouse, Yale became a proving ground for a generation of artists who emerged from Nashville's theatrical community and went on to local and national stages, as well as film and television.[52]

By the end of 1939 and the beginning of 1940, the playhouse was doing better than ever under Kleibacker's leadership, staging more and more elaborate productions, like the first two-story set designed for the Sidney Kingsley production of *Men in White* (1933) in February.[53] The playhouse was able to continue building improvements, adding new entrance doors, giving the building's exterior and interior fresh coats of paint, adding new lighting, a stoker, stage floor cloth, beam spots, and a re-planned basement that included costume and drafting rooms. By the end of October, they were under an installment deed contract with M. A. Lightman to buy the building for $14,500, with principal and interest notes each paid over five installments, resolving on December 1, 1943.[54]

During the 1940s, Ward-Belmont professor Catharine Winnia played a key role in maintaining student engagement with the Playhouse. She helped cultivate interest among students from institutions that lacked comparable training, facilities, or access to live entertainment. The Playhouse supported this outreach by offering discounted student season tickets, which were sold through campus bookstores, a practice that continued into the 1950s.[55]

WARTIME CHALLENGES AND OPPORTUNITIES

Season 6 (1940/1941) brought both success and controversy under Kleibacker's leadership. The opening production, *Margin for Error* (1939) by local playwright Clare Boothe Luce, staged October 15 through 19, was a political satire on Nazism later adapted into a 1943 film. At the time, Boothe Luce was a rising literary figure and former Ward-Belmont student. By the 1930s, she had gained national acclaim as a playwright and was married to Henry Luce, the influential publisher of *Time*, *Life*, and *Fortune* magazines.

The cast featured Esther Rezek, a former resident of Vienna, in the role of Frieda. Her fluent German was praised for adding authenticity to the production. However, with the war just surpassing its first year at the time of the staging of *Margin for Error*, some locals were torn over the social commentary

FIGURE 4.13. Cast performing a musical number from *H.M.S. Pinafore* on the stage of the Nashville Community Playhouse, April 17, 1941. Musical director Alan Irwin conducts the orchestra, with three of the thirteen musicians visible. *Nashville Banner* Archives Collection. Courtesy of the Special Collections Division, Nashville Public Library.

FIGURE 4.14. Rehearsal for the Nashville Community Playhouse production of *Mr. and Mrs. North*, April 7–11, 1942. The playhouse's orchestra pit is visible below the cast. Delbert Mann is pictured at center, preparing to throw an object. Delbert Mann Collection. Courtesy of Vanderbilt University Special Collections.

of the play, provoking backlash. Promotional posters featuring swastikas were removed from several businesses, and the theater received threatening phone calls.[56] While many Nashvillians opposed fascism, the response to the production suggested a limited tolerance, or understanding, of the provocative imagery and political satire of the play during this tense wartime period.

In April 1941, with the war drawing away much of Nashville's male talent into military service, Kleibacker mounted a grand production of Gilbert and Sullivan's comic opera *H.M.S. Pinafore* (1878). Staged in collaboration with the Ward-Belmont Conservatory, the musical was under the direction of Alan Irwin, dean of the conservatory. The production featured a fifteen-piece orchestra, a cast of eight principals, and a chorus of forty voices, a majority of whom were women and girls.

The show opened on April 21 and ran through April 29, beginning with a preview performance for soldiers stationed at Camp Forrest in Tullahoma, Tennessee. Due to strong demand, it was held over for two additional nights.[57]

On December 7, 1941, the Empire of Japan attacked the United States' Pacific Fleet at Pearl Harbor, prompting the US entry into World War II. The attack had a profound national impact and a unique local resonance in Nashville: It was first spotted by native Nashvillian Cornelia Fort, who was

FIGURE 4.15. Cast of the Nashville Community Playhouse production of *Mr. and Mrs. North*, April 7–11, 1942. The play, based on stories appearing in *The New Yorker* magazine by Frances and Richard Lockridge, featured Delbert Mann and Mary McComas (far left) in the leading roles, with Frank Sutton as the cop, Sam Reynolds as the photographer, Israel Kaufman as the detective, Al Patterson as the chief investigator, Welbourne Brown as the corpse, and Gene Kittrell as the Fuller Brush Man. Delbert Mann Collection. Courtesy of Vanderbilt University Special Collections.

airborne with a student pilot that morning when they narrowly avoided a midair collision with one of the Japanese aircraft leaving the scene, making them some of the first eyewitnesses to the attack.

At the Nashville Community Playhouse, the impact of World War II was immediate. In the winter of 1942, director Fritz Kleibacker enlisted in the US Army, departing to serve as a lieutenant.[58] He was one of many Playhouse members who extended their civic contributions to the national war effort.

Just months before his departure for the war, Fritz Kleibacker staged one of his final productions at the Playhouse. In April 1942, he directed the theater's forty-sixth production, *Mr. and Mrs. North* (1941), a comedic noir based on characters created by Frances and Richard Lockridge. Delbert Mann received top billing in the role of Mr. North, while Frank Sutton appeared as Policeman Cooper.

Leadership during the war years shifted frequently, with several guest directors stepping in to maintain operations. Among them were longtime contributors Inez Alder and Catharine Winnia, who had been deeply involved in the Playhouse's educational and artistic programming.[59]

Despite the wartime disruptions, the Playhouse maintained strong momentum, buoyed by its designation as a "vital recreational organization" by military service leaders stationed in the area.[60] Thousands of enlisted personnel were encouraged to attend or participate in productions, further integrating the theater into the city's wartime cultural life.

The most attended production of the 1940 through 1945 period was Clare Boothe Luce's *The Women* (1936), which ran from January 27 to 31, 1942, with two additional performances on February 2 and 3 due to high demand. According to internal Playhouse records, the show drew 3,032 attendees over seven performances.[61] Attendance was so high the theater hung a sign outside the box office each night reading "standing room only."[62]

Premiering on Broadway in 1936, *The Women* became a national hit before its publication in 1937. Its sharp satire of upper-class women's lives resonated strongly with wartime audiences, particularly as traditional gender roles were in flux during the early 1940s. Like the later film adaptation, a milestone in featuring an all-female cast, the Playhouse production included thirty-five women, likely a first for both the company and the city. This created significant opportunities for broader community participation, drawing in many well-known local actresses. The large ensemble cast activated wide social networks, contributing to the show's remarkable turnout. Local servicemen stationed in Nashville also supported and promoted the production, which aligned with the national push for patriotic and morale-boosting entertainment during the war's early years.

Kleibacker and NCP again drew national media attention when *Theatre Arts* published a feature on them in July 1942. In the article, he articulated the civic mission of the Playhouse, stating: "Their contribution to public morale is indispensable. This is the supreme opportunity for the non-professional theatre to come of age; to prove to the public at large it is not a plaything of the few but an integrated, mature enterprise necessary to the lives of the many—a real community theatre serving the needs of the community."[63]

ARTISTIC MATURITY AND FACILITY UPGRADES

Over the course of the 1940s, programming at the Nashville Community Playhouse evolved from middlebrow fare like *Cradle Snatchers* (1925) and Noël Coward's *Tonight at Eight-Thirty* (1936) to more ambitious and socially resonant works, including Shakespeare's *The Tempest* (1611), Maxwell Anderson's *Joan of Lorraine* (1946), and Lillian Hellman's *The Little Foxes* (1939). This artistic maturation coincided with the sustained leadership of Raymond Johnson, who succeeded Fritz Kleibacker as director. Johnson guided the Playhouse through a period of structural and creative expansion, strengthening its reputation as a serious cultural institution.

By Season 9 (1943/1944), sustaining membership had exceeded six hundred, and audience attendance was on the rise. Seasons 10 (1944/1945) and 11 (1945/1946) focused on consolidating this momentum, laying the foundation for what would become the Playhouse's most prolific period.

Season 12 (1946/1947) marked the artistic high point of the decade for the Nashville Community Playhouse, with an ambitious slate of fifteen productions, including the John Colton and Clemence Randolph play *Rain* and Shakespeare's *The Taming of the Shrew*. This period of creative momentum was matched by a series of significant facility upgrades. The auditorium was outfitted with five hundred new seats, replacing the previous four hundred and increasing overall capacity. New wine velvet velour proscenium curtains replaced the originals from 1925, and a new inner false proscenium was constructed. The stage lighting system was modernized with updated fixtures, pulleys, and counterweights to enhance production quality.

Renovations extended throughout the building. The box office was relocated, likely to the side of the building near the parking lot, where it remains today. A new ladies' lounge was added, and the lobby was updated with fluorescent lighting and an electric drinking fountain. Photo murals of past productions were installed to commemorate the company's growing legacy. Backstage, new dressing rooms were built beneath the stage, complete with red floors, gray walls, mirror-lit fixtures, and showers.[64] These improvements reflected not only the Playhouse's popularity but also its evolving commitment to professional-caliber theatrical production.

Season 15 (1949/1950) brought even more growth than the company. By September 1949, the playhouse had annexed a new structure onto the building they called "Kane's Warehouse" in honor of technical director Wyman Kane. It contained dressing rooms and prop storage, and functioned as a rehearsal stage when the theater's main stage was being used for other purposes, like for the Children's Theatre. This addition was initiated under the direction of Robert L. Gwinn at a cost of $5,000.[65]

In the September 1947 issue of *Theatre Arts* magazine, Raymond Johnson reflected on the Playhouse's growth and its relationship with the Nashville

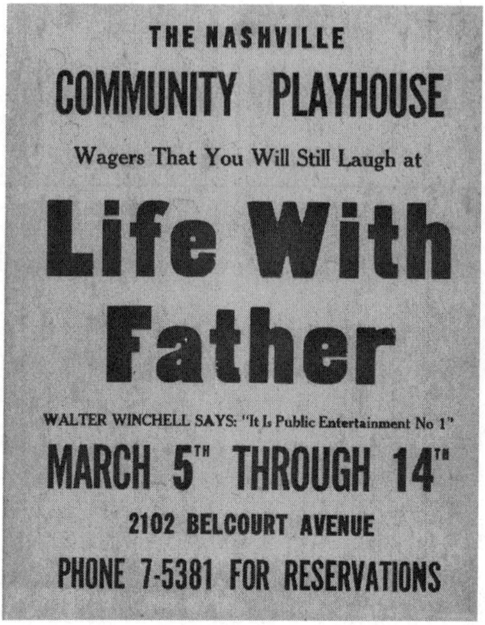

FIGURE 4.16. Poster for *Life with Father*, 1952–1953. Directed by Howard Orms and produced by the Nashville Community Playhouse during its eighteenth season. The play by Howard Lindsay and Russel Crouse, originally written in 1939, ran for ten days between March 5 and March 14, 1953. Courtesy of Belcourt Theatre.

Children's Theatre. He described the two institutions as having "endured family life under the same roof," evolving into true community enterprises composed of volunteer workers from all walks of life. Though serving different age groups, both organizations shared a common goal: to offer the community the highest-quality theater possible by harnessing local talent. Johnson noted with pride that, after fourteen seasons, the Playhouse had become a fully self-supporting community theater with more than four thousand sustaining members. It operated out of its own building, produced six major productions per season, and maintained a budget that supported a full-time director, technical director, and business manager.[66]

FINANCIAL STRAINS AND TRANSITION

Yet despite this robust community support, the Playhouse faced persistent financial challenges. The precise causes remain unclear, in part due to a lack of surviving institutional records. While the 1945/1946 season ended with a modest profit of nearly $2,800, the years that followed saw mounting deficits—$1,360 in 1947/1948, more than $6,300 in 1948/1949, and approximately $4,600 by 1954.

These ongoing financial strains, likely the result of rapid growth that outpaced revenue, gradually undermined the Playhouse's long-term stability.

ALUMNI AND LEGACY

By the early 1950s, leadership transitioned to Howard Orms, another Yale-trained director who maintained high artistic standards amid financial struggles. Kleibacker himself moved into television, directing Nashville's first live television broadcasts of the Grand Ole Opry on WSM-TV. Fellow Playhouse alumnus Fred Coe also transitioned successfully to television, becoming an influential producer known for works like *The Miracle Worker* (Arthur Penn, dir., 1962). Other notable alumni included Dinah Shore, Delbert Mann, and Sarah Cannon (a.k.a., Minnie Pearl), all of whom launched major careers after early experiences on the Playhouse stage.

In 1958, the Nashville Community Playhouse sought a new institutional plan: a merger that might unburden their mounting debt and declining

FIGURE 4.17. Howard Orms standing outside the Community Playhouse entrance facing Belcourt Avenue, early 1950s. Howard Orms Collection. Courtesy of Missouri State University Special Collections and Archives.

revenues, reestablish their relationship and trust in the wider community, and reinvigorate interest in live theater on a proscenium stage. This transition marked the end of an era of community-based drama at the Belcourt, but set the stage for new artistic ambitions and professional aspirations.

Ultimately, the Nashville Community Playhouse established the city's first sustainable model of civic theater rooted in education, collaboration, and community investment—a bridge from amateur enthusiasm to professional standard, a legacy that shaped the city and region's theater practice.

THEATRE NASHVILLE (1958–1965)

The theater ghosts of seasons past must be whooping it up jubilantly backstage and in the aisles. . . . Something wonderful and electric, it seems, is happening at The Playhouse. Its spirit is stirred; its energies are quickened. There is a feeling in the air that has been absent in recent years, a fresh and exciting mood that says theater in Nashville is on its way up again!

—CLARA HIERONYMOUS, *The Tennessean*, October 5, 1958

On June 22, 1958, local businessman Gilbert Dickey Jr. founded Theatre Nashville to elevate the city's theater scene by offering paid roles to actors and administrators. The initiative represented a formal merger between two active companies: Circle Players, based at 4102 Hillsboro Road, and the Nashville Community Playhouse, which had long operated out of the Belcourt Theatre. A new board of directors was formed, comprising four members from the general community and two from each theater company. Dickey served as board president, with the presidents of Circle Players and the Community Playhouse serving as vice presidents. The merger agreement included a contingency: if Theatre Nashville earned more than $10,000 during its first year, the two founding companies would permanently dissolve into the new organization. If not, they would resume separate operations.[67]

GENE FEIST'S VISION

In August 1958, the group appointed Gene Feist as its first artistic director. Feist, a Brooklyn native born in 1923, brought extensive training and national experience to the role. After serving as an aircraft mechanic in the Pacific during World War II, where he also directed soldier stage productions, he earned a BFA in directing and playwriting from Carnegie Institute of Technology and an MA in educational theater from New York University. He also studied with renowned method acting coach Lee Strasberg and worked as managing director of the Sharon Connecticut Playhouse.[68]

Feist's appointment signaled Theatre Nashville's intention to professionalize. In October 1958, the company undertook the Belcourt's seventh renovation, repainting the auditorium and lobby white and the proscenium arch gold, a color it retained for decades. The project also included a new roof and boiler.[69]

AMBITIOUS FIRST SEASONS

Theatre Nashville's first season (1958/1959) opened with an ambitious lineup: *The Matchmaker* (Thornton Wilder, 1954), *Separate Tables* (Terence Rattigan, 1954), *Cat on a Hot Tin Roof* (Tennessee Williams, 1955), *Children of Darkness* (Edwin Justus Mayer, 1930), *The Crucible* (Arthur Miller, 1953), *A Clearing in the Woods* (Arthur Laurents, 1957), *The Boy Friend* (Sandy Wilson, 1953), and *Six Characters in Search of an Author* (Luigi Pirandello, 1921).[70] The programming emphasized psychological realism, metatheater, and social critique. Notably, *Separate Tables* was staged in December 1958, just five days before the release of its film adaptation, directed by Nashville native and Community Playhouse alum Delbert Mann.

In its second season (1959/1960), Theatre Nashville expanded its repertoire with works that explored identity, transformation, and generational conflict. Productions included *Look Back in Anger* (John Osborne, 1956), *Orpheus Descending* (Tennessee Williams, 1957), and *Fallen Angels* (Noël Coward, 1925).[71] These plays reflected a desire to engage contemporary social themes while maintaining popular appeal.

Despite successful productions and critical praise, Theatre Nashville faced internal tensions. Feist raised concerns about unprofessional conduct by Circle Players members, interference and overreach by the Theatre Nashville board, and financial strain and irregularities on both sides.[72]

By April 1959, Circle Players had formally withdrawn from the partnership. The Community Playhouse continued, rebranding under the *New* Theatre Nashville (NTN) banner and retaining Gene Feist as artistic director. The company launched a long-range development plan that included sixteen productions over two years, a membership campaign, the founding of a new performing arts school, and a major remodeling effort.[73]

In September 1959, Theatre Nashville completed its ninth renovation of the Belcourt. A one hundred–seat micro-theater called The Upstairs was added in the balcony, and structural improvements included new acoustical cement walls, permanent side stages, and a removable apron over the orchestra pit. The auditorium received 375 new mustard and gray upholstered seats, and a concession stand was installed in the lobby, a first for the theater. The theater's exterior was redesigned in a New Orleans style by technical director Robert Barnes, a look that was refined three years later, and remained part of the building until the Belcourt's Capital Campaign renovation in 2016.[74]

That same fall, Feist launched the New Theatre School of Performing Arts. The school offered classes for children and adults and introduced a summer stock apprenticeship program. Faculty included Kathe Feist, Joy Zibart, Patti Jacobs, Shirley Dunn, Bill Moss, and Dan Fitzgerald. Students from Nashville and beyond received training in acting, makeup, stage management, and theater operations.[75]

In January 1960, the board approved an $8,000 replacement of the building's air conditioning system.[76] A fundraising campaign sought $10,000 in local investments to cover the cost. Kathe Feist led the effort, but many potential donors declined, citing concerns about the organization's financial stability.[77]

Although the company had secured 1,200 season memberships, the debt from successive renovations and short-term bank loans left Theatre Nashville in financial distress.[78] The summer 1960 production of Ira Levin's *No Time for Sergeants* (1955) was well received, but internal conflict between the Feists and the board escalated. On July 31, 1960, Gene Feist was dismissed by the board.[79]

BOARD CONFLICT AND LAWSUITS

In September 1960, Gene and Kathe Feist filed lawsuits against NTN, seeking unpaid wages and contractual bonuses. The litigation extended over eight years, finally concluding in Chancery Court in 1968. During that period, the original corporate entity was dissolved, and its remaining assets were liquidated.

Shortly after Feist's dismissal, the organization underwent a complete financial and legal reorganization. It terminated its existing corporate structure and re-formed as a new nonprofit corporation, though it retained the name NTN. This restructuring effectively severed legal continuity with the entity under which Feist had been hired, making it difficult to pursue claims tied to the original organization. The eventual sale of the building extinguished any remaining cash assets, as proceeds were used to settle outstanding debts. The prolonged delay in litigation, combined with the dissolution of the original entity, compounded the sense of injury and made financial recovery nearly impossible for the Feists.[80]

Gene Feist's personal papers, donated to the New York Public Library in 2004, contain extensive documentation related to his tenure at Theatre and New Theatre Nashville. These records shed light on the central issue of the legal dispute between the Feists and the board: control over financial decision-making. The core conflict revolved around two questions: who was responsible for generating revenue, and who had the authority to manage expenditures. The documents also shed light on the board's counterclaims, chief among them the accusation that Gene Feist was uncooperative and lacked the financial competence required to lead the organization.

According to the Feists, all major financial decisions had been mutually discussed and formally approved by the board. They asserted that box office returns and programming revenues were sufficient to sustain operations, but that the board failed to act on fundraising leads and neglected essential administrative tasks such as issuing payments on time. The documentation they retained suggests a detailed and sustained effort to defend these claims.

The dispute escalated with Feist's allegation that the board chair orchestrated a deliberate campaign to remove him. This included holding unauthorized meetings and calling official sessions on short notice, often scheduled during production hours or without notifying key board members. He further claimed that the board chair misrepresented the circumstances of his dismissal to the press.

The Feists' decision to preserve these records and make them publicly accessible underscores their desire for reputational vindication. The conflict exposed fundamental rifts in the organization's governance structure, transparency, and financial management, issues that remained unresolved even after Feist's departure. Feist's story is both a cautionary tale and a testament to the enduring struggle to balance creative vision with organizational sustainability in the nonprofit theater landscape.

DECLINE AND DEPARTURE

Despite its progressive vision under Feist, Theatre Nashville preserved strong ties to its local theatrical lineage. Longtime performers like Sam Tarpley, whose career began with the Nashville Little Theatre Guild in the 1920s, remained active, and more than a dozen actors and crew brought experience from earlier Belcourt-based groups such as the Nashville Experimental Theatre and Nashville Children's Theatre.

Between 1958 and 1965, Theatre Nashville staged forty-three plays and mounted 492 performances over six seasons at the Belcourt Playhouse. Their programming reflected the social and political awareness of the era. Productions addressed themes such as identity, repression, and psychological trauma. Notable works included *Cat on a Hot Tin Roof* (1955) by Tennessee Williams, a play engaging themes of masculinity and LGBTQ+ identity. Longtime member Gene Nash wrote and choreographed and helped stage *Stock and Trade*, a country music revue, in 1960. The show was likely the first of its kind to originate in Nashville and a precursor to the musical revues that would later define the city's entertainment identity through Opryland USA theme park from 1972 to 1997. The production featured twenty dance routines and eighteen original songs, and was signed into pre-production for intended runs in Las Vegas and off-Broadway in New York City, though those plans did not seem to materialize.[81]

Under Feist's leadership, the Belcourt underwent extensive renovations. Technical upgrades improved stage capabilities, and the installation of a New Orleans–style facade modernized the theater's appearance. Yet despite these advancements, persistent financial instability led to the company's departure from the Belcourt in 1965, ending nearly forty years of community-based live theater in the building.

Theatre Nashville's legacy endures in its efforts to professionalize performance, expand civic dialogue, and diversify representation on Nashville's stages. Its programming, outreach, and institutional reforms reshaped the city's cultural landscape and set new standards for community engagement through the performing arts.

THE END OF THE PLAYHOUSE ERA

FROM 1926 TO 1965, the Belcourt Theatre served as far more than a venue, it was the central stage for community-based theater in Nashville. Over the next four decades, it hosted a succession of theater companies, including the Nashville Little Theatre Guild, Nashville Children's Theatre, Nashville Experimental Theatre, Nashville Community Playhouse, and New Theatre Nashville, each contributing to the city's evolving theatrical and civic identity.

These organizations repeatedly adapted the Belcourt to meet their changing needs. Physical modifications included a movable orchestra pit, upgraded lighting systems, costume and prop storage areas, and flexible stage extensions. These architectural changes mirrored broader institutional shifts toward greater professionalism, educational integration, and civic engagement. Together, these groups transformed the Belcourt into a versatile performance space capable of supporting everything from intimate experimental works to large-scale ensemble productions.

More than a performance venue, the Belcourt became a civic crossroads. It served schools, churches, charities, and neighborhood organizations, with its location in Hillsboro Village, adjacent to major educational institutions, ensuring steady engagement across lines of age, class, interest, and eventually, race. Its programming balanced traditional classics with socially relevant contemporary works, reinforcing the theater's role as a responsive and inclusive cultural hub.

Each company that called the Belcourt home faced the recurring challenge of balancing artistic ambition with financial sustainability, a tension still familiar to regional theaters today. Yet each left a lasting impact, bridging amateur enthusiasm with professional standards, educational outreach with adult drama, and artistic tradition with social innovation.

By the time New Theatre Nashville ended its tenure at Belcourt in 1965, the American theater landscape was entering a new era. Federally funded regional theaters, identity-based ensembles, and interdisciplinary experimentation were emerging across the country. But many of these developments had early antecedents on the Belcourt stage, positioning Nashville not as peripheral, but as an early incubator of national theatrical trends.

The Belcourt's nearly forty-year history as a home for these theater organizations underscores its profound civic and cultural legacy. Fueled by volunteerism, community investment, and artistic risk-taking, the theater helped shape Nashville's cultural identity. Institutions like the Nashville Children's Theatre continue this legacy today, affirming the enduring influence of a neighborhood theater transformed into a citywide engine for culture and civic life.

5

BEING THE OPRY'S STAGE

CORRECTING THE HISTORICAL RECORD

FOR DECADES, IT'S BEEN WIDELY believed that the Grand Ole Opry was housed at the Hillsboro between 1934 and 1936.[1] Since 1993, those dates have been displayed on a historical marker on the exterior of the Belcourt Theatre. So, when Opry historian Brenda Colladay brought a *Radio Wave* article to my attention that suggested a different date, I was caught off guard; I'd had no reason to question what I assumed was a settled fact, a fact that was quite literally written in stone. But I recognized the importance of the Belcourt and the Opry (both of whom were celebrating a centennial birthday) agreeing on shared facts. I started to research and what I found is that the actual timeline begins in late 1935, *not* 1934.

You can trace the misunderstanding regarding the Opry's tenure at the Hillsboro back to Chet Hagan's 1989 book *Grand Ole Opry*. In it, Hagan references an October 21 issue of *Broadcasting* magazine that allegedly announced WSM's move to Hillsboro on October 27, 1934:

> Saturday night [the date would be Saturday, October 27, 1934] WSM officials move to the Hillsboro Theatre in Nashville where many will be accommodated. Three different sets of colored tickets will be issued to admit a person to one hour of the Grand Ole Opry. Already the demand for the first night is taxing the capacity of 2,400 which may now see the WSM Opry. WSM has never charged for admittance to its Opry.[2] (Brackets in the original.)

However, Hagan's quote was actually lifted from a *Radio Wave* newspaper article dated November 7, 1935, that does not contain the statement Hagan made in the bracketed edit. The full article reads:

> The famous WSM Grand Ole Opry has again outgrown its old clothes. Last February when the new WSM auditorium-studio was completed, WSM officials felt they had solved the problem of accommodating the crowds which assemble each Saturday night for the event, people who came from a dozen different states weekly and from as far-distant points as 1,000 miles. From February to July, the audience was admitted to the Opry in the new auditorium-studio, which has a capacity of 500. Three color tickets were issued, each admitting a person to one hour of the WSM Opry. Thus, 1,500 were taken care of each Saturday night.
>
> After a summer of no-audiences, the Opry again opened its doors and this time even the large auditorium-studio of WSM proved inadequate. Saturday night, WSM officials moved the Grand Ole Opry to the Hillsboro Theater in Nashville where many will be accommodated. Three different sets of colored tickets will be issued to admit a person to one hour of the WSM Opry. Already the demand for the first night is taxing the capacity of the 2,400 which may now see the WSM Opry weekly. WSM has never charged for admittance to its Opry.[3]

Additionally, there is an issue of *Broadcasting* magazine discussing the move using similar language, and it too is not dated in 1934. It is dated November 1, 1935, and states:

> WSM, Nashville, has moved its Grand Ole Opry to the Hillsboro Theatre, the new 500-capacity auditorium-studio having proved inadequate despite the fact that three sets of visitors are admitted to each of the weekly programs. In the theatre 2,400 will be able to see the show each Saturday.[4]

These primary sources make clear that the Opry did not make the move in October 1934 but rather in November 1935.

How did the wrong date end up on the historical marker, then? Four years after its publication, Hagan's book was cited in the paperwork approving Belcourt's historic marker. At the time, the book was newly released, with Opryland USA holding the copyright. Certainly it makes sense that people would have trusted that an author working with Opryland would have known when the Opry was at the Hillsboro. However, Hagan's book lacks a bibliography or primary source citations, aside from photo captions referencing archives. Tracing the origins of the 1934 date in brackets through Hagan's book would have led nowhere then, and may not have even raised much doubt at the time.

The last location of the Opry before coming to Hillsboro was WSM's Studio C, which opened in November 1934. If the Opry had already relocated to Hillsboro a month prior, as Hagan suggested, it would mean the show had two homes simultaneously—an unlikely scenario. It would have been confusing for the producers and the audience. Furthermore, contemporary Nashville newspapers documented the opening of Studio C in 1934, further supporting the notion that the Opry remained there for a year before moving to Hillsboro. Of course, additional evidence to corroborate this claim comes from the *Radio Wave* article, because it confirms that the Opry moved to Hillsboro on November 9, 1935.

If determining when Opry's first show at the Hillsboro Theatre was historically confused, then determining its final show at the venue also required additional research.

The Opry later moved to a larger venue, the Dixie Tabernacle in East Nashville, with multiple scholars pinpointing June 13, 1936, as the date of its debut there. This suggests that the final show at the Hillsboro Theatre took place on Saturday, June 6, 1936. This conclusion is supported by a ticket housed at the Tennessee State Museum, dated June 6, 1936, for an Opry performance at the Hillsboro.[5]

Additionally, newspapers show that between June 4 and June 6, 1936, the Dixie Tabernacle was hosting a Church of God Convention each night, making it unlikely that the Opry had already transitioned to the new venue that same weekend.[6] As before with the radio station, it would have been messy to do the show straddling two venues. The show was professionalized at that stage, which seems to suggest that the transfer between venues would have been more seamless than that.

Further evidence supporting this timeline comes from the death of Opry star Humphrey Bate on June 12, 1936. His daughter, Alcyone Bate Beasley, later recalled in an oral history: "The Tabernacle. We moved out there in

1936, I remember that well, because, as I said, my father died. He died in '36, June '36, and the week he died, they opened the next week out at the Tabernacle. That's the reason I know when we opened out there."[7] Additionally, an obituary for Bate published in *The Tennessean* states that he had been scheduled to perform on the Opry the night after his death for a "special" installment.[8] If this installment referenced the Opry's debut at the Dixie Tabernacle, as seems likely, given that the show was well-rehearsed by this point after months at the Hillsboro, it may have been delayed due to his passing. This would further support the theory that the transition to the new venue occurred on either June 13 or June 27, 1936.

One important point to clarify is the format of the show during this period, as conflicting accounts have emerged over the years. Some people say three shows. Some say two shows. Both camps agree the shows were split into smaller sets. A ticket dated June 6, 1936, indicates it was for the second show, which ended at midnight.[9] This suggests there were two shows—not three, as reported in newspaper articles and Hagan's book. This is further supported by weekly newspaper schedules, which confirm that final performances concluded no later than 11:50 p.m.

Hagan's book describes the show as being divided into three sets, requiring three separate tickets, with a total capacity of 2,400. In contrast, Charles Wolfe states that the show was split into two sets, requiring two tickets, yet still with a capacity of 2,400.[10] This suggests both Wolfe and Hagan were likely referencing the same *Radio Wave* article, but that Wolfe might have been looking at other sources, like ticket stubs.

However, the ticket is the winning evidence. If you're measuring crowds by set, using *Radio Wave*'s math, Hillsboro's capacity was around 800. By the ticket equation the room held roughly 1,200. Additionally, there's also mention of a 1,100 seat capacity including a balcony for the opening day of the theater.[11] Two shows, multiple sets is the correct math.

The ability to pinpoint the Opry's time at the Hillsboro with greater accuracy underscores the evolution of historical research. In the late twentieth century, scholars like Hagan and Charles K. Wolfe relied on going to and looking through physical archives, personal collections, and institutional repositories such as those at the Country Music Hall of Fame and Museum and the Center For Popular Music. While these methods produced invaluable scholarship, they were also prone to human error and limited by the accessibility of primary sources.

Twenty-first-century digital databases, optical character recognition (OCR) technology, and collaborations between institutions like the Library of Congress, Wisconsin Center for Film & Theater Research, and the Internet Archive allow historians to cross-reference materials with greater speed and precision. What took weeks or months of archival digging in the past can now be accomplished in a matter of seconds, minutes, or hours. Sometimes it also means it's hard to narrow down broad historical questions, as one can sometimes suffer from too much information and too many options. This technological shift is what enabled Colladay and me to correct the long-standing date discrepancies surrounding the Opry's tenure at the Hillsboro.

At first glance, correcting a date by a year may seem like a minor revision in the grand narrative of the Opry. However, history should be built on accuracy in as best a way as it can be determined. The story of the Opry is one of deep cultural significance, and ensuring the integrity of that story matters to historians, country music scholars, and fans of the show and the theater alike.

Napoleon Bonaparte is often credited with saying, "History is a set of lies agreed upon." Whether he uttered the words or not, the sentiment captures the malleability of historical narratives, and it also serves as a reminder of the historian's responsibility to seek truth. The Opry's tenure at Hillsboro is not just a footnote; it is part of Nashville's living history. By setting the record straight, we ensure that the story of country music's most iconic institution, and Belcourt Theatre as its first official stage, is preserved with the clarity and respect it deserves.

For seven months, the Hillsboro Theatre was ground zero for a seismic shift in American culture. As the home of the Grand Ole Opry, the theater's stage helped the show transition from a loose, informal format to a polished, structured production. This shift marked a turning point for country music, transforming it from a regional style into a national entertainment force, and Nashville, still defining its cultural identity, took a major step toward becoming the country music capital of the world.

RADIO BEGAN IN THE NEIGHBORHOOD

BEFORE HILLSBORO THEATRE COULD PLAY host to a cultural phenomenon like the Opry radio show, the radio itself had to become a cultural phenomenon. Like moving images on film, radio was technically invented in the 1890s, but it took more than a few decades for it to transform from a novelty to an essential part of American life. By the 1920s, radio had evolved as a mass media tool, and the people and neighborhoods surrounding Hillsboro were instrumental in its cultural and technological advancement.

Throughout the decade, Nashville's hometown stations, WSM, WLAC, and WDAA, filled the airwaves, their signals crackling through living rooms across the city. Listeners tuned in for everything from jazz, blues, and classical performances to local dance bands, political speeches, news updates, and lectures. Radio dramas, whether original works or adaptations of stage plays, blended docudrama, fiction, and comedy, bringing stories to life in a format tailor-made for the medium.

Perhaps not surprising for a city already bursting with musicians and other creatives, and inundated with multiple respected universities, Nashvillians were early adopters of radio technology and media. They were also key innovators of the medium in more ways than one. Nowhere was this more evident than in the neighborhoods surrounding Hillsboro Village, which became ground zero for radio's big boom, shaping how the emerging medium would evolve both locally and nationally.

Nashville's broader music infrastructure was developing, and on April 18, 1922, Ward-Belmont College's associate vice president, Dr. Clayton E. Crosland, became the first person to broadcast on Nashville radio: "This is Ward-Belmont, Nashville. W-A-R-D—B-E-L-M-O-N-T. We have today installed a radio sending station and will tonight broadcast the concert by Mr. Philip Gordon, the distinguished American pianist."[12] Behind the scenes, a sixteen-year-old high school student named John DeWitt Jr. helped construct the station's antenna, an early contribution from a young mind who would go on to become a pioneering figure in developing radio and radar technology.[13] As a result of this innovation, the city's radio stations began shaping regional tastes.

HOW THE OPRY BEGAN

THE GRAND OLE OPRY BEGAN in 1925 inside WSM, the radio station launched by the National Life and Accident Insurance Company. Named after its motto, "We Shield Millions," WSM quickly became one of the South's most powerful stations. Its success grew with the hiring of George D. Hay, a former journalist and showman who introduced old-time music to new audiences.

FIGURE 5.1. Portrait of Opry stage manager Vito Pellettieri, c. 1930s. Courtesy of the Grand Ole Opry Archives.

FIGURE 5.2. Color-coded ticket for the Grand Ole Opry at the Hillsboro Theatre, c. 1930s. Likely from the last performance at the Hillsboro Theatre before the show moved to the Dixie Tabernacle in East Nashville. Courtesy of the Tennessee State Museum.

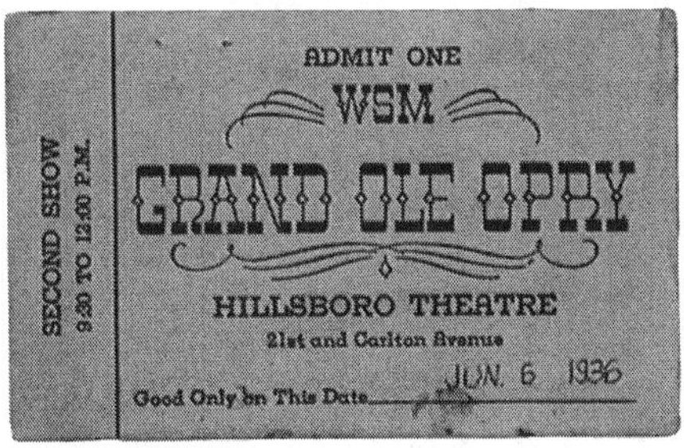

Hay booked fiddler Uncle Jimmy Thompson in 1927, and the response was overwhelming. That year, he formalized the Opry as a weekly Saturday night broadcast. The show quickly outgrew its studio space, prompting the move to the Hillsboro in 1935. The move brought changes, largely thanks to Hillsboro's stage manager Vito Pellettieri, who introduced time slots, ticketing systems, and structured transitions.

THE 1927 WATERSHED

BY 1927, THE HILLSBORO THEATRE had stopped showing silent films. Unlike other local venues, like the nearby Belmont Theatre, that transitioned to sound films, the Hillsboro pivoted to live performances, becoming home to the Nashville Community Playhouse and the Nashville Children's Theatre.

Before country music became a recording industry juggernaut, it thrived on the growing ubiquity of a radio in every American home. Nashville had the talent but lacked recording infrastructure until after World War II, when professional studios began popping up in the Belmont-Hillsboro-West End neighborhood corridor, including the area between 16th and 17th Avenues South, since dubbed Music Row. Between 1953 to 1955, Owen and Harold Bradley operated a studio near the Hillsboro Theatre, recording Kitty Wells,

FIGURE 5.3. Cast of the Grand Ole Opry on stage at the Hillsboro Theatre, c. 1935. The theater's proscenium arch is visible. Courtesy of the Country Music Hall of Fame and Archives.

Bill Monroe, and the Stanley Brothers.[14] But early on, much of country music's recorded history came from itinerant executives who set up makeshift studios across the South.

In 1927, Victor Records executive Ralph Peer recorded Jimmie Rodgers and the Carter Family in Bristol, Tennessee. These sessions, known as the "Big Bang of Country Music," helped define the genre by introducing the world to the sounds of Appalachia and the broader Southern musical diaspora. In 1927, George Hay renamed the "Barn Dance" to the "Grand Ole Opry" as part of a broader effort to promote the show nationally. He used his industry contacts to get WSM artists into Columbia recording sessions, capitalizing on the growing popularity of "old-time" or "hillbilly" music.

That same year, Opry performers Sid Harkreader and Grady Moore traveled to Chicago to record "Bully of the Town," part of a lineage that began with vaudeville performer May Irwin in the 1890s and continued through early country interpretations.[15]

Their decision to travel to Chicago to record signaled that Nashville musicians were no longer waiting for the music industry to find them; they were actively shaping it, asserting their place within it, and helping to build its infrastructure from the ground up. It also foreshadowed how country musicians, and the Nashville sound more broadly, would find new ways to weave itself into film culture, becoming a visible part of American cinema in the decades to come.

Peer made brief stops in Nashville in 1928 to record Opry acts, including DeFord Bailey, but didn't return. These early sessions marked Nashville's first commercial recordings and introduced Bailey's harmonica-driven sound to a broader audience. Bailey, born in 1899 in Smith County, Tennessee, developed his unique style after contracting polio. Moving to Nashville in 1918, he worked as a domestic laborer while studying performers at local Black theaters. His talent earned him a place at the Opry.

WHY THE HILLSBORO?

THE OPRY'S MOVE TO HILLSBORO was driven by necessity—a need for space. WSM's radio studios, its original home inside the National Life and Accident Insurance Company building, had become too small. Fans packed the insurance company offices where it aired, disrupting business. The Hillsboro Theatre offered a proper venue: one of the largest theatrical stages in the city, 1,100 seats, dressing rooms, a box office, a parking lot, and accessibility via a streetcar-sidewalk entrance. It was an ideal fit, and a temporary home that would have lasting impact.

FIGURE 5.4. Advertisement for WSM radio's clear channel, c. 1935. Courtesy of the Grand Ole Opry Archives.

Just days before the Opry's third Hillsboro broadcast on November 17, 1935, the Playhouse premiered its first production, the 1933 Tonkonogy play *Three Cornered Moon*. The theater had become a dynamic cultural venue.

Each Saturday night at Hillsboro, acts like the Delmore Brothers, Curt Poulton and the Vagabonds, Uncle Dave Macon, Sarie and Sallie, and DeFord Bailey took the stage, innovating future sounds of the genre before the show's first live theater audiences. The Delmore Brothers' harmony-driven sound laid groundwork for future brother duos like the Louvin

Brothers in the 1950s. The Vagabonds' hybridization of the country genre due to the pairing of other popular musical forms like Tin Pan Alley jazz set the tone for later country-pop crossover sounds from artists like Taylor Swift. Macon, a vaudeville veteran, blended music and comedy, while the sister-in-law duo Sarie and Sallie did on-air comedy sketches, all of which eventually led to Minnie Pearl. Bailey's harmonica performances blended old-time repertoire with the emergent sounds of the blues. Though he faced segregation on the road and marginalization within the show, Bailey remained the shows highlight as one of the most popular weekly acts.

The Hillsboro Theatre era marked the Opry's transformation into a professional entertainment institution. Performances were scheduled during prime-time hours, maximizing audience reach. With up to 1,756 shows during this stretch, the theater became a proving ground for artists and a testing ground for the Opry's evolving format.

THE OPRY OUTGROWS THE HILLSBORO

BY 1936, NASHVILLE HAD LAID the groundwork for its future as Music City. The Opry supported full-time performers, gave them national exposure, and catalyzed the city's music economy. Acts could now sustain careers from radio appearances, touring, and growing public recognition.

By mid-1936, the had Opry moved to the larger Dixie Tabernacle to accommodate growing crowds. Though short, the Hillsboro era left a permanent mark. Its innovations—structured performances, ticketing, and tighter production—became core elements of the Opry's identity.

6

BECOMING NASHVILLE'S ARTHOUSE

THE 1960S MARKED A PERIOD of sweeping transformation across the United States. Amid civil unrest and cultural upheaval, young Americans increasingly rejected traditional values, embracing activism, art, music, and fashion as vehicles for change. Protest movements, often associated with experimental drug use and postmodern ideologies, emerged in parallel with landmark campaigns for civil rights, gender equality, and sexual liberation.

Nashville, like many cities, became a focal point in this nationwide shift. The civil rights movement gained significant momentum beginning in 1960, when students from Fisk University, Meharry Medical College, American Baptist College, and Tennessee A&I State College (now Tennessee State University) organized sit-ins at segregated lunch counters. Tensions escalated after the bombing of civil rights attorney and city councilman Z. Alexander Looby's home. In response, demonstrators marched to city hall, prompting Mayor Ben West to publicly support desegregation. Leaders such as Diane Nash and John Lewis rose from these actions, helping to shape the national civil rights agenda and laying the groundwork for the Civil Rights and Voting Rights Acts of the mid-1960s.

Amid this backdrop of social change, the Belcourt Theatre evolved to meet the shifting cultural landscape. No longer just a venue for traditional stage productions, the Belcourt increasingly became a space for community dialogue and cultural experimentation.

FIGURE 6.1. Interior of the Belcourt Playhouse remodeled in summer 1962. Visible are the 344 Massey rocker lounger chairs.

FIGURE 6.2. Interior of the Belcourt Playhouse remodeled in summer 1962. Visible are the newly decorated greenery, lighting sconces, playhouse coats of arms, orchestra pit, and Massey rocker lounger chairs.

FIGURE 6.3. Interior of the Belcourt Playhouse remodeled in summer 1962. Visible are the new corner lounge and the iron staircase leading to the second-floor projection booth.

All three photos are from the article "Luxury Seating in Remodeled House," from the July 8, 1963, Boxoffice magazine. Courtesy of the Media History Digital Library, Wisconsin Center for Film and Theater Research at the University of Wisconsin-Madison and the Internet Archive.

TRANSITIONING FROM PLAYHOUSE TO CINEMA

BETWEEN JULY AND SEPTEMBER 1962, the Belcourt underwent a major physical and organizational transformation. Facing mounting financial difficulties, New Theatre Nashville rebranded the space as an "art movie house."[1] Unable to sustain ownership, NTN devised a strategy to lease the theater to a commercial operator while continuing to fundraise toward annexing a smaller proscenium theater adjacent to the main building. That fall, commercial

FIGURE 6.4. Exterior of the remodeled Belcourt Playhouse, summer 1962. Photograph likely from the same photo shoot published in the July 8, 1963, issue of *Boxoffice* magazine. Courtesy of Bob Grannis Photography.

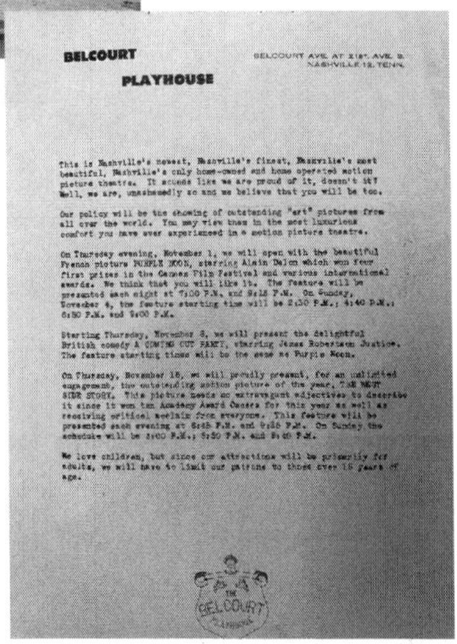

BELCOURT PLAYHOUSE

BELCOURT AVE. AT 21ST. AVE. S.
NASHVILLE 12, TENN.

This is Nashville's newest, Nashville's finest, Nashville's most beautiful, Nashville's only home-owned and home operated motion picture theatre. It sounds like we are proud of it, doesn't it? Well, we are, unashamedly so and we believe that you will be too.

Our policy will be the showing of outstanding "art" pictures from all over the world. You may view them in the most luxurious comfort you have ever experienced in a motion picture theatre.

On Thursday evening, November 1, we will open with the beautiful French picture PURPLE NOON, starring Alain Delon which won four first prizes in the Cannes Film Festival and various international awards. We think that you will like it. The feature will be presented each night at 7:00 P.M. and 9:15 P.M. On Sunday, November 4, the feature starting time will be 2:30 P.M.; 4:40 P.M.; 6:50 P.M. and 9:00 P.M.

Starting Thursday, November 8, we will present the delightful British comedy A COMING OUT PARTY, starring James Robertson Justice. The feature starting times will be the same as Purple Noon.

On Thursday, November 15, we will proudly present, for an unlimited engagement, the outstanding motion picture of the year, THE WEST SIDE STORY. This picture needs no extravagant adjectives to describe it since it won ten Academy Award Oscars for this year as well as receiving critical acclaim from everyone. This feature will be presented each evening at [illegible] P.M. and [illegible] P.M. On Sunday the schedule will be 3:00 P.M.; 5:50 P.M. and 8:40 P.M.

We love children, but since our attractions will be primarily for adults, we will have to limit our patrons to those over 16 years of age.

FIGURE 6.5. October 1962 press release for the first screenings as new arthouse Belcourt Cinema. Nashville Community Playhouse and Theatre Nashville Records. Courtesy of the Special Collections Division, Nashville Public Library.

operator Fred Massey began a ten-year lease of the Belcourt. Under the agreement, NTN would continue staging three plays a year in the original proscenium while relocating most of its activity to the nearby Children's Theatre.[2]

The $150,000 renovation introduced major structural and aesthetic changes to the building. The balcony was removed and converted into an upstairs office wing, accessed by a newly installed iron staircase. Seating capacity was reduced from 550 to 344 with the installation of new Massey Seating Company chairs. The orchestra pit was retained, while the auditorium was redecorated with greenery, lighting sconces, and a coat of arms bearing the venue's new branding, also added to both the theater's interior walls and the building's exterior. The lobby was enhanced with two redecorated terraces featuring café-style seating and a decorative fountain. Exterior archways were also added to the facade, adorned with framed movie posters. With these updates, the building was rebranded as the Belcourt Playhouse: "Sophisticated Entertainment in Superb Comfort."[3]

FIGURE 6.6. Advertisement for the Belcourt Playhouse's first film screening, October 31, 1962. Issued shortly before the theater's rebranding as the Belcourt Cinema. Courtesy of the *Nashville Banner*.

On Halloween night of 1962, the newly christened Belcourt Playhouse hosted its opening celebration and first official film screening since 1927: a preview showing of *Purple Noon* (1960), René Clément's French adaptation of Patricia Highsmith's novel *The Talented Mr. Ripley*.[4] Over the next few months, Massey's film programming quickly gained traction. His third offering, *West Side Story* (Jerome Robbins and Robert Wise, dirs., 1961), proved so popular it was held over for eighty-one days, spanning fall 1962 to winter 1963.

Despite Massey's early success, NTN continued to struggle. Their 1963 season failed to generate the revenue needed to reduce debt or fund their own theater space. To distinguish between the dual functions of the building, Massey branded live events under "Belcourt Playhouse" and films under the new moniker "Belcourt Cinema." However, public confusion about the theater's identity persisted.

Meanwhile, Massey's film lineup grew in both diversity and popularity, particularly among local youth who attended the neighboring universities and were beginning to occupy the aging apartments and single-family homes that had dotted the neighborhood since the 1920s. Screenings held over for weeks, drawing new audiences with titles that explored progressive themes. Among them were *A Taste of Honey* (Tony Richardson, dir., 1961), the cinema's first LGBTQ-themed film, and *David and Lisa* (Frank Perry, dir., 1961), about two institutionalized adolescents in love. *David and Lisa* ran for twenty-eight days.

By 1964, NTN's presence at Belcourt had diminished further. Only two of their five productions that year were held at the theater. Competing for space with Massey's expanding film schedule, NTN began staging performances at alternative venues, including Vanderbilt University and War Memorial Auditorium. Though they continued to receive strong attendance and press, the reliance on temporary venues exacerbated their organizational challenges. In response, New Theatre Nashville launched a capital campaign in 1964 to construct a new annex at the Belcourt: a 210-seat proscenium theater with a 20-by-24-foot stage. The effort was led by local theater figure and Community Playhouse alumnus Sam Tarpley.[5] Ironically, the proposed design, featuring concrete columns and a glass-walled facade, closely resembled the renovations that would be completed during Belcourt's 2016 capital campaign, offering an uncanny preview of changes yet to come.[6]

Even without a permanent home, NTN maintained high production standards and continued its commitment to social progress. In 1964, the company

FIGURE 6.7. Exterior of the Belcourt Cinema, February 1966. Visible in the poster windows are one-sheets advertising screenings of *Mondo Pazzo* (Mondo Cane No. 2), an exploitation documentary that ran from February 17 to March 2, 1966. Metropolitan Development and Housing Agency Slide Collection. Courtesy of the Metropolitan Government Archives of Nashville and Davidson County.

FIGURE 6.8. Hillsboro Village facing 21st Avenue from Blakemore Avenue after the demolition of the Belmont Theatre, 1961. The backside of the Belcourt Playhouse is visible. Metro Photographer Collection #864. Courtesy of the Metropolitan Government Archives of Nashville and Davidson County.

made a significant leap in racial integration. Following the passage of the Civil Rights Act, NTN desegregated the Belcourt Playhouse by opening casting for its production of *Show Boat* to Black performers.[7] Lloyd Lusk, head of the music department at Tennessee A&I State College, was cast as Joe. Sandra Dixon, a Fisk University student studying vocal performance, played Queenie.[8] These casting decisions marked the start of formal partnerships with historically Black institutions in Nashville. The show, produced by Massey, closed after an eleven-day run on September 6.

By 1965, New Theatre Nashville was in steep decline. Burdened by a second mortgage on the Belcourt and significant unsecured debts, the company's plan to build an addition onto the theater stalled. Despite strong leadership and community ties, the fundraising campaign failed to reach its goal.[9] They staged their final Belcourt production—the Joshua Logan and Oscar Hammerstein II musical *South Pacific*—from August 25 to September 5, with Massey again serving as producer.[10]

In August 1966, NTN relocated to a former Veterans Affairs building on White Bridge Road. The venue already housed a stage and dressing rooms and had previously hosted USO shows and live entertainment.[11] Despite modest renovations and five productions staged at the new location, disaster struck. A fire destroyed the venue, causing losses estimated between $30,000 and $50,000.[12]

FIGURE 6.9. Belcourt Cinema flyloft and branding visible from 21st Avenue South, c. 1960s. The Belmont Arts Building, which replaced the Belmont Theatre, is visible on the corner of 21st and Blakemore Avenues. MDHA Slide Collection. Courtesy of the Metropolitan Government Archives of Nashville and Davidson County.

Years of financial mismanagement, unstable leadership, and the final blow of the fire proved insurmountable. Faced with a property tax bill they could not pay, New Theatre Nashville ceased operations.[13]

In October 1966, Fred Massey officially purchased the Belcourt. The $50,000 sale cleared old mortgages, liens, and debts. There were no remaining profits, and Gene Feist, previously embroiled in litigation with NTN, received nothing in settlement. With ownership secured, Massey fully embraced art-house cinema as the Belcourt's new defining identity.[14]

BELCOURT CINEMA BEGINS

IN THE POST–WORLD WAR II ERA, the rising popularity of television led to a steep decline in movie theater attendance during the 1950s. Across the country, many once-grand movie palaces fell into disrepair or were demolished throughout the 1960s and 1970s. Nashville's Belmont Theatre—a former crown jewel of Hillsboro Village—met a similar fate. On March 8, 1961, it screened its final film: *As the Sea Rages* (Horst Hächler, dir., 1959), a German drama.[15]

The Belmont's closure marked the end of an era in Hillsboro Village, but also of a kind of cinema experience slowly dissolving in America: the end of the movie palace. Tony Sudekum's Crescent Amusement Company, which had long dominated local exhibitions, sold forty-six of its forty-seven remaining theaters to the Martin Theatre Company of Columbus, Georgia.[16] The Belmont, excluded from the deal, was acquired instead by Nashville developers H. R. Slaymaker and Wilbur F. Creighton III, who replaced the theater with the Belmont Arts Building, a four-story mid-century modern structure, an early sign of broader development pressures to come.[17]

During its final years, the Belmont had shifted toward programming foreign and independent films, and was increasingly described by local media as an "art theater." Its closure left a vacuum in Nashville's film culture at precisely the moment a new audience was emerging, one drawn to countercultural, international, and underground cinema. Fred Massey recognized this opportunity when he founded the Belcourt Playhouse in 1962.

After formally rebranding it as Belcourt Cinema in 1966, Massey struck a deal with the Martin Theatre Company to program the films. Martin picked up where the Belmont had left off, introducing foreign and independent titles to the Belcourt's screen. This marked the beginning of the venue's modern identity as an arthouse cinema. Even the concession stand reflected this new direction, offering imported European chocolates. The programming soon expanded to include experimental films, retrospectives of classic cinema, and works outside the Hollywood mainstream, attracting a growing community of cinephiles.

Massey's 1966 purchase of the Belcourt also launched Masco Enterprises, a theater chain that would grow to fourteen movie houses by 1974.[18] At the time, he also owned one of the country's largest theater seat manufacturing companies, as well as Fair Park, an amusement park at the Nashville fairgrounds that operated until 1987.

That same year, the boundaries of American cinema were being tested. Films like *The Leather Boys* (Sidney J. Furie, dir., 1964), which played the Belcourt in July 1966 and included explicit allusions to homosexuality, helped break down the long-standing Hollywood Production Code, a system of self-censorship in place since the 1930s. The Belcourt's increasing embrace of socially conscious and transgressive cinema contributed to a growing local interest in global film movements and the emerging "New Hollywood."

As film culture in Nashville shifted toward the avant-garde, pushback from city authorities was not far behind. On July 17, 1966, Sgt. Fred Cobb of the Nashville Police unilaterally shut down a screening of *Who's Afraid*

FIGURE 6.10. Box office sign for Belcourt Cinema Theater I, c. 1960s. Belcourt II would later signify the annexation of the second theater in 1968. Courtesy of Belcourt Theatre.

FIGURE 6.11. Box office sign for Belcourt Cinema advertising ticket prices. Courtesy of Belcourt Theatre.

of Virginia Woolf? (Mike Nichols, dir., 1966) at the Loew's Crescent Theatre, citing indecency. Cobb acted without authorization from police leadership or a formal censorship board. The action shocked audiences, particularly given the film's approval by the Motion Picture Association of America and its uncut showings in other major cities. Nashville officials quickly distanced themselves from Cobb's actions, acknowledging that they lacked legal basis.[19]

The incident sparked broader public debate. Later that month, local teenagers weighed in on whether Tennessee cities should establish film censorship boards. Their responses captured the generational tensions of the time. While some supported censorship as a means of protecting younger viewers, others opposed it on grounds of artistic freedom and personal autonomy. Many instead advocated for age-based ratings as a compromise solution.[20]

BELCOURT TWIN

Belcourt Cinema's early success screening foreign and independent films that could compete with larger theaters in town, like the Loew's Crescent, prompted Massey to expand. On December 15, 1968, a second auditorium,

FIGURE 6.12. Advertisement for Massey Seating Company's rocker lounger seats, 1968. Published in *Boxoffice* magazine. Courtesy of the Media History Digital Library, Wisconsin Center for Film and Theater Research at the University of Wisconsin-Madison and the Internet Archive.

known alternately as "Belcourt II" or the "Belcourt Twin," opened on-site. Designed by architect Francis P. Harper, the new theater reflected mid-century flair. Its color palette featured avocado green and turquoise blue with gold trim. Blue patterned carpeting covered the floors, while wood paneling lined the upper walls and green sound-dampening curtains hung below, suspended from stair-stepped sconces topped with gold lamps. Cascading ferns dotted the space, softening its modern edges.[21]

Seating consisted of 439 tangerine-colored Rocker-Loungers manufactured by Massey's own seating company. Marketed as the "most advanced" seats of the time, they were plush, oversized, permanently mounted rocking chairs, each with an ashtray built into the armrest, reflecting the era's still-permissive attitudes toward smoking in public. Without a balcony, Massey created a new "smoking lounge" in the rear of the theater, a space that, just four years prior, would have still been legally segregated in Nashville. Meanwhile, the original 1925 Hall, then referred to as "Belcourt I," increased its seating to 388, likely due to the removal of the orchestra pit. Additional parking was made possible by demolishing a nearby residential structure.[22]

The Twin's debut feature was *Elvira Madigan* (Bo Widerberg, dir., 1967), a Swedish-language allegory on 1960s dropout culture set in nineteenth-century Denmark. The film ran for twenty-nine days, a respectable performance and a fitting conclusion to a transformative year.[23]

The addition of a second screen played a crucial role in the Belcourt's longevity. Though multi-screen indoor theaters were not new in 1968, they remained uncommon.[24] The expansion allowed Massey to double his offerings, staggering showtimes to encourage double features while maintaining the same staff size. That year, the Motion Picture Association of America introduced a new ratings system—G, M, R, and X—to categorize films based on content. Although the Martin Theatre Company assured Nashvillians they would not exhibit X-rated films locally, Belcourt Cinema did screen some during this period.[25] Films were often classified as adult not due to explicit content like unsimulated sex acts, but rather because of their mature themes. Titles labeled "erotic" or "mature" had some of the most successful runs at the time. *I, a Woman* (Mac Ahlberg, dir., 1965), which ran for forty-two weeks,

FIGURE 6.13. Belcourt Cinema flyloft and branding visible from the west side of 21st Avenue South between Belcourt Avenue and Blakemore Avenue, December 1973. Courtesy of the Metropolitan Development and Housing Agency.

and *Carmen, Baby* (Radley Metzger, dir., 1967), which ran for an impressive fifty-six weeks, became the two longest-running films in this category *and* of the year in 1968.

The survival of neighborhood cinemas into the twenty-first century is rare, especially those originally built as single-screen venues. Many that endured did so by transitioning into adult theaters. By the 1970s, downtown Nashville was home to at least fifteen such venues screening 35mm and 16mm pornography. Establishments like Swinger's World (400 Broadway), Jolar Adult Cinema (404 Broadway), Ellwest Stereo Theatre (408 Broadway), and The Wheel (421 Broadway) became fixtures of Lower Broadway's adult entertainment district.

A common misconception among local lore is that the Belcourt was among these adult theaters. In reality, despite its progressive programming, the Belcourt never pivoted to hardcore pornography. Instead, it remained a hub for serious cinema, sustaining its place in Nashville's film culture through innovation, strategic expansion, and a clear artistic identity.

As historian and media producer Marc K. Stengel, whose great-grandfather Tony Sudekum founded Crescent Amusement Company, later reflected, the 1970s marked a turning point in local cinema culture that reflected larger trends in the exhibition space. "The suburbs were growing," Stengel recalled, "but downtown was evaporating as far as lifestyle . . . and [it] ended up with peep shows—a lot of bad behavior."[26] In contrast, the Belcourt offered an alternative: a forward-looking cinema dedicated not to titillation but to thoughtful, adventurous film.

The 1968 opening of the Belcourt Twin ensured the theater's survival by expanding its programming flexibility and boosting revenue. As Tennessee's first indoor, dual-screen cinema, the Belcourt established a new statewide standard for film exhibition, one that balanced innovation with cultural preservation.

BELCOURT CINEMA (1970S)

The 1970s marked a pivotal decade for Belcourt Cinema, as it solidified its reputation as Nashville's hub for foreign, independent, and countercultural films. Among its devoted patrons was Randall Brady, a lifelong Nashvillian, music lover, and film enthusiast, who first visited the theater in 1966 on a date to see *Julius Caesar* (Joseph L. Mankiewicz, dir., 1953), starring Marlon Brando. That visit marked his introduction to the Belcourt's emerging arthouse programming and sparked a relationship with the theater that has lasted more than five decades.[27]

Throughout the 1970s, Brady became a regular attendee, drawn to the theater's bold, alternative programming. He recalls seeing *200 Motels* (1971), the surrealist musical by Frank Zappa, which screened from February 18 to March 9, 1972. "Hillsboro Village was a place to hang out for a lot of 'long hairs' back in the day," Brady remembers. "You had some what they called 'head shops' and music shops down there—Sergeant Pepper's [music store] sold albums and blacklight posters. You'd go to a movie and just hang out. Go to a pub or something like that. There was a lot of action—a lot of younger people hanging out."

While the Belcourt flourished as a space for artistic exploration, the neighborhood around it became a flashpoint for broader cultural tensions. In October 1970, a high-profile controversy erupted at the nearby Pancake Pantry when owner Robert S. Baldwin denied service to Sam and Marsha Routh, a white couple with a baby, because the father "looked like a hippie." The incident sparked weeks of protest and resulted in twenty-one arrests and a lawsuit. Though no convictions were secured, the episode exposed the friction between Nashville's conservative establishment and the city's shifting cultural landscape, particularly in and around Hillsboro Village.[28]

For singer-songwriter, actress, and author Marshall Chapman, the Belcourt was deeply woven into the creative community she experienced during and after her time at Vanderbilt University (1967–1971). Chapman remained in

FIGURE 6.14. Protest at the Pancake Pantry Restaurant, Hillsboro Village, October 1970. Demonstrators picketed against the owner's policy of denying admission to "hippie" patrons. Syd Levine Demonstration Collection. Courtesy of the Metropolitan Government Archives of Nashville and Davidson County.

Nashville and became a fixture in its evolving music scene, collaborating with artists such as Rodney Crowell, Guy Clark, and John Prine. Her memories of the Belcourt are both professional and personal. "I lived at 3008 Dudley Avenue. Vanderbilt got that neighborhood condemned so they could supposedly grow," she recalls. "Guy and Susanna Clark were right up the street. Townes Van Zandt—one of the most brilliant songwriters ever to come through Nashville—he was in the neighborhood." Chapman remembers the Belcourt as a space for artistic exploration: "It was just where you'd go to see weird movies—films, like [Ingmar Bergman's] *Cries and Whispers* (1972)."[29]

From 1973 to 1974, during the final years of the Belcourt's X-rated programming era, theater management and programming were led by Gene Nash, a former actor, writer, musician, and director, and an alumnus of both the Nashville Community Playhouse and New Theatre Nashville. At the time, Nash was transitioning out of a brief but notable independent filmmaking career that had earned him local recognition, taken him to Hollywood, and secured national distribution. He had written, directed, and composed the soundtracks for two films that received national attention: *What Am I Bid?* (1967), a fictional country music film starring Tex Ritter and Faron Young; and *Dinah East* (1970), an X-rated feature praised by the *Los Angeles Times* as "hilarious camp on one level and poignant chronicle on another."[30]

Gene Nash became deeply involved in the logistical and political challenges of screening non-mainstream cinema in Middle Tennessee. During his tenure at the Belcourt, he addressed these issues publicly through interviews on WPLN and responses to columns in *The Tennessean*, highlighting the complexities of securing film rights and navigating the region's limited distribution infrastructure.[31] Nash also spoke candidly about the risks of programming controversial or countercultural films, and the careful distinctions the theater made under his leadership.

In one column, Nash cited the example of Frank Zappa's *200 Motels*, a screening that attracted a disruptive audience—vandals who destroyed twenty to thirty seats. The incident soured the theater's interest in similar live music documentaries and influenced the decision not to screen films like *Rainbow Bridge* (Chuck Wein, dir., 1971), which featured Jimi Hendrix and focused on the counterculture in Maui.[32]

Beyond administrative duties, Nash positioned himself as a cultural advocate. He worked to educate audiences about the inner workings of the film

FIGURE 6.15. Crowds outside the Belcourt Cinema for the first showing of *Last Tango in Paris*, July 27, 1973. Hundreds lined up to see the X-rated film starring Marlon Brando; many were turned away after both screenings sold out, with an estimated eight to nine hundred unable to obtain tickets. © Robert Johnson, USA TODAY NETWORK via Imagn Images.

promotion system, sometimes organizing curated screenings or pre-filmed celebrity introductions to deepen the artistic impact of the theater's offerings.[33] His programming expanded Nashville's cinematic horizons, encouraging audiences to engage with international, independent, and controversial films.

Nash was consistently a curator and educator, committed to raising cinematic literacy in Nashville despite ongoing challenges such as censorship, limited access to prints, and local skepticism toward art cinema. At the Belcourt, he became a defining figure in shaping Nashville's evolving film culture during a transformative era in American cinema.

That commitment to daring cinema reached a public climax on July 27, 1973, when the Belcourt Twin premiered *Last Tango in Paris*, starring Marlon Brando. The theater screened the uncut version of the controversial film, drawing crowds that lined up around the block.[34] Determined to get ahead of the controversy, Massey staged a prescreening of the film where he explained the difference between the censored and uncut versions of the film. He then conducted an audience survey and tallied that 90 percent of the audience was in favor of the uncut version, signifying its artist merits with Nashville audiences.[35]

It quickly became one of the most talked-about releases of the year. The timing was significant: just weeks earlier, the US Supreme Court had ruled that states could ban printed or visual material deemed to lack "serious literary, artistic, political, or scientific value," a vague enough statement that threatened to put the exhibition of arthouse films in peril. In response, local officials, including Nashville district attorney general Thomas Shriver, assistant attorney general Richard McCully, assistant police chief William St. John, and attorneys Tom Moon and Hayes Cooney, began drafting new state legislation to bring Tennessee's pornography laws in line with the updated federal standards.[36]

Roughly a month into the film's engagement, the Tennessee attorney general launched an investigation to determine whether *Last Tango in Paris* violated state obscenity laws, but never appeared at a screening.[37] Despite the scrutiny, the film was ultimately deemed permissible and remained on screen for sixty-three days, the longest theatrical run at the Belcourt that year.

The following year marked a turning point in leadership. On May 23, 1974, Fred H. Massey, founder of MASCO Theatres and the visionary behind the Belcourt's transformation into a leading arthouse venue, died of a heart attack while attending a convention in Williamsburg, Virginia. He was survived by his wife, Dorothy Sweeney Massey; daughters, Laura and Emily; and sons, Brett and Wade, who assumed management of the theater.[38] At the time of his death, MASCO operated a dominant chain of single- and twin-screen neighborhood and drive-in cinemas across Middle Tennessee, including Rivergate Cinema, Franklin Cinema, Columbia's Polk Theatre, Lebanon's Capitol Theatre and Cedar Drive-In, Shelbyville's Capri Twin Theatre and 41 Drive-In, and the Springfield Cinema.

Despite the loss of its founder, the Belcourt continued to flourish. In its first two decades as a cinema, the theater introduced Nashville audiences to groundbreaking filmmakers such as Ingmar Bergman and Akira Kurosawa, opening new cinematic worlds for thousands of viewers. Special screenings, retrospectives, and festivals became regular features, positioning the Belcourt not just as an entertainment venue, but also as a center for cultural dialogue and film education.

By the close of the 1970s, Belcourt Cinema had become more than a neighborhood theater; it was a cornerstone of Nashville's evolving artistic identity, shaped by the countercultural forces of the era and preserved by the dedication of its patrons and community.

7

NASHVILLE'S FILM CULTURE

LITTLE INK HAS BEEN SPILLED on Nashville's role in the first hundred years of American film culture. As the city's oldest neighborhood theater, a place for all the encompassing art forms, industry, and cultural experience surrounding films, the nexus of much of the city's place in creating in the medium of motion pictures, it is the Belcourt Theatre and the local people who support it who have given it meaning. The city's film culture encompasses the city being the topic of films, a site where films are made, and a place where filmmakers are produced, and how each—topic, place, and maker—has reflected and shaped cultural values, beliefs, and trends. The city and its people's contributions to filmmaking, though often overlooked, have been vital both locally, regionally, and nationally in transmitting culture, influencing attitudes, behaviors, and perceptions. Nashville as a topic of films has reflected the anxieties, beliefs, and values of the people producing the images, as well as the audiences that consume them.

Since the 1950s, most fictionalized films made in the city have been dramas, more than 150. And beginning in the 1970s, most of the filmmaking that has taken place inside Nashville has been narratively driven by some specific aspect of the city's specific or adjacent music culture. The lion's share of filmmaking in Nashville has centered around documentaries, mostly concert performances or biographical profiles on artists and the industry that supports them. Almost three hundred of these features have been made, many centering artists that have called the city home at some point in their lives.

1910S AND 1920S

AS NASHVILLE QUICKLY BECAME A major hub for film exhibition in Tennessee and the South, local interest in the filmmaking process grew. With the medium still in its infancy, Nashvillians began experimenting with film production, turning the city into both a creative site and a subject of early cinema. Residents became not only audiences and exhibitors but also filmmakers and performers, helping shape the foundations of a regional film culture. During the first quarter of the twentieth century, Nashville produced several notable figures from the silent era, including actors Alan Roscoe (1886–1933) and Cullen Landis (1896–1975), both of whom appeared in, and in Landis's case, also directed, more than one hundred films. By the 1910s, Nashville was emerging as a site of film production with ambitions that reached both regional and national audiences.

Among the first to bridge Nashville's literary and cinematic cultures was Opie Read, born in the city on December 22, 1852. A prolific writer, journalist, and humorist, Read gained national recognition for his storytelling, which often reflected the cultural tensions of the post–Civil War South.[1] Though his literary reputation has faded, his work played a formative role in introducing Southern themes to the silver screen. Read adapted his novel *The Starbucks* (William J. Bauman, dir., 1912) into a two-reel silent film produced by the American Film Manufacturing Company in Santa Barbara, California.[2] While the film was never shown in his hometown, it did screen in Chattanooga, marking one of the earliest instances of a Nashville-born author bringing local storytelling into the emerging medium of motion pictures.[3]

Read's influence continued into the 1920s with two additional film adaptations: *The Kentucky Colonel* (William A. Seiter, dir., 1920) and *The Jucklins* (George Melford, dir., 1921). Although neither was filmed in Nashville, *Jucklins*, inspired by Read's early years in nearby Gallatin and set in the city, was screened for three days at Nashville's Fifth Avenue Theatre.[4] These early adaptations positioned Read as a bridge between Nashville's literary culture and the rise of American cinema. His embrace of film as a storytelling medium places him at a key juncture in the city's cinematic history, even as his legacy remains entangled with the racial ideologies embedded in his work.

Simultaneously, Black performers in Nashville were also beginning to shape national stage and screen culture. While attending Fisk University in the 1910s, Irvin Colloden Miller, Flournoy Eakin "F. E." Miller, and Aubrey Lyles honed their craft on Nashville's theater stages, including the Bijou, before rising to national prominence. The vaudeville duo formed by F. E. Miller and Lyles during their student years became a lasting partnership that would help transform American theater and film. Later all three worked together on a self-scripted, -produced, and -starred-in 1921 Broadway production, *Shuffle Along*, which was groundbreaking, marking a turning point for Black performance on the national stage.

Its success helped launch a new era of Black-led theater and directly influenced the emergence of studio-produced Hollywood musicals in the decades to follow, culminating in films like *Stormy Weather* (Andrew L. Stone, dir., 1943), loosely based on the life of tap legend Bill "Bojangles" Robinson. Featuring an all-Black ensemble cast, including Lena Horne, the Nicholas Brothers, and Cab Calloway, the film also featured F. E. Miller, whose performance reflected the vaudeville style he had helped pioneer. Playing a version of himself, Miller appeared opposite actor Johnny Lee, who portrayed his late partner Lyles, bringing their local and national legacy full circle on screen.

Beyond narrative fiction, early documentary efforts also positioned Nashville as a visual subject in national exhibitions. In 1914, L. Bernstein of the Southern Industrial Film Company announced plans to produce a documentary promoting Nashville's civic beauty and economic promise.[5] The film was created for exhibition at the Panama-Pacific Exposition in San Francisco, a world's fair held to celebrate the opening of the Panama Canal and showcase American progress on a global stage. National film companies also recognized Nashville's appeal. That same year, the Bon Ray Film Company, based in Long Island, New York, sent cinematographer Otto C. Gilmore and director S. I. Conner to Tennessee as field representatives for the Tennessee Exposition Commission. Tasked with capturing twenty thousand feet of film across Memphis, Knoxville, Chattanooga, and Nashville, they dedicated seven thousand feet, the largest share, to the state capital.[6]

Their footage included 1,500 children gathered in Centennial Park, panoramic shots from the State Capitol, and multiple angles of the Hermitage, the former home of President Andrew Jackson.[7] The completed footage premiered the next year inside the Tennessee Building at the Panama-Pacific Exposition, itself modeled as an exact replica of the Hermitage.[8] These efforts introduced Nashville's landscape and cultural identity to a national audience, reinforcing the city's role in the early development of American cinema.

At the same time, local institutions were stepping into film production as well. The Crescent Amusement Company, best known for operating theaters across the South, began creating short films and newsreels that documented civic life. In 1914, Crescent staged a public filming event outside their Fifth Avenue Theatre, gathering hundreds of locals to be captured on camera as they entered and exited the building, premiering the footage three days later to the same local audience, inside the same theater.[9] This rapid production-to-exhibition cycle marked a local milestone in early film history. It demonstrated not only the city's growing appetite for cinema but also its emerging role as a producer of moving images, not just a consumer of them. Fred Carter was a cinematographer for the Crescent Amusement Company, which documented life in Middle Tennessee through newsreels. His 1914 footage of Nashville's suffrage parades and prohibition protests captured the city in motion, preserving moments of resistance and activism that were still new to the silver screen.[10]

Carter's films preserved moments of local activism on screen, capturing a spirit of civic engagement that has remained part of Nashville's identity for over a century. In 2020, the Nashville Public Library opened a permanent exhibit in its main branch dedicated to the city's pivotal role in the passage of the Nineteenth Amendment, which granted women the right to vote. Titled *Votes for Women: The Legacy of the Nineteenth Amendment*, the exhibit highlights the enduring impact of Nashville's suffrage movement and its place in the broader history of American democracy.

The city's growing film culture reached a milestone in 1915 with the release of *Sam Davis, the Hero of Tennessee*, the first feature film written, produced, and shot entirely in Nashville. Directed by S. I. Conner and written by Lillian Nicholson Shearon, the five-reel silent film was shot entirely on location using an estimated three hundred or more local actors.[11] The film dramatized the life and execution of Confederate soldier Sam Davis, portraying him as a martyr. The film served as a powerful example of Lost Cause mythology, romanticizing Davis's loyalty and presenting him as a Christlike figure, a narrative reflective of broader regional and national attitudes at the time.

Its cast featured members of Nashville's theatrical and civic community, including actors from the Stagecrafters Drama Club such as W. B. Shearon, Vanderbilt students Russell A. Rose and L. F. Sperry, and members of prominent entertainment families like Lucille and Clarence Sudekum, relatives of the Crescent Amusement Company's founders.[12] This collaboration between civic leaders, theater professionals, and early filmmakers signaled Nashville's arrival as a full participant in the new American film industry.

1920S AND 1930S

BY THE 1920S, THE HOLLYWOOD studio system had become a dominant force, drawing actors from across the country with the promise of stardom. Studios controlled nearly every aspect of filmmaking, from casting and production to distribution and exhibition, creating a vertically integrated system that left little room for feature film production outside of Hollywood. With major studios owning many of the theaters where films were shown, independent projects in cities like Nashville struggled to gain traction. As a result, no record exists of feature-length films being made in Nashville during the 1920s, apart from newsreels.

Still, the city remained creatively active, contributing to the industry through its talent rather than its business infrastructure. One notable figure was Carman Barnes, a teenage author and student at Ward-Belmont School between 1924 and 1925. While enrolled, Barnes wrote *Schoolgirl*, a provocative novel loosely based on her experiences at the school, including depictions of romantic and sexual relationships between female students. The book's controversial content and runaway success led to her expulsion from Ward-Belmont, and later from the school she transferred to.

Schoolgirl became an international bestseller and caught the attention of Paramount Pictures. In 1931, Jesse L. Lasky, first vice president in charge of production for Paramount Publix, announced that the eighteen-year-old Barnes had been offered a studio contract to adapt her novel for both stage and screen, with plans for her to star in the film.[13] Paramount, which was also home to stars like Tallulah Bankhead, saw in Barnes both literary and screen potential. However, the film was never greenlit, and her relationship with Hollywood fizzled shortly thereafter.

Though brief, Barnes's encounter with the studio system signaled a larger trend: Nashville's creative voices, and its evolving cultural identity, were beginning to register within national film circles, even if the city had not yet become a production center.

As the industry transitioned to sound in the 1930s, Nashville continued to produce actors who made their mark in Hollywood. Among the most notable was Nashville native Lucille La Verne (1872–1945), best remembered for voicing both the Evil Queen and the Witch in Walt Disney's groundbreaking animated feature *Snow White and the Seven Dwarfs* (1937). Her performance became a defining moment in early sound animation, establishing a new standard for vocal character acting. Fellow Tennessean and Grand Ole Opry member Zeke Clements also contributed to the film, lending his yodeling voice to the character of Bashful, uncredited but historically significant.[14]

At the same time, local theater remained a training ground for aspiring screen talent. A few actors from Nashville's stage scene, particularly those affiliated with the Nashville Community Playhouse, found their way to Hollywood during this time and in the decades to come. La Una Gay Parkes and Lona Andre both trained at the Playhouse and were selected as part of the WAMPAS Baby Stars program, a national promotional campaign run by the Western Association of Motion Picture Advertisers from 1922 to 1934 (excluding 1930 and 1933).[15] Each year, WAMPAS named a class of young women deemed poised for stardom. While not all achieved lasting fame, including Parkes, the campaign launched careers for several actors, including East Tennessee-born Jobyna Ralston, a 1923 WAMPAS Baby Star, featured in the first Academy Award–winning film, *Wings* (William A. Wellman and Harry d'Abbadie d'Arrast, dirs., 1927), and frequent co-star to silent film icon Harold Lloyd.

Parkes began her stage career in children's theater, appearing in *The Magic Tinder Box* (a Hans Christian Andersen adaptation in 1934), *Orgets in the Air* by Frances Fullerton Neilson in 1935, Harold Selman's adaptation of the *Cinderella* folk tale in 1935, *The Patchwork Girl of Oz* by Mrs. James Waller Marshall in 1933 and 1938, and Muriel Brown's *Oliver Twist* in 1940. She also worked behind the scenes in production and took adult roles in the Nashville Experimental Theatre and the Community Playhouse, including *Forsaking All Others* (1933) in 1934, *Stage Door* (1936) in 1938, and the 1934 Ayn Rand play *Night of January 16th* in 1938.

Lona Andre, selected as a WAMPAS Baby Star in 1932, signed a contract with Paramount the following year. Over a fourteen-year career, she appeared in forty-nine feature films, often taking supporting roles in major productions or leads in lower-budget fare. Her credits include *School for Girls*

(William Nigh, dir., 1934), where she co-starred with Lucille La Verne, and the exploitation film *Slaves in Bondage* (Elmer Clifton, dir., 1937).

By the close of the 1930s, Nashville Community Playhouse had emerged as a place where performers could prepare for the national stage and continue their impact on American film. Additionally, Nashville had secured its place as the epicenter of country music, largely due to the rising influence of the Grand Ole Opry. With the expansion of radio and the advent of sound in cinema, Hollywood began turning its attention to the city's musical culture. Opry performers, already beloved on stage and radio, began crossing into film, particularly in Westerns, bridging the gap between Nashville's live performance tradition and its emerging screen presence.

1940S AND 1950S

THE FIRST CREDITED OPRY STARS to appear on the silver screen were Gene Autry, Pee Wee King, and the Golden West Cowboys, who starred in *Gold Mine in the Sky* (Joseph Kane, dir., 1938). Just a year later, Hillsboro Theatre–era comedy duo Sarie and Sallie appeared in *In Old Monterey* (Joseph Kane, dir., 1939). Their transition from radio and live performance to film illustrated how country music entertainers, and Nashville itself, were becoming viable screen personalities in their own right, able to shape on-screen identities.

That momentum accelerated in 1940, when the Opry became the subject of a Hollywood-produced motion picture dramatizing the show's history and cultural influence. Titled *The Grand Ole Opry*, the film was produced and headlined by longtime announcer and co-founder George D. Hay. The production featured key Hillsboro-era acts, including Uncle Dave Macon and his son Dorris, and captured the Opry's rise following its relocation to a more professional setting at the Hillsboro Theatre.

These early portrayals signaled a broader cultural transition: Nashville was no longer just a regional entertainment hub. Its music, people, and performance culture were gaining national recognition, and the city was beginning to establish a brand in American popular culture. It also demonstrated that Nashville could produce talent and stories capable of contributing to the expanding and increasingly interconnected industries of film and music.

Meanwhile, the Hollywood studio system reached its peak during the 1940s. Controlled by five major studios, MGM, Paramount, Warner Bros.,

FIGURE 7.1. Delbert Mann receiving the Oscar for Best Director for *Marty*, 1955, at the 28th Academy Awards. Delbert Mann Collection. Courtesy of Vanderbilt University Special Collections.

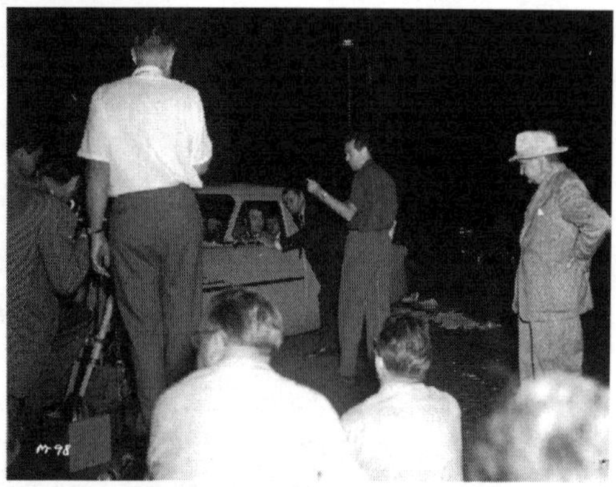

FIGURE 7.2. Director Delbert Mann (center foreground) with Community Playhouse and Children's Theatre alumnus Frank Sutton (seated in the driver's seat) on the set of *Marty* (1955), as the film's star Ernest Borgnine leans into the car window. Delbert Mann Collection. Courtesy of Vanderbilt University Special Collections.

FIGURE 7.3. Frances Rose Shore on the set of *The Dinah Shore Show*, National Broadcasting Company, New York City, 1955–1956. Ralph G. Morrissey Collection. Courtesy of the Tennessee Historical Society Collection, Tennessee State Library and Archives.

RKO, and Twentieth Century Fox, and three smaller studios, Universal, Columbia, and United Artists, the system continued to maintain its vertically integrated model, controlling production, distribution, and exhibition. World War II initially bolstered box office sales, but by the late 1940s, the industry faced significant challenges.

Nashville, like other cities, had studio-operated theaters such as the Paramount, a $400,000 movie palace on Church Street that opened in 1930.[16] However, Nashville remained largely outside Hollywood's production ecosystem, continuing primarily as a source of talent rather than a filming location.

During this time, several Nashville-born actors gained national attention. Howard Caine (1926–1993), discovered at age thirteen by Vendome Theatre employee Coleman Harwell, left for New York City to study acting but remained tied to his Nashville roots.[17] He appeared in Delbert Mann's 1953 television production of *Marty* for *Philco Television Playhouse*, a project that would later earn Mann multiple Academy Awards (for Best Screenplay, Actor, Director, and Picture) and the Palme d'Or for its 1955 film adaptation. Caine also acted in *Judgment at Nuremberg* (Stanley Kramer, dir., 1961), alongside Marlene Dietrich and Burt Lancaster.

Another Nashville native, Claude Jarman Jr., got his start at the Belcourt Theatre with the Nashville Children's Theatre, appearing in productions like Adam T. Rice's play *The Garden Circus* in 1944. Discovered by MGM while attending Eakin Elementary, he won a special Academy Award, "Outstanding Child Actor," for his performance in *The Yearling* (Clarence Brown, dir., 1946).[18]

James Craig (1912–1985), also from Nashville, built his career as a contract actor for Paramount and MGM, later transitioning into Westerns and television in the 1950s and 1960s. During this time, it was not uncommon for established Hollywood actors to mentor emerging actors into the complex star system. Nashville starlet Lucille Knox (1923–1990) was the recipient of this golden-age mentorship by Paulette Goddard, by then well known for her role in *The Women* (George Cukor, dir., 1939), a groundbreaking film notable for its all-female cast and its roots in the work of playwright Clare Boothe Luce.[19]

Dinah Shore, born Frances "Fanny" Rose Shore, began her career onstage at the Nashville Community Playhouse in Fritz Kleibacker-directed productions. Before becoming a household name as the top-selling female vocalist of the 1940s, Shore honed her stage presence locally, appearing in late-1930s

Playhouse productions such as *What Price Glory* (1924) and *Stage Door* (1936). This theatrical experience helped pave the way for her breakthrough in radio, film, and television, and in part fueled her subsequent success in major Hollywood studio musicals *Thank Your Lucky Stars* (David Butler, dir., 1943), *Up in Arms* (Elliott Nugent, dir., 1944), and *Make Mine Music* (Robert Cormack et al., dir., 1946). Over the course of her career, she appeared in more than ten feature films and hosted a string of popular television variety shows that spanned from the 1950s into the 1990s.

In *Three Guys Named Mike* (Charles Walters, dir., 1951), a romantic comedy centered on a flight attendant pursued by three suitors, Nashville served primarily as a backdrop. Scenes shot at Berry Field, Nashville's municipal airport, lent realism to the film's aviation theme but gave the city little narrative significance. In contrast, *Davy Crockett* (Norman Foster, dir., 1955) featured scenes at the Hermitage, Andrew Jackson's home, embedding Nashville more deeply into the storyline and linking it to broader national conversations about history, frontier mythology, and American identity. While these productions reflected Hollywood's occasional interest in Nashville, the city had yet to emerge as a true center for film production.

Meanwhile, the film industry was undergoing seismic changes. From 1946 to 1952, average weekly movie attendance in the US dropped rapidly, from about ninety million to fifty-two million.[20] Contributing factors included the rise of suburbanization, driven in part by the GI Bill, and the spread of television. The 1948 Supreme Court case *United States v. Paramount Pictures* forced studios to divest from theater ownership, ending vertical integration and reducing production output.[21]

International pressures also took a toll. In 1947, the British government imposed a 75 percent tax on American films, cutting studios off from a major market and threatening to reduce global profits by 20 percent.[22] In response to these complex and mounting pressures on the industry, the Council of Motion Picture Organizations launched "Movietime U.S.A.," a campaign that sent celebrities across the country to promote Hollywood at the grassroots level. From 1951 to 1953, the campaign included regional tours.[23]

In Tennessee, Claude Jarman Jr. and James Craig served as campaign ambassadors. They met with governor Gordon Browning and toured seventeen cities, using their local roots to bridge Hollywood and home.[24] At the same time, the Motion Picture Industry Council (MPIC) emerged to promote anticommunist messaging through cinema, positioning film as a defender of democracy during the Cold War.[25]

While film production lagged locally, television offered a new platform for Nashville talent. Dick Dudley (born Casper Bernard Kuhn Jr.) transitioned from the Children's Theatre to appearances on the Fred Coe–produced NBC series *Mister Peepers*, and as a guest announcer on *The Price Is Right*, one of the longest-running television shows in American history. Minnie Pearl and Dinah Shore, already established stars, appeared on NBC's documentary series *This Is Your Life*, further cementing the city's influence in helping emerging media.

1960S AND 1970S

DURING THE 1960S, ALUMNI OF Nashville's Community Playhouse and Children's Theatre continued to build careers as they transitioned from stage to television and film. Among them was puppeteer Tom Tichenor, who made his mark in New York City after his Nashville years.

Tichenor spent seven years in New York. In 1960, he auditioned his puppets for the Broadway production of *Carnival!*, a breakthrough that brought national attention. The production earned him a *Life* magazine cover story, a series of television appearances, and, in 1964, his own ABC show, *The Mysterious Magical Miracle Box* (1963–1967). At the same time, he was also performing on the WNBC-TV children's program *Birthday House* (1963–1967).

Others, like Fred Coe, moved into Hollywood film production. Coe's work included the Academy Award–winning film *The Miracle Worker* (Arthur Penn, dir., 1962) which also featured Little Theatre Guild co-founder Madge West Joseph. Coe continued collaborating with Patty Duke, star of *The Miracle Worker*, on the Golden Globe–winning *Me, Natalie* (Fred Coe, dir., 1969), strengthening his role as a connector between Nashville's theater scene and major studio productions.

While Coe found success in traditional studio films, a broader transformation was underway. The 1960s and '70s ushered in a wave of countercultural filmmaking led by directors like Francis Ford Coppola, Martin Scorsese, and Robert Altman. Rejecting conventional Hollywood formulas, these filmmakers embraced personal, boundary-pushing narratives. In Nashville, this era gave rise to a parallel trend: the "Hick Flick."[26]

The Hick Flick era became one of Nashville's most active periods in film production. Often produced on tight budgets by local talent, these exploitation films focused on Southern culture, regional stereotypes, and sensational themes. Distributed through neighborhood theaters and drive-ins, they found eager national audiences. Together with the rise of counterculture cinema, these films positioned Nashville as a distinctive voice in American film.

Hollywood also continued tapping into Nashville's influence. Studio films like *Hootenanny Hoot* (Gene Nelson, dir., 1963), featuring Sheb Wooley and Johnny Cash, and *The Fastest Guitar Alive* (Michael D, Moore, dir., 1967), starring Roy Orbison, were filmed in California but centered around Nashville's music stars, reinforcing the city's screen presence.

Within Nashville, country music insiders began producing their own films. Audrey Williams, wife of Hank Williams, launched Marathon Pictures Corporation in 1963 and produced films like *Country Music on Broadway* (Victor Duncan, dir., 1963), featuring herself, Hank Sr., and Hank Jr. These projects were essentially concert films, with little emphasis on plot. Marathon's second film, *Second Fiddle to a Steel Guitar* (Victor Duncan, dir., 1965), also shot in Nashville, included stars like Kitty Wells, Minnie Pearl, and Faron Young before the company dissolved.

Other locals followed suit. Albert C. Gannaway produced *Country Music Caravan* (1964), a revue-style film also shot in Nashville. These projects paved the way for a wave of music-centered productions tied to the city.

By the mid-1960s, the Ormond Organization had risen to prominence as pioneer auteurs of the Hick Flick genre, employing some of the biggest names in country music, Nashville's theater scene, and the local television production universe. Ron Ormond directed *Forty Acre Feud* (1965), starring Ferlin Husky and Del Reeves, and *Girl from Tobacco Row* (1966), starring Tex Ritter and Ralph Emery, utilizing WSM-TV and Bradley Studios cameraman Sid O'Berry to shoot it. More films and filmmakers followed: *Country Boy* (Joseph Kane, dir., 1966), with Skeeter Davis, and *Las Vegas Hillbillys* (Arthur C. Pierce. dir., 1966), featuring Ferlin Husky and Wilma Burgess.

These films often reused cast members and Nashville landmarks. For example, *That Tennessee Beat* (Richard Brill, dir., 1966), starring Pete Drake, co-starred Community Playhouse alum Sam Tarpley and Minnie Pearl, who would log many on-screen moments together during this time. *Hillbillys in a Haunted House* (Jean Yarbrough, dir., 1967), featured Sonny James and the

FIGURE 7.4. Promotional film still of Sam Tarpley (center) and Minnie Pearl (left) on the set of *Forty Acre Feud* (1965) with co-star Ferlin Husky (right). Belcourt Theatre Collection. Courtesy of Vanderbilt University Special Collections.

convertible famously owned by Webb Pierce, his "silver dollar" car, since displayed at the Country Music Hall of Fame. Others, like *Smokey and the Good Time Outlaws* (Alexander Grasshoff, dir., 1978), again featuring Sam Tarpley, continued the tradition into the next decade.

Throughout the 1970s, Nashville filmmakers continued producing exploitation films grounded in regional identity. As the decade progressed, Nashville evolved from a backdrop to a central on-screen character. The city's music, people, and culture became essential to storytelling. This visibility was bolstered by the continued popularity of independent Hick Flicks and the rise of made-for-TV movies in the 1980s. Whether through genre films or television, Nashville stayed in the national spotlight.

Sam Tarpley started the decade with *The Delta Factor* (Tay Garnett, dir., 1970), a spy thriller with a hillbilly bend shot in Nashville. The film followed CIA agents rescuing a kidnapped scientist, and its title song was penned by local songwriter Lawton Williams, a testament to the integration of Music City talent both on and off screen.[27]

Other music industry figures also explored filmmaking. Jack Clement produced the Southern Gothic slasher *Dear Dead Delilah* (John Farris, dir., 1972), starring Agnes Moorehead, best known for her role as Endora on the hit television show *Bewitched*, in her final role. The film, shot around

Nashville and Brentwood, premiered at the Paramount Theatre on Church Street and had a regional release across twenty nearby cities.[28] Initially rated X by the MPAA, it was later adjusted to an R, reflecting the hurdles faced by independent productions.[29]

Wes Bishop, born Charles Pellettieri and nephew of the Opry's first stage manager when it was resident at Hillsboro, was another local exploitation filmmaker. Starting with Circle Theatre, he partnered with Lee Frost to direct two drive-in hits: *The Thing with Two Heads* (1972) and *Dixie Dynamite* (1976).

The era's most iconic film, however, was Robert Altman's *Nashville* (1975). Using the city as both setting and subject, Altman crafted a sweeping narrative of twenty-four characters navigating politics, fame, and performance. The film culminated at Nashville's Parthenon with a shocking political assassination attempt, highlighting the blurred line between entertainment and violence.

Controversial upon release, the film drew criticism from Nashville leaders and country stars but received national acclaim. Today, it's considered a cinematic milestone. Among the cast were Karen Black and Keith Carradine, who had debuted in *A Gunfight* (Lamont Johnson, dir., 1971) with Johnny Cash. Nashville-based musician Steve Earle and, again, Sam Tarpley made uncredited appearances.

Earle later returned to the Belcourt Theatre in 2002 to stage his play *Karla*, under the artistic direction of Jeremy Childs and produced by Broad Axe Theatre, based on the life of Karla Faye Tucker, the first woman executed in Texas in over a century.[30] The following year, Earle joined the *Tell Us the Truth* tour with Billy Bragg, Lester Chambers, and American film director Boots Riley, representing the Communication Workers of America and Screen Actors Guild unions, promoting media regulation reform.[31]

Though the official local premier of *Nashville* took place at the Martin's 100 Oaks Theatre, Altman himself arranged a private press screening of *Nashville* at Belcourt Cinema, just before its national release. Coordinated with Johnny Rosen of Fanta Professional Services and Belcourt programmers, the event honored local cast and crew.[32] Since then, the Belcourt has helped preserve the film's legacy, hosting over thirty screenings with guests like Lily Tomlin and Keith Carradine, and panel discussions featuring screenwriter Joan Tewkesbury and Exit/In historian Stephen Thompson.

Another major 1970s film shot in the city was *W. W. and the Dixie Dancekings* (John G. Avildsen, dir., 1975), a heist comedy starring Burt Reynolds. Featuring Jerry Reed, Mel Tillis, Don Williams, and Motown singer Conny Van Dyke, the film celebrated Southern identity. At the time, Reynolds had recorded a country album, titled *Ask Me What I Am*, with Buddy Killen and the Nashville Cats, and was romantically linked to Dinah Shore.[33]

Set in the South with a country soundtrack, *W. W. and the Dixie Dancekings* reflected the decade's fascination with the "good ol' boy" image, a trend continued by *Smokey and the Bandit* (Hal Needham, dir., 1977). The film used Nashville as more than a backdrop; it embraced the city as a character, helping to define its cinematic identity for national audiences.

1980S AND 1990S

NASHVILLE RETURNED TO THE NATIONAL spotlight at the start of the 1980s with *Coal Miner's Daughter* (Michael Apted, dir., 1980), the acclaimed biopic of country music legend Loretta Lynn. Starring Sissy Spacek and Tommy Lee Jones, the film was shot across multiple locations, including the Ryman Auditorium, where Lynn is depicted performing on the Grand Ole Opry stage.

Like Robert Altman before him, director Michael Apted incorporated local talent into the production. Among the cast was Alice McGeachy (1929–2011), a member of Nashville's Circle Theatre who had spent nearly four decades with the company.[34] Her participation reflected the filmmakers' intention to root the story in authentic regional voices and performance traditions. The film bridged local culture with national cinematic recognition, making Nashville both a setting and a subject.

Nashville's most unexpected pop culture phenomenon of the era, and likely, most well known of the twentieth century, is the Ernest P. Worrell franchise, a comedic universe that lasted from 1980 to 1998 and included television commercials, ten feature films, and a network television series. Created by actor Jim Varney and the Nashville-based agency Carden & Cherry, the character became a national sensation. Varney earned an Emmy Award for his performance and also voiced Slinky Dog in Disney's *Toy Story* franchise.

Hey Vern, It's Ernest!, a CBS spin-off, aired for one season in 1988 and gained a following through reruns in the early 1990s. Filmed in both Nashville

FIGURE 7.5. Invitation for local crew and press for the premiere screening of *Ernest Scared Stupid* (1991) at the Belcourt Theatre. Courtesy of Alec Klapper.

and Burbank, it featured Bruce Arntson as Mike the Clown and Existo the Magician. The Existo character inspired the cult film *Existo* (Coke Sams, dir., 1999), shot in Nashville and starring local theater figures like Jeremy Childs, Barry Scott, and David Alford. In 1999, Scott returned to the Belcourt stage after a thirty-year hiatus with his performance in *Stuff*. Alford, co-founder of Mockingbird Theatre, later appeared in local films *Stoker* (Park Chan-wook, dir., 2013) and *Closer to God* (Billy Senese, dir., 2014).

Co-written by Arntson and Coke Sams, *Existo* garnered national media attention, including coverage in *Variety*. Its soundtrack, composed by Arntson, laid the groundwork for *The Doyle & Debbie Show*, co-starring Jenny Littleton. A satirical musical about iconic country duos, the show ran nearly every week from 2006 to 2020 at the Station Inn (402 12th Ave. S.). It became a staple of Nashville entertainment, earning TV appearances including on *Late Night with Conan O'Brien*.

Ernest films have often returned to the Belcourt for special screenings, keeping the character's legacy alive. Like Altman's *Nashville*, the Ernest franchise became part of the city's cultural identity, offering a grassroots, offbeat alternative to mainstream representations.

During the 1990s, Nashville cultivated a modest but steady film industry. With state support, enthusiastic local talent, and its blend of music and character-rich settings, the city attracted both studio and television productions. Notable among these were *Ernest Goes to Jail* (John R. Cherry III, dir., 1990), *Ernest Scared Stupid* (John R. Cherry III, dir., 1991), and HBO's *Against the Wall* (John Frankenheimer, dir., 1994), which depicted the 1971 Attica prison uprising and employed hundreds of local extras while generating over $1 million for the local economy.[35]

Many of these productions were filmed at the Tennessee State Prison, active from 1898 until its 1992 closure. Its Gothic architecture made it a popular filming location for movies like *Framed* (Phil Karlson, dir., 1975), *Nashville* (Robert Altman, dir., 1975), *The Green Mile* (Frank Darabont, dir., 1999), and *Walk the Line* (James Mangold, dir., 2005).

Another significant film was *The Thing Called Love* (1993), directed by Peter Bogdanovich. Set in Nashville's country music scene, it was shot at local landmarks like the Bluebird Café and Drake Motel. While the film drew criticism for not using songs by established Nashville songwriters, it featured cameos by Trisha Yearwood and Pam Tillis, and starred River Phoenix, Dermot Mulroney, and Sandra Bullock, who performed their own music.

The Wachowskis' *The Matrix* (1999) used Nashville's skyline in its opening chase scene, incorporating the Stahlman Building, adorned with WKDF's neon-red call letters, and the "Batman Building" via green screen. Though shot mainly in Sydney, the film subtly embedded Nashville into its visual identity.

Barry Levinson's *Wag the Dog* (1997) included aerial shots of downtown Nashville, including the John Seigenthaler Pedestrian Bridge and 1st Avenue North, with scenes featuring Willie Nelson filmed in a local studio. The score, composed by Mark Knopfler, was recorded at Ocean Way Nashville, which occupies a former church and the 1914 childhood home of American playwright Tennessee Williams.[36] Ocean Way (17th Ave. S.) has since recorded scores for *O Brother, Where Art Thou?* (Joel and Ethan Cohen, dirs., 2000), *Harriet* (Kasi Lemmons, dir., 2019), and *Trolls Band Together* (Walt Dohrn and Tim Heitz, dirs., 2023).

In the 1990s, Nashville also produced one of its most important independent filmmakers: Harmony Korine. Known for his provocative, antimainstream style, Korine's films challenge conventional narratives and reflect a punk, DIY sensibility. Raised in Nashville after an early childhood in California, Korine attended Hillsboro High School and was introduced to film by his PBS documentary filmmaker father.

Korine's short film *A Bundle a Minute* (1991) earned him early admission to NYU's dramatic writing program, where he met Larry Clark. At nineteen, Korine wrote the screenplay for *Kids* (1995), a raw portrait of urban youth that gained immediate attention.[37] The film quickly became a landmark of youth-centered independent cinema, helping define Korine's reputation for creating unsettling, atmospheric works that blur the lines between art and exploitation.

His filmmaking style draws from New Punk Cinema and shares ideological roots with Dogme 95, the minimalist movement that promotes low-budget production, fragmented narrative structures, non-professional actors, and post-continuity editing, led by Lars von Trier and Thomas Vinterberg.[38]

Both the New Punk Cinema and Dogme 95 movements sought to strip away the excesses of studio filmmaking in favor of raw, minimalist storytelling. Harmony Korine's work embraces these same principles; his films reflect not only his personal artistic ethos but also key elements of Nashville's entertainment subculture.

Korine's breakout success marked a continuation of a larger pattern in the city's cinematic history. Just as the Ormond family's Hick Flicks of the 1960s and the Ernest P. Worrell franchise of the 1980s brought locally rooted, idiosyncratic cinema to national audiences, Korine demonstrated that Nashville could once again produce original, auteur-driven films outside the established industry centers of the East and West Coasts.

His directorial work frequently draws from the city's environments and subcultures. *Gummo* (1997), though set in a fictional Ohio town, was shot entirely in and around Nashville. The film highlights neighborhoods like West End, Richland Park, and The Nations, capturing them just before waves of redevelopment and gentrification began to reshape the city's landscape. Today, *Gummo* serves as both an unsettling narrative and a visual time capsule of Nashville at the close of the twentieth century.

2000S AND BEYOND

AS THE 2000S BEGAN, Harmony Korine continued to produce films that challenged convention and deepened his ties to Nashville's cinematic identity. At the same time, the city began attracting higher-budget mainstream productions, including *Hannah Montana: The Movie* (Peter Chelsom, dir., 2009),

FIGURE 7.6. Polaroid photograph of former *Nashville Scene* editor Jim Ridley with filmmakers Gaspar Noé and Harmony Korine at the Belcourt Theatre, 2010. Taken during filming of the German documentary television series *Durch die Nacht mit . . .* (*Into the Night with . . .*), directed by Bruce LaBruce. Courtesy of Garland Gallaspy.

starring Franklin, Tennessee, native Miley Cyrus. Much like Disney's *Davy Crockett* decades earlier, the Hannah Montana character transitioned from a television hit to a feature film, reaffirming Nashville's relevance in youth-oriented pop culture, particularly when the character reflects Southern identities grounded in aspects of the city's character.

Korine's *Trash Humpers* (2009), shot entirely in Nashville, stands in stark contrast to this commercial project. Deeply embedded in the city's underground arts scene, the film follows a group of elderly sociopaths and features a cast drawn from local talent. Among them are songwriter Chris Gantry, known for his work with Kris Kristofferson, Mel Tillis, and Shel Silverstein; comedian and musician Chris Crofton; and experimental rock vocalists Paul Booker and Dave Cloud. The film's lo-fi aesthetic and unsettling narrative reflect Korine's ongoing commitment to outsider storytelling.

Trash Humpers premiered at the Belcourt Theatre in 2010, with Korine in attendance to introduce the film. The Belcourt has since preserved a 35mm archival print and continues to circulate the film to theaters nationwide, helping maintain its cult status.

Across the 2010s, both independent and major studio film productions continued to be made in Nashville. One of the biggest names in independent filmmaking during this decade is horror writer-director Billy Senese.

Today, the Belcourt remains a vital hub for local filmmakers and Nashville-born talent. As of 2025, the theater maintains active ties with local figures such as comedians and actors John Early and James Austin Johnson, a cast member on *Saturday Night Live*, who support the theater as members attending screenings and as allies who engage the public by occasionally introducing films, continuing the theater's long-standing tradition of fostering local voices within the national cinematic conversation.

8

LOSING THE BELCOURT

BY THE 1980S, THE BELCOURT Cinema stood as a weathered fixture in Nashville's cultural landscape. Once a vibrant space for silent films, community theater, and alternative cinema, it had become a relic in a rapidly changing world. As urban redevelopment accelerated and economic pressures mounted, the theater struggled to maintain its relevance. Once central to Nashville's film scene, the Belcourt teetered on the edge of obsolescence.

Nationally, the 1980s brought sweeping transformations. The US economy shifted from manufacturing to services. Cable TV, MTV, and CNN redefined media, while the Reagan era marked a rightward political turn. The AIDS crisis, the attempted assassination of President Reagan, and the *Challenger* disaster left lasting marks on the American psyche. Technological advances, particularly in computing, began reshaping everyday life.

In cinema, the rise of multiplexes and corporate consolidation challenged small, independent theaters. Nashville's Belcourt was no exception. It had once flourished as the city's premier arthouse venue, but by the late 1980s, the landscape had shifted. Megaplexes, backed by studio blockbusters, dominated distribution. Demographic changes in surrounding neighborhoods further complicated Belcourt's ability to retain audiences.

Survival, not innovation, defined this period. The Belcourt continued to lean into repertory, foreign, and independent film programming to stay afloat. This pivot mirrored national trends in alternative cinema and reaffirmed the theater's commitment to a distinct cultural identity.

To longtime patrons, the Belcourt remained more than just a movie house. For singer-songwriter and actress Marshall Chapman, it was a beloved constant despite its physical decline. "In the eighties the Belcourt really fell into disrepair," she recalled. "I can't believe they didn't condemn it. Plaster would fall in your hair while you watched a movie."[1]

Chapman's connection to the theater would come full circle decades later, with her appearances in *Love Song* (So Yong Kim, dir., 2016) and *Novitiate* (Maggie Betts, dir., 2017), both of which premiered at the Belcourt. But in the 1980s and '90s, she, like many locals, was simply a fan, going on dates to watch whatever avant-garde films were still being shown with her husband.[2]

Industry-wide, the 1980s marked a dramatic consolidation of theatrical exhibition. Multiplexes changed the game, allowing chains to offer more films and more showtimes. Studios increasingly favored these venues for

FIGURE 8.1. Water spots on the ceiling of the Belcourt Theatre, 2015. The stains illustrate decades of cumulative moisture problems caused by roof leaks, plumbing issues, and poor ventilation.

FIGURE 8.2. Cups from concessions lining the window sill in the second-floor office to catch water from a leaking roof, 2015.

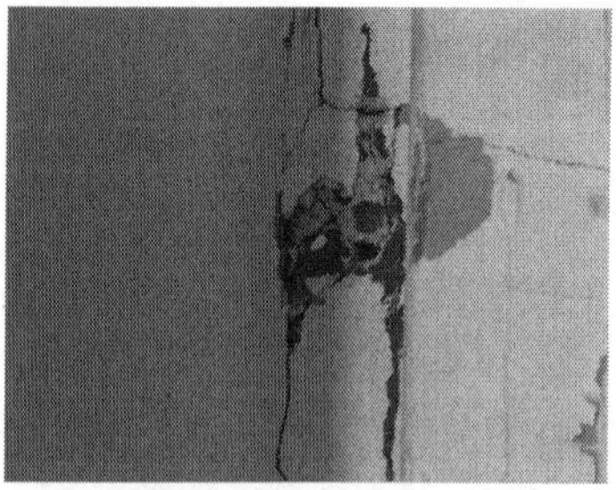

FIGURE 8.3. Chipping paint in the Belcourt Theatre, 2015. The layers likely reveal the theater's second renovation, a 1930 refresh that introduced a white, green, and red motif alongside window boxes and wrought-iron lamps above the lobby entrance.

FIGURE 8.4. Original theater fly loft showing extreme decay, 2015. Likely installed as early as 1927, the deteriorated structure had become a major hazard to the building's infrastructure and safety, leading to its later removal.

exclusive distribution of big-budget blockbusters, a model popularized by the success of *Jaws* (Steven Spielberg, dir., 1975). This left smaller theaters fighting over less-promoted, less-profitable fare.

By the 1990s, neighborhood cinemas like the Belcourt faced existential threats. Chains had the scale to negotiate better deals with studios. Independent theaters had to adapt or close. The Belcourt, with its mixed programming of Hollywood hits and foreign films, attempted to strike a balance. Programming titles like *The Blues Brothers* (John Landis, dir., 1980), *Friday the 13th* (Sean S. Cunningham, dir., 1980), and *The Tin Drum* (Volker Schlöndorff, dir., 1979) exemplified its effort to retain broad appeal.

Still, this hybrid strategy faltered. Films like *La Cage aux Folles* (Édouard Molinaro, dir., 1978) and *2001: A Space Odyssey* (Stanley Kubrick, dir., 1968)

FIGURE 8.5. Chipped paint and plaster of the Belcourt Theatre proscenium arch, 2015. The layers reveal the theater's various playhouse eras. The black paint beneath recalls the period between 1937 and 1958, when proscenium arches were often painted black to align with the minimalist aesthetic of experimental and black box theatre while serving practical lighting purposes.

FIGURE 8.7. Ornamental plaster medallion by the G. Mattei Ornamental Plaster Co., 2015. Designed by Raffaelo Mattei, the piece was one of the original theater's crown jewels and remained obscured inside the second-floor offices for decades.

FIGURE 8.6. Crumbling plaster in the back hallways of the Belcourt Theatre, 2015. Layers of paint reveal multiple eras of remodel.

All photographs in Chapter 8 by Will Morgan Holland except as noted; all come from the Belcourt Theatre Collection, courtesy of Vanderbilt University Special Collections.

FIGURE 8.8. The crumbling exterior of the Belcourt Theatre, 2015. The New Orleans–style facade was originally designed and installed in 1959 by Theatre Nashville technical director Robert Barnes.

sustained the arthouse audience, but blockbusters such as *The Blue Lagoon* (Randal Kleiser, dir., 1980) increasingly defined its second-run status.[3] The theater's niche was narrowing.

At the time, home video had yet to become ubiquitous. Theatrical screenings remained the best post-release option, temporarily buffering the Belcourt. That edge vanished quickly.

In 1982, Carl Patrick acquired Martin Theatres, the fourth-largest motion picture exhibitor in the nation and the largest in the Southeast, which had leased the Belcourt since 1974 following the death of founder Fred Massey. Patrick rebranded Martin as Carmike Cinemas and embraced a cost-efficient strategy focused on small-town, second-run theaters. This model extended the life of properties like the Belcourt but often deprioritized investment in their upkeep.[4]

Patrick had led Martin Theatres since 1968 before becoming CEO of Fuqua Industries, which had absorbed Martin in a wave of mergers. This corporate lineage echoed broader industry consolidation. Martin had previously expanded in 1961 by acquiring forty-six of Crescent Amusement Company's forty-seven theaters. The lone holdout, the Belmont, was repurposed into a 38,000-square-foot multi-office penthouse by developer William F. Creighton.[5]

FIGURE 8.9. Original projection room of the 1925 Hall at the Belcourt Theatre, 2015. A toilet was installed in the 1960s for projectionist James William "J. W." Young, allowing him to take breaks without leaving his post. Visible are former technologies such as the film projection platter system (right foreground) and guillotine shutters (on the projection ports). Photographer unknown.

The multiplex era arrived decisively in Nashville in 1987 with the opening of AMC's fourteen-screen Fountain Square complex. Offering exclusive distribution rights and modern amenities, the new venue quickly drew audiences away from older, independent theaters.[6] Neighborhood legacy cinemas like the Belcourt, single- and twin-screen houses, struggled to compete. The rise of multiplexes marked a turning point, introducing direct and aggressive competition that hastened the Belcourt's decline and reshaped the city's exhibition landscape.

As multiplexes dominated the exhibition market, access to screens for independent and foreign films, especially outside major hubs like New York or Los Angeles, became increasingly limited. In Nashville, the Belcourt remained one of the few reliable venues for such content. Yet even this distinction was not enough to reverse its declining fortunes. Despite the city's growing number of theaters, dozens of significant independent films each year bypassed local screens entirely, or, if shown, received poor projection quality and minimal promotion, and vanished quickly from the schedule.[7]

Critic Jim Ridley captured the moment starkly in his *Nashville Scene* article "Attack of the Megaplexes": "The megaplexes, like Godzilla, are consuming everything in their path."[8]

The Belcourt's struggles extended into the early 2000s. Studios like Sony Pictures Classics, once supportive, withdrew due to pressure from chains like Regal, which threatened to pull films from their regional screens if independents like the Belcourt were serviced.[9]

Programming shifted to high turnover. Runs of one to four weeks became the norm. Midnight movies and curated series returned, offering a nod to earlier eras and helping sustain niche interest. By the mid-1990s, the Belcourt had fully embraced its alternative identity, showcasing LGBTQ+ films and other underrepresented stories.

Notable successes included *Four Weddings and a Funeral* (Mike Newell, dir., 1994), which ran for sixty-three days; *The Incredibly True Adventures of Two Girls in Love* (Maria Maggenti, dir., 1995), for twenty-three days; and *Bound* (Lana Wachowski and Lilly Wachowski, dirs., 1996), for twenty-one days. These films cultivated loyal audiences but couldn't offset the financial challenges of maintaining an aging building.

By the mid-1990s, Belcourt's physical condition was deteriorating, and structural issues grew dire. Ceiling damage caused falling debris. Audiovisual systems lagged behind competitors. In 1996, water damage forced a partial shutdown by the city's Department of Codes.[10] One hall reopened within days, the second after six weeks, while the water damage could be repaired.[11] Though operations resumed at the end of August 1996, the disruption highlighted the fragility of the theater's business model.

A more existential threat emerged in 1997: the expiration of the land-use ordinance protecting Hillsboro Village's zoning. Without legal safeguards, developers eyed the property. That October, Carmike exited, ending a two-decade run. The end of the Belcourt Cinema era was fittingly marked by its final screening, *Kiss Me, Guido* (Tony Vitale, dir., 1997), an LGBTQ+ film. That same month, a new chapter began. Charlie Hawkins and the Watkins Institute of Art & Design formed Belcourt, LLC, purchasing the theater from the Massey family.

Rebranded as Watkins Belcourt, the theater recommitted to arthouse programming. Its debut featured *The Myth of Fingerprints* (Bart Freundlich, dir., 1997) and *The Full Monty* (Peter Cattaneo, dir., 1997), the latter enjoying a strong twenty-eight-day run. Because the theater was affiliated with the institute's newly established Film School, Watkins also used the space to showcase student films, integrating education with exhibition.[12]

The Belcourt's decline through the 1980s and '90s reflected national shifts: multiplex dominance, distributor consolidation, and changing audience habits. Yet its resilience under Watkins-Belcourt laid the groundwork for a twenty-first-century revival. Despite overwhelming odds, the Belcourt endured, a testament to the lasting power of independent film and community-driven cinema.

9

SAVING THE BELCOURT

THE BELCOURT THEATRE WASN'T supposed to survive.

Between 1925 and 1962, the building underwent at least nine minor renovations, with no major restoration efforts for another three decades. Meanwhile, Middle Tennessee weathered four significant tornado outbreaks, any of which could have reduced the aging structure to rubble.[1] Structurally and aesthetically, it was hardly the most robust landmark in Hillsboro Village, certainly not compared to the more solidly built Belmont Theatre. But with some good luck, both managed to withstand decades of natural disasters. One ultimately fell victim to the city's first wave of urban renewal, but that demise befell the grand movie palace the Belmont, not the cobbled together neighborhood theater that could.

By 1961, the Belcourt could have easily met the same fate. The Nashville Community Playhouse, which had operated there for years, was struggling financially, burdened by the costs of its own remodeling efforts. Selling to developers, as Belmont Theatre had done, would have been the obvious escape route. Yet somehow, against financial strain, time, and the elements, the Belcourt remained standing, a survivor in a city eager to modernize at the cost of its past.

By the late 1990s, Nashville's last functioning neighborhood theater stood on the edge of oblivion, caught in the sweeping forces of urban development, economic downturns, and the entertainment industry. Though the Belcourt had installed dual screens in the 1960s, the culture of cinema surrounding the aging "twins" had outgrown the need for independent theaters, many of which were single-screens. By then, consumers in America had been watching pornography on VHS in the privacy of their own on-screen televisions since the 1980s, and the ubiquity of the World Wide Web on a home's other single-screen—the personal computer—was already emergent. What use were single-screens theaters anymore? Belcourt Cinema had once been a beacon, a place where students from Vanderbilt and Belmont walked down the street for a weekend double feature, where cinephiles first discovered Lynch and Bergman, and where generations of Nashvillians gathered beneath the Belcourt Avenue box office awning. But by 1998, the crowds had thinned. The popcorn machines had gone cold. By January 28, 1999, the doors were locked.

Jim Ridley, longtime film critic for the *Nashville Scene*, captured the moment in his elegiac January 21, 1999, article "Fade to Black: Can the Watkins Belcourt Be Saved?" The Belcourt was up for sale, and in a rapidly developing city where old buildings were being razed for condos and retail space, its fate seemed sealed.

"[This] imminent loss is troubling for more reasons than just movies," Ridley wrote.

> Off the top of my head, I can think of a dozen reasons why Belcourt should be saved. Because it's a piece of our history. Because the cutting edge of an art form as democratic as film shouldn't be the exclusive property of bicoastal snobs. Because it makes Nashville a richer place. Because going to the movies is a relatively cheap thing that can bring you in contact with other people and make your life a little better for two hours—sometimes a lot better.

What happened next wasn't just the story of a theater; it was the story of a city at a crossroads. What kind of Nashville would emerge in the twenty-first century? One where history and culture were expendable? Or one where a community could rally to save something that felt, at its core, irreplaceable?

The answer, as it turned out, would be written not by developers, but by a scrappy band of young organizers, a few deep-pocketed believers, and a grassroots movement that refused to let the screen go dark.

For much of the twentieth century, the Belcourt had been a survivor. Through the decades of organizational changes, the Belcourt endured shifting cultural trends and entertainment industry upheavals. But the 1990s

FIGURE 9.1. Hillsboro Village from 21st Avenue, 1998. Belcourt Cinema branding, once visible on the flyloft in the 1960s, is faintly visible after years of fading. Mayor Purcell Papers. Courtesy of the Metropolitan Government Archives of Nashville and Davidson County.

FIGURE 9.2. Jim Ridley cover story for the *Nashville Scene*, 1999. Courtesy of the Center for Popular Music, Middle Tennessee State University.

brought a different kind of threat, one it wasn't prepared to fight alone.

The rise of multiplexes had transformed the way people went to the movies. Where the Belcourt once served as a neighborhood hub, and when it was a new suburb, its own local destination, Nashville audiences now flocked to sprawling theater complexes like the Hollywood 27, which boasted more screens, better seating, and the latest in THX sound systems. Small, independent cinemas struggled to compete. It wasn't that people stopped loving the Belcourt, at least nostalgically. It was that they stopped noticing it; they took it for granted.

Carmike Cinemas, which had operated the Belcourt since the 1980s, was itself struggling in the era of corporate theater chains. When Carmike relinquished its lease in the fall of 1997, a group of private investors, consisting of Massey's heirs and old guard real estate maverick Charlie Hawkins, purchased the theater for $1.4 million.[2] Then Watkins College of Art, which housed a

FIGURE 9.3. Save the Belcourt poster for the Belcourt YES! campaign, 1999. Printed poster by Hatch Show Print. Courtesy of the Country Music Hall of Fame and Museum Archives.

FIGURE 9.4. Exterior of the Belcourt Theatre with campaign posters displayed in the frames, February 17, 1999, taken between the building's listing for sale and the creation of the nonprofit that would sign the first lease with Charlie Hawkins with option to buy. Photograph by Katherine Bomboy. Courtesy of Julia Sutherland.

growing film studies program, stepped in with a plan to turn the Belcourt into an arthouse venue, using the theater's programming as a cooperative branch of their educational offerings, doing things like showing short student films before screenings of studio features.

But the economics didn't work. One problem they faced was that distributors had little incentive to loan first-run independent films or archival prints of repertory films to a nonprofit theater with equipment that hadn't been updated in thirty-five years, which could easily damage prints and at the very least offered an unreliable viewing experience for the customer. Julia Sutherland recalled that, "often films were broken in the middle."[3] The Belcourt was forced to book older prints and second-run titles, drawing only a fraction of the audience it needed to survive. "Where [Hollywood 27] has really hurt us is in movies we've had to share," said David Hinton, then dean of Watkins.[4]

By 1999, the experiment had failed and the theater was losing money at upward of $7,000 a month.[5] Watkins shuttered its operations, and the property owner, Charlie Hawkins, put the theater up for sale at $1.85 million.[6] The message was clear: If no buyer stepped forward, the last historic neighborhood theater in Nashville would soon be converted into high-end retail or apartments, just as Tony Sudekum's former grand art deco movie palace, the Tennessee Theatre, had been before it.[7]

That's when Jim Ridley's "Fade to Black" article hit newsstands.

The feature in the *Nashville Scene* was a gut punch to Nashville's film lovers. It painted Belcourt's closure as not just the loss of a building, but a sign of a city losing its cultural identity. The piece struck a nerve, especially with Tom Wills, a Nashville artist and film enthusiast, who read it and immediately decided to show up at a public meeting organized to discuss the theater's future. Organized by Nashville native Julia Sutherland, who had then recently moved back to her hometown, the meeting took place at a small black box theater space in the upstairs attic of neighborhood coffee shop Bongo Java, Sunday afternoon, January 24, 1999.[8]

There, in front of a small group of professors, instructors, musicians, and filmmakers, Sutherland jumped onto a makeshift stage and asked a question that would change everything: "Hey kids, do you want to save Belcourt?"[9]

The day Julia Sutherland stood on that stage at Bongo Java, the energy in the room shifted. Until that moment, the Belcourt's closure had felt like another inevitable casualty of Nashville's rapid development. But suddenly, there was a spark, an idea that maybe, just maybe, the theater could be saved.

FIGURE 9.5. The historic 1925 Hall, February 17, 1999. Photograph by Katherine Bomboy. Courtesy of Julia Sutherland.

The group that formed in the aftermath was young, scrappy, and relentless. They called themselves Belcourt YES!, and while most of them had no experience running a theater, let alone financing a multimillion-dollar rescue effort, they had something just as important: unshakable conviction.

Sutherland recalled years later, "All we cared about was that we lived here, and our families lived here, and we wanted our children to live here. We just couldn't let it go. So it became a lot bigger than just us."[10]

But belief alone wouldn't save Belcourt. The first hurdle was time. The building was officially for sale, and real estate developers had already started making offers. The grassroots team of Belcourt YES! needed a strategy—and money—fast.

Enter Scott and Mimi Manzler. A Nashville couple born and raised in Cincinnati, Ohio, who met in high school and later married, eventually settling in Nashville after Scott completed his MBA at Vanderbilt University, the Manzlers followed Belcourt's early struggles with concern. The couple's deep love for education, the arts, and cinema, and their desire to preserve independent film culture led them to play a pivotal role in the Belcourt YES! campaign and beyond. Most importantly, they were philanthropic businesspeople, and they understood that what the grassroots group needed most was time and donations.[11]

Scott, a devoted cinephile and former freelance writer for *No Depression* and the *Nashville Scene*, was deeply invested in the film programming and the financial sustainability of the theater. Mimi, with a background in education and community engagement, took on public outreach, event planning, and fundraising, helping to establish key initiatives like children's programming, community film discussions, and the Belcourt's first major fundraisers. Together, their work and the tens of thousands of dollars worth of donations made to the nonprofits over time were instrumental in stabilizing operations long-term.[12]

By November 1999, the group had engendered enough trust that they were able to sign a ten-year lease with Hawkins, buying them enough time to try to raise capital to hopefully purchase the building once and for all.[13]

The lease wasn't cheap: $85,000 upfront, a daunting sum for a scrappy operation run by a handful of idealistic twenty-somethings fueled by idealism and a growing, but not fully sturdy, base of community support.[14] To keep the doors open, they launched fundraisers, including an Academy

FIGURE 9.6. Belcourt YES! co-founder Tom Wills standing in front of Save the Belcourt yard signs and poster for the benefit screening of the locally produced *The Misadventures of Amy Everhart*, May 1999. Courtesy of Julia Sutherland.

Awards viewing party that later evolved into Belcourt's A Red Carpet Evening, which in most recent history is responsible for raising over 2.5 percent of the theater's annual budget.[15] Membership sales became a key revenue stream, while screenings, like *The Misadventures of Amy Everhart* (1999), a locally produced film by director Samuel E. Stumpf and co-producer Jane Stumpf, helped sustain the cause by increasing patronage. Jane Stumpf, daughter of former Nashville Community Playhouse actor and vice president Robert L. Gwinn (1948–1949), remembers the era as a whirlwind of relentless hustle, deep community support, and the thrill of being part of something bigger than herself. One of her most vivid memories was a fundraiser attended by a political celebrity and wife of then–vice president Al Gore: "I just [have] a memory of the very first 'Dinner and a Movie' that we had for Park Center. Tipper Gore was here and we had the Klieg lights out front. It was such fun—that excitement, 'scintillation' would be a wonderful word [to describe it]." She continued, "The lights and that excitement that . . . she wasn't a movie star, per se, [but] it was thrilling."[16] Every community tie, every high-profile sighting, every ticket sold, every dollar raised played a crucial role in sustaining the theater's future and legacy.

Even with the lease secured, the long-term future of the Belcourt still remained uncertain. Without permanent ownership of the building, the theater was always one bad financial quarter away from closure. That's where Nashville-native studio artist, film historian, and nonprofit leader Tom Wills stepped in.

Wills became instrumental in building community around the new nonprofit, hosting free screenings and music events, including the Early Bird Club, a private Saturday morning film series featuring prints from his rare personal archive of 16mm films. Wills would later go on to co-found *The Contributor*, a nonprofit street newspaper focused on addressing homelessness that gives unhoused people entrepreneurial and creative opportunities as writers and distributors of the paper. His work at the intersection of arts, social justice, and historic preservation has left a lasting impact on Nashville's cultural landscape.

Wills had been one of the first to answer Ridley's call to action in "Fade to Black," attending that fateful Bongo Java meeting and throwing himself into the fight to save the theater. Wills, who comes from a family deeply embedded in the city's history, also had a fateful tie to the building's history. Wills's great-great-grandfather had been one of the founders of the National Life and Accident Insurance Company, the parent company of WSM radio station and subsequent owners of the Grand Ole Opry during the 1930s when it had been housed in the old Hillsboro Theatre.[17]

Wills later realized that activism alone wouldn't be enough. The Belcourt needed something more concrete: a financial safety net. Former board member and Belcourt YES! organizer F. Clark Williams remembered this moment. "[Stephanie Silverman's predecessor], Steve Small, did a good job of getting us financially stabilized and operationally sound, and he was able to convince the board that we could purchase the theater from Tom Wills."[18]

In the fall of 2003, Wills made a bold move by putting his life savings on the line for the theater. He made a direct offer to the owners, matching the competing bid while also covering the theater's outstanding rent, personally purchasing the Belcourt and holding it in trust for the nonprofit group to buy back at a later date. This plan ensured that the building wouldn't be snapped up by developers if the group fell further behind in their lease or the owners decided to sell, and bought the organization time to secure more stable funding. The deal was struck, and Wills became the owner, ensuring the Belcourt remained a theater rather than another commercial development.

Confident that the nonprofit model was working, Scott Manzler, in cooperation with the board, approached then-director Steve Small and property owner Tom Wills in a triangulated negotiation to secure a stair-step plan that would provide an economic pathway to building ownership while leaving enough mileage for the group to continue raise the necessary funds along the way.[19] To secure its long-term future, Wills structured a new lease agreement that required the nonprofit to gradually take on financial responsibility, including taxes and upkeep, eventually leading to full ownership. This strategic move protected both the theater's mission and his own investment, creating a sustainable path for Belcourt's survival.[20]

"I just didn't want to see it disappear," Wills later said. "I believed in what they were doing, but I also knew that without ownership, their hands were tied."[21]

His investment gave Belcourt what it had never truly had before: an empowered path to more permanent stability. With ownership secured and the nonprofit structure taking shape, the Belcourt group turned its attention to the theater's programming. What would the new theater be? Gone were the days of struggling to compete with multiplexes for the latest Hollywood releases. Instead, the Belcourt would reinvent itself as Nashville's home for repertory, foreign, and independent cinema. They booked arthouse films that weren't playing anywhere else in town. They grew their live music events and theatrical performances, and continued to build their reputation for film by leaning into unusual programming and community engagement, like hosting silent films with live orchestral accompaniment.[22]

By the early 2000s, the Belcourt's transformation was taking hold. Attendance steadily increased, memberships grew, and the theater began shifting from a struggling venue into a recognized cultural institution. A milestone came on November 5, 2007, when Belcourt Theatre Inc. purchased the property from Tom Wills. This acquisition brought long-term security and renewed stability to the organization.

Even then, resources remained thin. The theater operated with little cash on hand, a small and underpaid staff, and screenings that sometimes drew modest audiences. Yet despite these challenges, the Belcourt had survived, and for the first time in years, its future looked promising.

The fight to save the theater wasn't over.

Against all odds, the grassroots movement that had formed in response to the theater's near-demolition had successfully transformed the Belcourt into something new: a nonprofit arts center dedicated to repertory, foreign, and independent cinema. It was a departure from its past as a neighborhood movie theater that still harkened back to the old playhouse days when the community rallied to keep it afloat several times through the Great Depression, World War II, and the debt-heavy latter years before the purchase from Massey that kept the building alive and built a foundation for arthouse in Nashville. No longer was the Belcourt trying to compete with the Regal Hollywood or Green Hills megaplexes. Instead, it had once again carved out a niche as Nashville's premier destination for film lovers who wanted something different, something they couldn't get at a corporate-owned theater.

But with success came a new challenge: sustainability. In theory, a nonprofit cinema allowed the Belcourt to operate without the same profit pressures that had doomed it in the 1990s. But in practice, financial stability remained elusive. Ticket sales alone wouldn't be enough to keep the doors open. The Belcourt had to get creative.

It launched a membership program, offering discounted tickets and special screenings for subscribers, a model borrowed from other independent theaters across the country like Coolidge Corner in Boston, Massachusetts. It expanded live events, hosting everything from concerts to panel discussions to experimental film screenings. And it forged partnerships with local businesses and donors, securing grants and sponsorships to help offset operating costs.

Still, there were growing pains. The historic building was old, and maintenance was expensive. Plumbing issues led to flooding in the lobby. The theater's aging projectors required constant repairs. And while the programming was strong, some skeptics wondered whether a city like Nashville, better known for country music than arthouse cinema, could sustain a venue like the Belcourt long-term.

Then came the Great Recession.

When the global financial crisis hit in 2008, independent cinemas across the country faced an existential threat. Would audiences still spend money on movies when they were cutting back on everything else? For the Belcourt, the timing was precarious. The nonprofit model had proven viable, but it wasn't necessarily guaranteed. The theater's ability to stay afloat still depended on the generosity of the community.

Stephanie Silverman, who took over as executive director in 2007, later recalled the pressure of keeping the Belcourt running in those uncertain years: "The hardest part [was] the physical plant [operations] hurdles. Almost everything else we [had] overcome. But when the lobby is literally raining from plumbing issues? You just have to move buckets around and wait."[23]

Despite the challenges, the Belcourt endured. The theater's reputation as a cultural cornerstone of Nashville kept it going. The city's growing creative class, filmmakers, musicians, and artists, embraced it as their own. And unlike its near-death experience in the 1990s, this time, the Belcourt had a safety net: a dedicated staff, a board of directors, and a community that refused to let it fail. The Belcourt Theatre's journey from near-demolition to a thriving nonprofit arts institution was more than just a story about saving a building. It was about saving a piece of Nashville's soul.

The fight to preserve Belcourt wasn't just about nostalgia. It was about what kind of city Nashville wanted to be. Would it be a city that paved over its history in the name of profit? Or one that protected its cultural landmarks, even when doing so required a fight? Thanks to the relentless work of grassroots organizers, philanthropists like Tom Wills and the Manzlers, and the thousands of Nashvillians who showed up—bought tickets, became members, donated money—the answer, for now, was clear.

But the battle for independent theaters was far from over.

Even as the Belcourt emerged stronger than ever, new challenges were on the horizon. Streaming services were changing how people consumed movies. Corporate multiplexes were consolidating power. And as always, the forces of urban development loomed large.

Belcourt survived failure, turned seventy-seven years old, and then kept going. They owned the building, but they needed to make plans for the future, again. On the eve of their ninetieth birthday, the organization asked itself, "Could the Belcourt survive another twenty years? How about fifty years?"

This time, they needed to think bigger than ever before. They needed to figure out how to secure the future of the building so it could survive to celebrate one hundred years and beyond. If its history had proven anything, it was this: Never underestimate the power of a city that refuses to let its last picture house fade to black.

WHEN COMMUNITY THEATER CAME BACK

PROPOSALS WERE SUBMITTED BY MOCKINGBIRD Theater Company, Circle Players, ACT I, and Nashville Shakespeare Festival.

The stage lights flickered to life, illuminating a space that had once been dark for decades. The Belcourt Theatre, a historic landmark nestled in

Nashville's Hillsboro Village, had been saved from demolition by the sheer will of its community. And now, for the first time in thirty years, actors stepped back onto the stage once more. Their names were Jim Reyland, Kimberley LaMarue, Barry Scott, and Matt Carlton.[24] Reyland recalled how neglected the old 1925 Hall was by 1998.

> [We thought], "This place needs some work." So the first thing we did was we raised the screen, and we opened up the stage to look at what we had to perform on. And there hadn't been a stage production there in twenty-five or thirty years. Our [next] thought was, "[Look at] all the junk behind the screen." And we [said], "Well, there's some of our set!"[25]

For Belcourt, who had signed their first lease with Charlie Hawkins under Belcourt YES! in March of 1999, Reyland's production was more than just a return to live performance. It was a declaration; one that underscored the power of independent theater, the resilience of community spaces, and the never-ending struggle to carve out a home for the arts in a city increasingly shaped by commercial interests.

Jim Reyland's three-day run of his original play *Stuff* in March of 1999 became the first theatrical production performed on the historic stage since the 1965 New Theatre Nashville production of *South Pacific*, setting the stage, quite literally, for what was to come.[26] Soon after, Olde Worlde Theatre Company, helmed by Richard Stein, a man whose theatrical journey had carried him from street performances in Denmark to the heart of Nashville's grassroots theater revival, found a home at the Belcourt, bringing a new era of performance with it.

The return of live theater to the Belcourt reflected a broader historical struggle: the fight for independent performance spaces in an era dominated by commercial entertainment.

For much of the twentieth century, small, locally driven theater movements emerged as a reaction to the monopolization of the arts. The Little Theatre Movement, which began in the early 1900s, sought to create spaces where artists could experiment outside of Broadway's commercial constraints. These grassroots theaters fostered new talent, emphasized artistic freedom, and, crucially, relied on community support to survive.

By the late twentieth century, these theaters and theatrical companies faced an existential crisis. Funding was inconsistent, real estate costs soared, and securing permanent venues inside major metropolitan areas became increasingly difficult. The struggle was particularly pronounced in Nashville, where the city's rapid growth during the late 1990s made it harder for small theater groups to find stable footing.

"The challenge for any community theater is always the space," said Bobby Boucher, a longtime performer with Olde Worlde Theatre. "The Belcourt gave us a home, a place where we could create without worrying about where we'd be next season."[27] For independent theater companies like Olde Worlde, the Belcourt's stage was a rare and invaluable resource. It provided not only a performance venue but also a connection to a rich theatrical history that had been nearly erased.

The force behind Olde Worlde Theatre was Richard Stein, a theater artist, director, and educator whose passion for movement-based performance defined his career. Born in Brooklyn, New York, in 1956, Stein fell in love with the performing arts at an early age, drawing inspiration from the street theater he witnessed in Denmark as a teenager. That moment sparked a lifelong fascination with physical storytelling.[28]

Stein's path was unconventional. Rather than following a traditional theatrical route, he left college to train in mime and commedia dell'arte, studying under renowned instructors like Tony Montanaro. His work was deeply influenced by avant-garde theater, improvisation, and European performance traditions.[29] In the early 2000s, he brought that sensibility to Nashville's children's theater scene, founding Olde Worlde Theatre. From 2000 to 2016, he directed and produced more than sixty-five shows at the Belcourt Theatre, making him one of the most prolific performers in the venue's history. Stein's legacy at the Belcourt remains a defining chapter in Nashville's rich history of community-driven theater.

His adaptations of classic nineteenth-century fairy tales, such as *Hansel and Gretel* and *Jack and the Beanstalk*, were known for their slapstick comedy, audience interaction, and inventive staging, creating performances that felt spontaneous and alive. "We didn't use scripts the way traditional theater does," Stein recalled. "The stories evolved through performance, through character work, through play."[30] This improvisational approach made Olde Worlde a favorite among Nashville audiences, particularly children.

Bobby Boucher, one of the company's most beloved performers, was a natural fit for Olde Worlde's playful, interactive style. A Nashville native born in 1962, Boucher had spent his early years performing comedy for friends and family, honing a talent for improvisation that would define his stage career. His connection to the Belcourt stretched back to his childhood, when he attended screenings of *Monty Python and the Holy Grail*.[31]

Boucher joined Olde Worlde Theatre in 2006 and remained a key member until the company's final show in Nashville in 2019. Known for his over-the-top comedic timing and ability to transform into wildly eccentric characters, he played a range of roles, from villains to bumbling sidekicks, in productions like *Hansel and Gretel*, *Cinderella*, and *The Wizard of Oz*. His performances were defined by their physicality, humor, and an innate ability to engage young audiences. Beyond acting, Boucher played a crucial role behind the scenes, contributing as a director, set designer, and graphic artist. His ingenuity was evident in his stage gags, such as a wrecking ball effect or a Velcro-based costume mishap, that became audience favorites.[32]

For sixteen years, Olde Worlde Theatre brought laughter, wonder, and a sense of play to the Belcourt. But, like so many community-driven artistic endeavors, it eventually reached a crossroads. In 2019, the company held its final performance in Nashville, marking the end of a chapter in the theater's long history.[33]

The struggle remains. Across the country, small theater companies continue to fight for funding, for space, and for the right to exist in an industry that often prioritizes profit over artistic expression. The story of the Belcourt's return to live performance serves as a reminder that these struggles are not new, nor are they insurmountable.

The stage at the Belcourt may have once again gone dark for regular live performances, but its impact lingers in the memories of those who took part in its revival. For Stein, for Boucher, and for the countless actors, directors, and audience members who filled that space with life, it was more than just a theater. It was a home.

And for Nashville, the lesson remains: Theaters, like the communities that sustain them, must be fought for. Because without them, something vital is lost: a space where stories are not just told, but truly lived.

THE CONCERT ERA

BY THE LATE 1990S, the Belcourt was saved, its stage a living artifact imprinted with the footsteps of some of the greatest legends in country music's early history. Back in the mid-1930s, when the stage hosted the Grand Ole Opry, performers regularly played to packed houses without much need for additional promotion. The show was skyrocketing in popularity and all the musicians had to do was show up.

That history, though decades removed, was still palpable in the creaky wooden floors, and the warm glow of the stage lights. But nostalgia alone wasn't enough to keep one of the city's oldest stages alive and relevant. The theater had been physically saved by the work of Belcourt YES!, but the effort wasn't just about keeping the doors open; it was about reimagining what the space could be. And at the time, the theater not only needed more than film screenings to meet the needs of the community stakeholders asking for diversified programming, they needed it to stay financially viable, as they had yet to secure the kind of reputation with filmmakers and distributors they needed to get regular repertory prints and new films to screen, or the customer base to support it alone. Belcourt needed an identity that both honored its past and secured its future. And that's when the music returned.

The Belcourt's rebirth as a concert venue wasn't just about filling seats, it was about tapping into a lineage. The same stage that once hosted Grand Ole Opry icons like DeFord Bailey, Sid Harkreader, and Uncle Dave Macon was now welcoming a new generation of Americana artists, indie rockers, and singer-songwriters who were reshaping Nashville's musical identity at the turn of the century. From Gillian Welch and Dave Rawlings to Bright Eyes, Todd Snider to Marianne Faithfull, Lambchop to Cowboy Junkies, Iris Dement to Jello Biafra, the Belcourt became more than a movie house; it became a proving ground for artists who blurred the lines between folk tradition and modern storytelling.

One era-defining concert took place on September 25, 2006, when Solomon Burke played songs from his album *Nashville*, backed by an all-star lineup including Emmylou Harris, Patty Griffin, Gillian Welch, and Dave Rawlings. A titan of mid-twentieth-century soul and R&B, Burke was best known for his 1955 single "Cry to Me," which famously appeared in *Dirty*

Dancing. Burke's Belcourt performance was one of the most star-studded in the venue's history, rivaling the grandeur of its 1930s Opry days, and eventually culminating in the release of a live concert film.

When the Belcourt reopened in June 2000, after seventeen months of closure, the building was improved, still fumbling a bit with old systems and infrastructure, but the organization was a newborn baby, yet to find its footing.[34] The Belcourt YES! campaign had given it a second life, but financial sustainability remained an open question. As an independent cinema, it lacked the deep-pocketed marketing budgets of national theater chains, and in the early 2000s, independent film was in a precarious position. Streaming hadn't yet taken hold, but multiplexes were dominating, and the arthouse audience wasn't large enough to single-handedly keep the Belcourt afloat. The solution? Look beyond the screen.

It was music, specifically, Nashville's rapidly evolving Americana and indie-rock scene, that helped usher the theater into its next chapter. At a time when the music industry was experiencing its own seismic shifts—Napster, the decline of major label dominance, and the rise of DIY touring and small independent labels—the Belcourt became a critical space for artists on the fringes. However, it also attracted major acts who were on the incline of their careers and legacy artists still popular and influential in the popular music zeitgeist.

From the very beginning, the Belcourt's stage had cultural weight. It wasn't just another room on a tour itinerary, it was a stage that had once held Grand Ole Opry legends, a space that carried a certain reverence. This made it an attractive venue for a new generation of musicians, many of whom were blending traditional country and folk influences with a modern edge. Artists like Gillian Welch, Todd Snider, and David Mead played early shows there, their music echoing through the historic walls.

By the early 2000s, the Belcourt was hosting a steady stream of concerts that would, in hindsight, read like a roll call of Americana and indie-rock royalty. In 2000 alone, the lineup included performances from Warren Zevon, Radney Foster, Alex Chilton, and Victoria Williams. The following years would bring Norah Jones, Cowboy Junkies, Patty Griffin, and Ralph Stanley. It wasn't just established names; this was a place where new artists could step onto a historic stage and play to an audience that actually listened.

For musicians, playing the Belcourt wasn't about selling out a massive venue or chasing radio play, it was about playing in a space with soul. Mary Gauthier, who played seven different times on Belcourt's stage, her first on October 23, 2002, opening for Guy Clark, remembers the experience vividly. "I don't clearly remember my own performance—I was probably a nervous wreck," she admitted. "But I remember Guy. I remember sitting in the green room with him. I watched the master work. That was my education."[35]

The Belcourt also provided something increasingly rare in the early 2000s: a venue where the performance itself was the main attraction. In an era when big-label country music was leaning toward arena spectacle, the Belcourt remained a listening room at heart. There were no beer-soaked bar crowds, no deafening chatter. The setting allowed songwriters to tell stories, to hold an audience with just a guitar and their voice.

For an artist like Tim O'Brien, a veteran of bluegrass and folk, the Belcourt was a place where history and intimacy met. "I love this place," O'Brien said. "I love the fact that it was home to the Opry, but that it's still here, still evolving."[36]

Belcourt's stage was also a place for artists to engage with national and community-based social issues, using their music as a conduit to organize, teach, and rally resources to help solve social problems. Other notable concerts underscored the intersection of music and activism. The *Tell Us the Truth* tour in 2003, featuring Billy Bragg and Steve Earle, as well as benefit shows like the 2005 concert for the Nashville Peace and Justice Center, and the 2008 fundraiser for the Lost Boys of Sudan (a group of young Sudanese men displaced or orphaned during the country's more-than-three-decade civil war beginning in the 1980s) cemented the Belcourt's role as a platform for social justice and political discourse.

But the Belcourt's success as a music venue wasn't just about the artists; it was about the people behind the scenes who curated and booked these shows. That's where Jim Pitt and Rick Whetsel come in.

What happened at the Belcourt wasn't accidental. It was the result of careful booking, an understanding of where Nashville's music scene was headed, and a willingness to take risks. Pitt and Whetsel weren't just putting on concerts, they were shaping an era.

With the Belcourt gaining financial stability progressively each year thanks in large part to successful concert programming that brought in needed revenue (like many venues, mostly in bar sales) and helped build an audience for the new theater, the next challenge was maintaining that momentum while securing the theater's place as a cornerstone of independent film culture. But before that could happen, the venue needed gatekeepers—people who could not only bring in the right acts, but could also connect Nashville's local music culture to a wider, national scene.

That job fell to two men with deep roots in the industry, men who knew how to spot talent before the rest of the world caught on. Jim Pitt didn't just fall into the music business, he built his career from an early love of music and a keen eye for artists on the verge of breaking. Born in Bridgeport, Connecticut, Pitt grew up in a household surrounded by music. His father played piano and organ, his sisters collected records, and the New York radio waves brought him everything from the Beatles to classic Broadway soundtracks.[37] But it wasn't just music he was obsessed with, it was the way music was presented. He studied liner notes, learned the names of club bookers and radio programmers, and absorbed how artists were discovered.[38] This obsessive attention to detail paid off when he landed his first major booking job.

By the late 1980s, Pitt was working as a talent booker for NBC's *Saturday Night Live*, a role that put him at the intersection of music and pop culture. One of his most famous bookings? Nirvana's January 11, 1992, performance on *SNL*, the band's first appearance on the show and a defining moment in their career. The band had just broken into the mainstream with the release of their major label debut, Geffen records' *Incesticide* (1992), and the performance is still considered one of *SNL*'s most iconic performances. Pitt's *SNL* boss, Lorne Michaels, remembers the booking cementing Nirvana's status as a generation-defining band. "David Geffen called me about Nirvana because they were on his label, and he said, 'I don't know what's happening, but you know, last week they sold 60,000 records, and this week they sold 140,000, so something is happening."[39]

Years later, Pitt had another defining moment when he booked Norah Jones at the Belcourt just before she became an international sensation. "She was still just this rising artist, and it wasn't clear yet how big she was going to be," Pitt recalled. "Then suddenly, *Come Away with Me* blew up, and she was playing every major venue in the country. That Belcourt show became one of those moments where people later said, 'I can't believe I saw her there before she got huge!'"

Pitt's ability to spot talent before the rest of the world caught on was a crucial asset for the Belcourt during its early revival. Booking the right artists wasn't just about selling tickets, it was about crafting a reputation. Under his company, Acme Booking, the Belcourt became a venue where artists could perform in an intimate, historic space before ascending to larger stages.

While Pitt had a national scope to his work, Rick Whetsel was deeply embedded in the fabric of Nashville's independent music scene. Originally from Pittsburgh, Whetsel moved to Nashville in 1991, drawn by its raw, eclectic music culture.[40] Unlike the city's more corporate country industry, Whetsel gravitated toward the rock and alternative scenes bubbling under the surface.

Before working with Belcourt, he had made his mark in the late 1990s as part of Great Big Shows, one of Nashville's most important live music promotion companies. He played a key role in booking for Dancing in the District, an outdoor concert series that brought major national acts to downtown Nashville. It was during this time that he helped introduce My Morning Jacket to Nashville audiences, booking the band when they were still an underground name.[41]

Whetsel's relationship with Belcourt started in an unexpected way. In the early 2000s, when the theater was still finding its footing as a new nonprofit arts center, he was approached by Charlie Hawkins and Julia Sutherland, two figures instrumental in the theater's nonprofit transition. They saw an opportunity in Whetsel's connections and vision. "When Charlie and Julia first brought up the idea of me working with the Belcourt, I was hesitant," Whetsel recalled. "At that time, the theater was still trying to find its identity again. But I saw the potential. This was a space with history, real history. It wasn't just another venue."[42]

For Whetsel, working with the Belcourt wasn't just about filling dates on a calendar, it was about curating a musical experience. His expertise in booking meant he knew which artists would resonate with the theater's acoustics, its audience, and its atmosphere. Rick had this ability to know which acts would fit the Belcourt. He wasn't just throwing shows together, he was building a local audience.

Together, Pitt and Whetsel turned the Belcourt into more than a theater; it became a proving ground for some of the most important artists of the early 2000s. Omaha, Nebraska, auteurs and Saddle Creek indie label artists

Bright Eyes played one of their most intimate early Nashville shows there with M. Ward on September 25, 2002. Gillian Welch and David Rawlings used it as a home base for their folk revival sound on multiple occasions, clocking seven solo or guest appearances between 2001 and 2006. Local indie artists like Todd Snider and Kim Richey and others played crucial early gigs that helped them build a following in their home city, Snider accruing five appearances between 2000 and 2005, and Richey tallying four between 2002 and 2010.

At a time when Nashville's mainstream music industry was focused on arena country, and the Contemporary Christian Music industry was preoccupied with how they were going to make praise and worship songs sound like mainstream pop music, Belcourt became a sanctuary for artists who didn't fit that mold. It was a venue where an artist like Patty Griffin could perform a stripped-down acoustic set one night and a group like Lambchop could push the boundaries of indie rock the next.

The impact of Pitt and Whetsel's work went beyond just the Belcourt. The city itself was changing, with Nashville's indie and Americana scenes gaining national attention. The future success of artists like Jason Isbell, Sturgill Simpson, and Kacey Musgraves owe something to the groundwork laid by the local indie Americana scene that flourished at the Belcourt during that first decade of the 2000s.

The Belcourt emerged from its uncertain early years with the help of music programming and a committed community. Concert rentals brought in audiences and energy, giving the theater a stronger footing even as it remained financially fragile. Behind the scenes, the challenges were stark. Management sometimes delayed payroll tax payments for months, a risk that could have closed the theater at any moment. Yet the steady income from concert rentals, and the concessions sales they generated, provided both cultural momentum and much-needed financial relief.

This era proved critical. The revenue and visibility created by music programming gave Belcourt the stability to imagine a future beyond survival. Without the influx of concertgoers during these years, the theater might not have endured long enough to transition into a nonprofit arthouse cinema at all. For Pitt and Whetsel, it was about doing their part to help a new community organization keeping the lights on while doing a job they loved. But in retrospect, their work made popular music history.

Today, the Belcourt is firmly established as one of the country's premier independent cinemas, but its success is inseparable from the music that once kept it alive. The early 2000s were a defining era, not just for the Belcourt, but for Nashville's broader cultural identity. Pitt and Whetsel's work helped redefine what the city's music scene could be, proving that Nashville wasn't just Music City, USA, in the traditional sense. It was a place where old and new, past and present, country and indie, could collide in ways that shaped the city's future.

The Belcourt's stage, once home to the fiddles and banjos of string band performers and barn dance bands, and of hillbilly, and sadly, Blackface comedy, had become a place where Mary Gauthier and Tim O'Brien could carve out their own legacy. And at the center of it all were two bookers who saw not just a struggling theater, but a stage with a future.

In the early years just beyond the first decade of the 2000s, the Belcourt Theatre had firmly reestablished itself as an essential space in Nashville's cultural landscape. No longer teetering on the brink of closure, it had become a thriving nonprofit cinema, a premier destination for independent film, and a beloved concert venue that had played a crucial role in elevating the city's indie and Americana scenes.

But as much as Belcourt's survival was a triumph, it was also a reminder of the challenges that independent cultural spaces face in a rapidly changing city.

By 2012, the Belcourt's focus had fully shifted back to cinema, as it had when the building became Belcourt Cinema back in the early 1960s. Concert programming, once the financial backbone of the theater's survival, had become less necessary as the nonprofit secured stable funding through grants, donations, and a growing audience of dedicated filmgoers.

On Christmas Eve 2015, the theater closed its doors. This time, for growth, not failure. In 2016, the theater underwent a massive renovation, expanding its screening spaces and restoring much of the building's historic architecture, ensuring that it would survive another hundred years.

This shift wasn't a rejection of the musical culture that had sustained the theater for so long, but rather an evolution. The Belcourt had always been a space of reinvention: first as a silent film house, then playhouse and home to the Grand Ole Opry, later as an arthouse cinema, and in the 2000s, as a concert venue that helped define an era of Nashville's independent music scene. Now, it was embracing its identity as a nonprofit dedicated to cinema, ensuring its longevity for future generations.

Like many longtime patrons who had been instrumental in the theater's musical rebirth and community members who worked to save the theater at the turn of the century, for Rick Whetsel, the transition was bittersweet. "The Belcourt had done exactly what it needed to do—use music to stay alive," he reflected. "But it was never meant to be just a concert venue. It was always about something bigger."

For those who were there in the early 2000s, when the Belcourt was more than just a movie theater—when it was a place where music history was being made, night after night—it will always be more than just a screen in a darkened room.

It will be a stage. A stage that saved itself, with a little help from its friends . . . and maybe a few ghosts.

"A building like that is always going to feel haunted."

—RICK WHETSEL

"When you look up [from the stage] you can just imagine everything that has happened . . . [everything] that has wafted up to these rafters."

—JIM PITT

"I will say that the stage . . . there is a sensation, or at least a reverence for those who have stood on it. You conjure it. It could be your own imagination, it probably is, but you conjure it. And you realize, I'm walking behind those who are no longer here, who helped develop this art form and create something in this world that mattered."

—MARY GAUTHIER

10

BECOMING NASHVILLE'S FILM CENTER

THE BEGINNING OF THE REVIVAL (1999–2003)

AT THE CLOSE OF the twentieth century, the Belcourt Theatre stood at a crossroads. Once a bustling neighborhood cinema and performing arts venue, it had fallen into dormancy, shuttered and facing an uncertain future. But in March 1999, a grassroots effort, spearheaded by a newly formed nonprofit, Belcourt YES!, breathed new life into the historic building.[1] Their goal was straightforward yet ambitious: preserve the Belcourt, restore it as a cultural gathering place, and ensure its future as a home for cinema and community.

On June 3, 2000, following a seventeen-month closure for planning and repairs, the Belcourt reopened under the stewardship of Belcourt YES![2] Its programming slate reflected its eclectic identity: repertory film screenings, live concerts, theatrical performances, community events, and private rentals. In this formative period, the organization emphasized accessibility and experimentation, laying the foundation for the institution it would eventually become.

Reopening, however, did not yet mean stability, and one of the people most responsible for turning the Belcourt from a rescued building into a functioning institution was Steve Small. He arrived at the Belcourt in 2003, when the theater had reopened but was still far from secure. He came not from arthouse exhibition, but from a broader entertainment background that included artist management, live production, television, and music business operations. That experience proved invaluable. As managing director,

Small learned the mechanics of exhibition from the ground up while handling the less glamorous work that kept the theater alive: staffing, licensing, concessions, rentals, audience development, and day-to-day operations. He also helped the Belcourt broaden its programming mix, understanding early that specialty film alone would not sustain the institution. Concerts, family programming, rentals, community events, and bar service all became part of a practical strategy for survival. Just as importantly, Small helped the organization navigate serious institutional threats, including tax and management problems that could easily have derailed the early nonprofit. In those fragile years, he served as a bridge figure, helping convert grassroots passion into a workable operating model and laying the groundwork for the more stable film center that would follow. Small's work helped steady the institution during its most precarious years, but long-term security still depended on solving the larger question of the building itself.[3]

That new stability depended not only on ownership arrangements, but also on board members and donors willing to treat the Belcourt as an institution worth sustaining for the long term. Among the most important of those figures was H. G. Webb, who became one of the Belcourt's most consequential stewards in the years after reopening. Drawn first by the campaign to save the theater and then by the repertory programming he found there, Webb joined the audit and finance committee and later served multiple terms on the board. He brought to the Belcourt a background in investment management, corporate finance, and long-range planning, and he approached the theater with the same seriousness. In the leanest years, that often meant literal survival: Webb recalled moments when he and Nina were helping cover payroll and times when the theater remained afloat only through a fragile combination of donor support, bank relationships, and landlord patience. Over time, his role expanded from emergency stewardship to strategic leadership. He helped guide the Belcourt toward fiscal stability, supported the eventual building purchase and renovation, and, through the Mansker-Webb Screening Room, helped make the post-renovation business model more flexible and sustainable. His legacy was not only generosity, but judgment. With that emerging financial and structural footing in place, the Belcourt could begin defining itself more clearly through the people shaping what audiences encountered on screen.[4]

A key turning point came in October 2003, when Tom Wills, a philanthropist and co-founder of Belcourt YES!, purchased the building. He entered into a five-year lease agreement with the nonprofit, offering them the opportunity to buy the building at cost once they had raised the necessary funds. This act of stewardship secured a future for the Belcourt beyond temporary tenancy, giving the organization stability to define its mission more clearly.

Among the staff at the time was Toby Leonard, who joined the Belcourt team in 2003. Born and raised in Nashville, Leonard's relationship with the theater began as a patron. He vividly recalled attending a showing of *Chariots of Fire* (Hugh Hudson, dir., 1981) in 1982, during its 119-day run, one of the longest in Belcourt's history. Once he became an employee, he started out in the box office and concessions, but Leonard gradually took on programming duties, learning the ropes under then-programmer Michael Arendt. By 2005, he had curated his first series, a retrospective of director Werner Herzog, which marked the beginning of his curatorial influence.

ART HOUSE CONVERGENCE AND SUNDANCE FILM FESTIVAL (2005–2007)

IN THE WINTER OF 2005, Toby Leonard, by this time the Belcourt's programming director, received an invitation that would expand Belcourt's role from a local institution to a voice in the national independent cinema landscape. The Sundance Film Festival invited a small group of fourteen theaters, including the Belcourt, to a new initiative as part of a year-long twenty-fifth anniversary celebration of their Sundance Institute.[5] This gathering, convened by Sundance artistic director John Cooper and programmer Connie White, recognized Belcourt for its quality film programming and commitment to building local audiences for independent film. Calling their selected theaters the "unsung heroes of independent film," Cooper and White brought together the fourteen mission-driven cinemas to explore strategies for strengthening the visibility and viability of independent film.[6]

Though the initial idea, to bring Sundance titles to hometown screens, proved difficult due to distribution limitations, the meeting sparked lasting relationships. With leadership from the Michigan Theater in Ann Arbor, the group began meeting annually, giving rise to the Art House Convergence. What began as a little more than a dozen theaters in a Sundance conference room would grow into a national movement, hosting over five hundred attendees by 2019 and representing nearly one hundred theaters.[7]

For Leonard and the Belcourt, these gatherings were transformative. They provided new frameworks for sustaining independent cinemas and encouraged the transition from for-profit venues to nonprofit models, ensuring long-term organizational stability. They also offered access to funding avenues for infrastructure, education, and outreach.

Leonard's participation positioned Belcourt at the heart of this emerging movement, and his creative leadership placed the theater squarely within a growing national movement of independent film exhibition. As his programming expanded and audiences steadily increased, the Belcourt's reputation began to spread beyond Nashville. Distributor reports soon listed the theater among the top-grossing US venues for certain limited-release titles—an unexpected distinction that even Leonard had not initially recognized.[8]

This visibility and financial success marked the critical forward momentum needed to begin stabilizing, and eventually growing. The Belcourt was no longer simply Nashville's neighborhood cinema; it had become a recognized player in the national and local exhibition landscape. Leonard achieved this prominence by creating a sustainable programming framework that could serve as a model for other independent theaters. His mix of first-run and repertory titles, innovative series structures, and recurring program anchors, such as *Music City Mondays*, gave the Belcourt a distinct identity.

Through this approach, Leonard established the foundation that defined the theater's programming in its first decade and beyond. His creativity and discipline provided the Belcourt with an operating structure strong enough to support growth, setting the stage for its broader success.

Programming gave the Belcourt its intellectual shape, but its growing identity also depended on the staff members who made that programming visible, legible, and technically possible. One of those figures was Matt Polman, who joined the Belcourt in 2004 and grew with the institution over the next two decades. He came to the theater through Watkins Film School, where he had learned to handle film as a loader on 16mm productions, and was trained in the booth at a moment when the Belcourt was still fully film-based, improvised, and uncertain. Polman quickly became fluent in the practical craft of exhibition, from 35mm platter systems to 16mm presentation, but his role soon widened. Using downtime in the booth, he began designing flyers and graphics, taught himself Photoshop and the principles of layout, and gradually took on more and more of the theater's visual identity. Over time, he became the person behind much of the Belcourt's public face: posters, slideshows, signage, website updates, marquees, and promotional graphics. His contribution was often invisible precisely because it worked so well. As the Belcourt matured, Polman helped give it continuity, polish, and a recognizable look across changing technological eras. That combination of curatorial ambition and growing institutional coherence soon translated into measurable momentum.[9]

The year 2006 marked a turning point for Belcourt YES!. In January, the organization recorded its first month in the black. By September, it had begun the process of exercising its option to buy the theater, and by year's end, the purchase was complete.

A NEW ERA OF LEADERSHIP (2007–2015)

IN JANUARY 2007, BELCOURT WELCOMED Stephanie Silverman as its new executive director. With a background in theater marketing and development, Silverman brought fresh energy to the organization and a strong sense of its potential. Her introduction to the Belcourt had been as a moviegoer in the neighborhood; by the time she stepped into the leadership role, she was entering a theater in the midst of success, with *Pan's Labyrinth* (Guillermo del Toro, dir., 2006) drawing extended runs and substantial box office.[10]

Silverman's immediate focus was stabilization. In its early years, the Belcourt had operated largely through the efforts of volunteers and a small, informal staff. One of Silverman's first tasks was to professionalize the organization's operations, a process that included difficult but necessary transitions in leadership culture. She worked to shift control from the founding volunteers of Belcourt YES! toward a staff-led, institutional model, sometimes facing resistance, but ultimately succeeding in building a foundation for long-term growth.[11]

That process of stabilization depended not only on leadership at the top, but also on staff members whose day-to-day work made the organization more durable from within. Elle Long was one of those figures. She joined the Belcourt in 2007, first in a hybrid front-of-house and office role, and stayed as the theater grew from a relatively small, manual operation into a far more structured institution. In those early years, membership cards were printed, assembled, and mailed by hand, and the organization's ambitions were still modest by later standards. As the audience expanded, so did Long's responsibilities.

Long eventually became the membership and administrative manager, overseeing member relations, office administration, volunteer coordination, and many of the small but essential systems that keep a nonprofit cinema functioning. Her work also extended into fundraising culture through the Red Carpet Evening, where she helped shape the event's logistics and silent auction as it evolved into a more polished annual gala. Long's role was largely behind the scenes, but its impact was concrete: she helped the Belcourt professionalize its internal operations, support substantial membership growth, and build the kind of organizational continuity on which later expansion depended. As the staff structure strengthened, Silverman and her colleagues were able to sharpen the theater's public identity with greater confidence.

Under her direction, the Belcourt refined its identity, moving away from its earlier "Film, Music, Theater" branding. The theater's programming had already begun reducing live performances in favor of more consistent film curation. Silverman embraced and formalized this shift, positioning the theater not just as a venue that showed films, but as a film center: a civic and cultural space dedicated to cinema as an art form.[12]

This rebranding gained momentum during successful programming events, such as a Terrence Malick retrospective, where a screening of *Badlands* (1973) unexpectedly drew an audience of 130.[13] In contrast to earlier showings that might have attracted only a few attendees, these turnouts demonstrated a growing appetite for curated film experiences, and confirmed that the theater's evolving identity was resonating with the public.

Later that year, on November 5, 2007, the Belcourt reached a landmark milestone: It finalized the purchase of the building from Tom Wills. The acquisition secured Belcourt's permanent home and underscored its transformation from a grassroots experiment into an established institution with a long-term vision. Securing the building answered one question of survival, but it did not by itself explain how the Belcourt became Nashville's film center. That transformation happened most clearly through programming.

PROGRAMMING THE REVIVAL: HOW THE BELCOURT BECAME NASHVILLE'S FILM CENTER

SAVING THE BELCOURT WAS ONLY the first step. The harder task came after the doors reopened.[14]

When the nonprofit revived the theater in 2000, it did not inherit a fully formed film center. It inherited a historic building, a strong wave of civic goodwill, and a set of unanswered questions about ownership, sustainability, and mission. The institution that emerged from the rescue effort was still fragile, under-resourced, and trying to determine what kind of cultural organization it would become. Reopening on June 3, 2000, with symbolic twenty-five-cent tickets was a triumph—the Belcourt was alive again. It was not yet secure.

That distinction matters because Belcourt's transformation into Nashville's film center did not happen all at once. It happened through programming.

FIGURE 10.1. Exterior of the Belcourt Theatre before rebranding as "Nashville's Non-profit Film Center," July 2, 2006. Photograph by Julia Sutherland. Belcourt Theatre Collection. Courtesy of Vanderbilt University Special Collections.

Not abstractly, and not only through mission statements or donor appeals, but through repeated acts of curation that taught audiences how to use the theater again. In the early years of the nonprofit, the Belcourt was still trying to be several things at once: a venue for new releases, a home for live music, a space for theater, and a site where repertory cinema might once again take root. This was less a contradiction than a practical response to instability. The organization was testing formats, audiences, and rhythms of use while trying to determine what would hold.

The reopening-day lineup captures that transitional moment well. On screen were *The Muppet Movie* (James Frawley, dir., 1979), Tom Tykwer's *Winter Sleepers* (1997), and Mike Hodges's *Croupier* (1998), a slick British thriller starring Clive Owen before he became an international star. The variety of that bill reflected Belcourt's eclectic identity in its earliest nonprofit phase. It was trying to welcome broad audiences, serve adventurous viewers, and signal that this was not simply a restored old house but a newly active cultural institution. Of those three titles, *Croupier* proved the most consequential. It played for roughly two and a half months and became the organization's first major hit of the nonprofit era. Its success was not only financial. It demonstrated that Nashville audiences would support sustained runs of specialty cinema if the programming was smart and the context was right.

That first success did not immediately resolve the larger question of repertory identity. In the early 2000s, Belcourt's approach to repertory was still provisional. Week-long runs were common, supplemented by what would later become known as Weekend Classics, usually Saturday and Sunday noon screenings. These efforts were modest in scale, but they were foundational in method. They allowed the Belcourt to begin rebuilding not just attendance, but audience literacy. Repertory at this stage was a way of teaching the public what kind of institution the Belcourt wanted to be.

This was where underwriting and early curatorial support proved essential. Titles such as Robert Bresson's *Au Hasard Balthazar* (1966), along with other demanding arthouse selections shown in the early 2000s, were made possible in part by Nashville Premieres, an independently operating group of Belcourt founders who underwrote original programming while the nonprofit found its footing. Their support helped build an audience for more challenging cinema and for newly circulating prints of underseen classics before the Belcourt could fully sustain such programming on its own.

Initial programmatic support also came from in-house staff and board members. At the time, programming was handled by a committee. Scott Manzler played a leading role, driven both by force of personality and by the philanthropy he contributed to keep the theater going. Tom Wills loaned out prints from his personal archive of 35 and 16mm films. Other key participants included front-of-house staffer Shawn Shepherd, who oversaw the booking process; Toby Leonard; Mark Mays; F. Clark Williams; and others who moved in and out of the committee over time. That support is easy to overlook in hindsight, but it was crucial. Institutions do not become film centers simply by aspiring to be one. They require a period of transition during which audience development can catch up with curatorial ambition.

A title like *I Am Cuba* (1964), programmed in 2001, reveals what was already emerging in those years. Directed by Mikhail Kalatozov, the film linked the Belcourt to the ongoing work of preservation and rediscovery that was reshaping repertory culture nationally. The theater's exhibition conditions at the time may have been imperfect, but the curatorial instinct was firmly in place. The Belcourt was beginning to position itself not simply as a place to replay the canon, but as a place where audiences could encounter restoration culture, international cinema, and neglected masterworks in a shared public setting. That ambition would become one of the clearest marks of its identity.

As the decade progressed, the programming became more confident and more formally adventurous. Bela Tarr's *Sátántangó* (1994), a seven-and-a-half-hour work of slow cinema running 37,204 feet on 35mm, screened from December 8 through 10, in 2006 and returned again in 2019. A film like *Sátántangó* was not just another repertory booking. It was a statement about what kinds of cinematic experiences Belcourt believed Nashville could sustain. Its twelve-part structure, its durational demands, and its reputation as a landmark of international art cinema made it exactly the sort of title that separated a serious film institution from a venue merely rotating old favorites. By showing it, Belcourt was helping create the audience it needed for the next stage of its own development.

At the same time, Belcourt's path toward becoming a film center was never defined by film alone. One of the most distinctive aspects of the early nonprofit era was the continued interplay between cinema, music, and live event culture. That overlap did not distract from the Belcourt's identity. It helped build it. The theater was still, in effect, learning how to function as a nonprofit arts center in a city whose cultural energy often moved through music first. The 2009 screening of *Anvil! The Story of Anvil* (Sacha Gervasi, dir., 2008) demonstrates how porous those categories could be. After the documentary screening, the band performed live, with Lips Kudlow sliding beneath the rising screen and launching directly into a set. The evening extended into the lobby and beyond. It was part screening, part concert, part communal happening. Events like that kept the Belcourt visible, lively, and legible as a place where culture was experienced collectively rather than passively consumed.

That same elasticity also shaped Belcourt's relationship to cult and midnight cinema. Nobuhiko Obayashi's *House* (1977), which passed through the Belcourt between 2009 and 2010 and returned again in 2013 and 2019, offers an especially telling example. The film's American revival moved through informal circulation, fan subtitle culture, and then above-board repertory exhibition, with one of its first legitimate screenings arriving at the Belcourt as part of the Midnight Movies series. The theater's hand-designed screenprint by local artist Sam Smith for that engagement was later adopted by Janus Films and the Criterion Collection for the film's theatrical and Blu-ray circulation. Whether or not the Belcourt caused the film's full-scale rediscovery, it clearly functioned as one of the places through which that rediscovery gained shape and momentum. This was programming as not just exhibition, but cultural intervention.

By the early 2010s, the repertory program had moved beyond one-off revivals and niche midnight shows into more ambitious thematic structures. Smaller director-centered or actor-centered bookings, often housed within Weekend Classics, gave way to large-scale series built around broad historical or regional arguments. The first major example was Visions of the South in spring 2011, a four-week survey of twentieth-century films depicting life in the southeastern United States. Bringing together twenty-two films spanning seventy-five years, the series marked a shift in Belcourt's institutional confidence. It was no longer only reviving important films. It was framing them interpretively, inviting audiences to see cinema history comparatively and to think about the South as both lived place and cinematic construction.

The opening-night selection, Elia Kazan's *Wild River* (1960), made that shift especially legible. Newly restored at the time by 20th Century Fox and shown in 35mm, the film is set in the post-Depression Tennessee Valley and was shot northeast of Chattanooga. It concerns a TVA administrator sent to clear land for flooding by a new dam, where he confronts local resistance and becomes involved with the granddaughter of an elderly landowner who refuses to sell. In the context of Visions of the South, *Wild River* was more than a strong repertory title. It became a way to connect national film history to Tennessee's own historical landscape. That move, from general film culture to locally resonant programming, is one of the clearest ways the Belcourt became Nashville's film center rather than merely Nashville's arthouse.

The programming around Terrence Malick's *The Tree of Life* (2011) pushed this evolution further by linking repertory thinking to contemporary release strategy. In the month leading up to the film's summer run, Belcourt programmed Malick's earlier features, effectively creating an in-house retrospective that prepared audiences for his new work. This was a curatorial move as much as a commercial one. It assumed that a current release could be enriched by historical framing, and that viewers would respond to the chance to encounter a filmmaker's body of work as a whole. The result was one of the longest runs in the theater's modern history. *The Tree of Life* played for fifty-six days, the strongest sustained performance since *Croupier*. That kind of run confirmed that curation was not simply a matter of taste. It was an audience-building tool and a defining feature of the Belcourt's exhibition model.

The following year only reinforced that lesson. In 2012, Wes Anderson's *Moonrise Kingdom* was a major draw, in keeping with the long-standing popularity of Anderson's work at the Belcourt. But around it, the theater mounted an all-35mm Hitchcock series, a complete touring Robert Bresson retrospective with prints imported from France, and a sixteen-film Studio Ghibli retrospective made possible by the renewed circulation of that library through GKIDS Films. Soon after came The Light and Sound Machine, a multi-year partnership with Third Man Records built in part around 16mm changeover capability. By this point, the Belcourt was operating on several levels at once: as a destination for new specialty releases, as a serious repertory house, as a partner in archival-format exhibition, and as a collaborative institution embedded in Nashville's broader cultural life.

The second half of the 2010s brought a different but equally important kind of validation. Documentaries became a major force in Belcourt's programming and audience growth. Raoul Peck's *I Am Not Your Negro* (2017), built from James Baldwin's unfinished writings on Medgar Evers, Malcolm X, and Martin Luther King Jr., arrived at a moment when documentary form and political urgency were reinforcing one another. The film became part of a larger documentary wave that included *Kedi* (Ceyda Torun, dir., 2016), *Loving Vincent* (D. K. Welchman and Hugh Welchman, dirs., 2017), *RBG* (Glen Simister, dir., 2018), *Free Solo* (Jimmy Chin and Elizabeth Chai Vasarhelyi, dirs., 2018), and *Three Identical Strangers* (Tim Wardle, dir., 2018). Many of these films played for weeks or months, a level of sustained documentary interest that had become increasingly rare. The Belcourt was not only responding to national trends. It was helping localize them, making Nashville one of the places where documentary cinema remained a central public form.

The industrial context of those years also mattered. The MoviePass era altered viewing habits across the country and intensified attendance at the Belcourt just as the theater was emerging from renovation with stronger operational footing.[15] In 2018, films like *The Shape of Water* (Guillermo del Toro, dir., 2017), *I, Tonya* (Craig Gillespie, dir., 2017), and *Phantom Thread* (Paul Thomas Anderson, dir., 2017) all played for months, sometimes leaving regular patrons wondering if the theater would ever show anything else. Lines wrapped around the block. Whatever portion of that surge can be credited to subscription culture, the larger point remains the same: the Belcourt had reached a stage where it could convert national film buzz into sustained local attendance across multiple kinds of specialty cinema.

No title demonstrates that better than Morgan Neville's *Won't You Be My Neighbor?* (2018). It became the highest-attended run of the Belcourt's tenure, not only as the modern nonprofit of the last twenty-five years, but one of the most successful across its earlier arthouse life under Belcourt Cinema as well. The demand was so high that the theater opened the film on both downstairs screens, an unusual move that resulted in repeat sellouts and, at one point, the highest gross in the country. This was a remarkable benchmark, not simply because the film was popular, but because it showed that the Belcourt had become an institution capable of outperforming theaters in much larger markets when the right film met the right audience in the right setting.

Repertory, however, remained central to the theater's identity even during these years of contemporary success. The Belcourt continued to stage genre festivals and large-scale series, including noir, samurai, and western programs.

In 2018, Essential Westerns, a twenty-six-film series underwritten and shaped in part by H. G. Webb, brought that repertory muscle into full view. That program followed an earlier Westerns series from 2009, when technical limitations still affected access to archival 35mm materials. By 2018, the Belcourt had both the equipment and the audience to program with greater depth and confidence. Sam Peckinpah's *The Wild Bunch* (1969), one of Webb's favorites, stood as a fitting emblem of that stage in the institution's life: a film about the end of one era and the uneasy emergence of another, shown in a theater that had survived by doing exactly the same.

Then came *Parasite* (Bong Joon Ho, dir., 2019), a film that brought together many of the forces the Belcourt had spent nearly two decades consolidating: adventurous audiences, international cinema, repertory-informed viewers, strong word of mouth, and a distributor pipeline that could carry a specialty title from Cannes to the Academy Awards. *Parasite* opened at the Belcourt on October 25, 2019, and ran continuously until March 8, 2020, for a total of twenty weeks, becoming yet another of the longest runs of the modern era. Its success confirmed the theater's place in the national specialty ecosystem, but it also reaffirmed something local. By then, the Belcourt had created a public for whom a Korean-made dark comedy winning the Palme d'Or did not feel like difficult programming. It felt like the kind of event the Belcourt was built to host.

A week later, the emergent global COVID-19 pandemic halted that momentum. On March 15, 2020, the Centers for Disease Control and Prevention recommended against public gatherings of fifty or more people, and the Belcourt closed for the foreseeable future. That same week, Kelly Reichardt's *First Cow* (2019) opened at the theater, only to become one of the most significant missed opportunities of the nonprofit era because of its timing. Released in four US theaters on March 6, 2020, the film was pulled from distribution by A24 on March 15. Nashville-based musician William Tyler, who provided the film's soundtrack, had been scheduled to make a rare live musical appearance at a special screening at the theater on March 31, but the event was canceled. The Belcourt then worked to remain active through online screenings via a makeshift streaming channel and a revived series of drive-in nights in the parking lot—an echo of earlier outdoor screenings from the early 2000s-era. Even there, *First Cow* nearly slipped away again when wind made its inflatable-screen presentation unwatchable. If *Croupier* marked the first successful run of the nonprofit era, *First Cow* revealed the fragility of the theatrical culture the Belcourt had spent twenty years rebuilding.

Seen across the full arc from 2000 to 2025, the Belcourt became Nashville's film center not because it abandoned its earlier identities, but because it learned how to integrate them into a coherent institutional mission. It used live music and events to stay active while the nonprofit model stabilized. It used repertory to cultivate audience literacy and distinguish itself from multiplex culture. It used contemporary releases to demonstrate that difficult or specialized films could thrive in Nashville. It built partnerships, expanded curatorial ambition, and translated local loyalty into national reputation. In that sense, the modern Belcourt's rise has been neither accidental nor purely symbolic. It has been built screening by screening, series by series, run by run.

By the time the theater entered its third decade as a nonprofit, the transformation had become unmistakable. The Belcourt was no longer simply a rescued building or an independent cinema surviving against the odds. It had become what earlier generations of Nashville filmgoers had long lacked and what the city had, in many ways, been preparing for all along: a film center rooted in local history, responsive to its moment, and capable of placing Nashville in a national conversation about what moviegoing, preservation, and public culture could still be.

FIGURE 10.2. Poster for a concert fundraiser to replace outdated theater seats, autographed by participating artists, May 5, 2009. Courtesy of Belcourt Theatre.

As programming grew more ambitious, audiences became more engaged, and the Belcourt Theatre matured into a full-fledged film center, its leadership recognized that exhibition alone was not enough. To fully serve its mission, the theater needed to become a space where cinema could be actively explored, discussed, and taught. This vision came to life in the early 2010s with the formal development of the Belcourt's education and engagement programming, a growing pillar of the institution's public role.

This strategic shift was driven by the work of two key staff members: Allison Inman,

FIGURE 10.3. Close-up of the Belcourt Theatre box office facade, 2010. Belcourt Theatre Collection. Courtesy of Vanderbilt University Special Collections.

who joined Belcourt in 2010 as director of Education and Engagement, and Zack Hall, who became Education and Engagement coordinator in the years that followed. Together, Inman and Hall laid the groundwork for what would become one of the theater's most impactful areas of growth.

Inman, with a background in communications and public programming, brought structure and intention to Belcourt's outreach efforts. She helped define the theater's educational mission as one that extended beyond schools and into the broader public sphere. Early initiatives included student matinees and classroom visits as part of the theater's Mobile Movie Theater, designed to make film more accessible to a broader and younger audience and to introduce critical thinking through cinema.[16]

Inman also expanded adult engagement efforts, developing programs that connected film content to contemporary issues and created entry points for broader community participation. This often included guest speaker series, filmmaker Q&As, thematic panels, and collaborations with local universities, nonprofits, and civic groups. Under her leadership, Belcourt began to foster a more intentional conversation between film and public life, helping audiences connect what they saw on screen with the world around them.[17]

As Allison Inman laid the foundation for the Belcourt's education department, Zack Hall joined and brought renewed energy to youth and school-based programming. Building on existing partnerships, Hall expanded the theater's engagement with K–12 educators by developing High School Film Club, a program designed to help students incorporate cinema into their educational experience.[18] Open to all students regardless of prior film knowledge, the club created a space for young people to watch films together and discuss them with peers, fostering a welcoming environment where diverse perspectives were encouraged.

Hall and Inman's most significant contributions centered on youth-oriented programming that emphasized media literacy and critical viewership. Through curated screenings and workshops, both guided students to think analytically about film, not just as entertainment, but as a powerful cultural force that shapes identity, perception, and public discourse. Under their leadership, the Belcourt became a trusted partner in arts education, regularly hosting school groups for educational programs aligned with classroom goals.

Importantly, Hall and Inman also prioritized outreach to underserved schools and communities, ensuring that the Belcourt's offerings were accessible and inclusive programs through partnerships with local organizations like Martha O'Bryan Center, Metro Parks DisABILITIES Program, Oasis Center, Room in the Inn, and Waves Inc. Their work helped embed the Belcourt more deeply into the educational landscape of Nashville, advancing its mission to use film as a tool for learning, equity, and civic engagement.

In 2014, Hall has also played a pivotal role in reintroducing Science on Screen to the Belcourt, a national program funded by the Alfred P. Sloan Foundation and the Coolidge Corner Theatre that pairs science fiction and science-focused films with live presentations by scientists and researchers. By 2015, Zack Hall had assumed full responsibility for programming Belcourt Midnights, bringing a curator's instinct to the theater's late-night offerings.[19] His work built upon the Belcourt's tradition of adventurous cinema while expanding its appeal to new audiences. The series underscored Belcourt's commitment to bridging cinematic storytelling with public education and intellectual inquiry.

Hall's editorial eye shape also gave new shape to how audiences experienced screenings during this period. As the editor of trailers and pre-show reels, he layered in humor, deep-cut references, and a fan's reverence for cult genres. His programming choices for Belcourt Midnights reflected more than just a love of horror or exploitation; they reflected an acute understanding of the communal energy generated by watching these films in a packed theater at midnight. For the annual 12 Hours of Terror marathon, Hall orchestrated an all-night experience for horror enthusiasts, blending rare 35mm prints, thematic progressions, and unannounced titles to build suspense and sustain audience engagement.[20]

Through their work, Allison Inman and Zack Hall helped redefine educational programming at the Belcourt as a form of creative authorship. Their initiatives reflected the theater's broader mission: to balance scholarly engagement with subcultural celebration. Whether Hall was curating a horror marathon or connecting scientists with science fiction films, each event was conceived not just to screen movies, but to shape how audiences watched, thought about, and remembered them.

Together, Inman and Hall laid the groundwork for a robust and sustainable education department. Their efforts aligned Belcourt's programming with its identity as a community-centered, nonprofit film center, making it not only a place to experience cinema, but a place to learn from it, reflect on it, and connect through it.

CAPITAL CAMPAIGN AND RENOVATION (2015–2016)

BY THE EARLY 2010S, THE Belcourt Theatre had secured organizational stability and was gaining recognition as a regional and national leader in film exhibition. However, as its audience base expanded and programming ambitions grew, the limitations of its physical space became increasingly apparent. Aged infrastructure, failing systems, and limited accessibility posed serious challenges. To realize its vision as Nashville's premier film center, the Belcourt would need to reinvest in its home. Planning for a capital campaign began around 2013, driven by urgent facility needs, deteriorating seating, an unreliable HVAC system, and a failing roof, among others. What began as a response to deferred maintenance soon evolved into a bold opportunity: to reimagine and redefine the Belcourt's future.

Silverman understood that in order to raise the capital needed, a larger team would need to be assembled. Silverman hired Brooke Bernard as development director in 2013. Bernard's professional path brought her to Nashville as a student at Watkins Institute of Art's Film School. After graduating, Bernard began her career in film production, where she developed an expertise in narrative features and independent cinema, eventually co-founding her own film production company, Nomadic Independence Pictures, and producing films like *The Colonel's Bride* (Brent Stewart, dir., 2010).[21]

Executive director Stephanie Silverman recognized that, though she had no prior experience in nonprofit fundraising, Brooke Bernard could serve as a vital bridge between the independent film industry and nonprofit exhibition. Bernard brought to the role a producer's toolkit: project management, fundraising acumen, and stakeholder communication, skills that proved essential during a pivotal phase of the Belcourt's institutional development.[22]

Her operational strengths aligned with the creative momentum already underway at the theater. By 2010, Belcourt programmer Toby Leonard was applying indie-rock logic to film booking, forging a new model of distribution that bypassed traditional theatrical circuits by partnering with record label Drag City to release Harmony Korine's *Trash Humpers* (2009), a Nashville-shot feature that tested a new strategy: delivering independent films directly to like-minded arthouse cinemas, completely sidestepping negotiations with megaplexes.[23]

Working in close collaboration with Silverman and the board of directors, Bernard cultivated new and expanded donor relationships, secured major gifts, and developed strategic messaging that clarified and energized the campaign's vision. In doing so, she achieved what no prior iteration of the Belcourt, whether as cinema or playhouse, had ever fully accomplished in its hundred-year history: a capital campaign that successfully aligned institutional identity, community support, and long-term sustainability.

Her work was foundational to the campaign's success. Bernard helped articulate not only the theater's structural needs—new seats, improved HVAC, and updated technical systems—but also its evolving civic role. She emphasized the Belcourt's function as a cultural anchor, framing it as a space for education, discourse, and access to global cinema. She recalls the campaign period as both intense and energizing, marked by a deep commitment to stewarding a historic space while envisioning its future.

Bernard's fundraising work was matched by an equally important communications effort, one that helped the Belcourt explain both its needs and its civic value to a broader public. That work was led in significant part by Cindy Wall, who joined the Belcourt around 2013 or 2014 as the organization prepared for its largest modern capital campaign. Wall came with a background in political media, documentary production, nonprofit campaigns, and institutional communications, experience that made her especially well suited to a moment when the theater needed not just money, but a persuasive public narrative.

Her early portfolio was unusually broad, spanning both development and communications, and she helped shape the case for support, refine campaign language, and bring greater editorial discipline to the Belcourt's public messaging. Wall also centralized communication workflows, strengthened newsletter and social-media strategies, and helped make the theater more legible to people beyond its most devoted regulars.

Her contribution was strategic as much as stylistic. She helped the Belcourt articulate why renovation mattered, not merely as deferred maintenance, but as an investment in a civic institution whose role in Nashville had outgrown its aging infrastructure. With Bernard driving development and Wall helping shape the campaign's public voice, the renovation effort took on a clarity and momentum the institution had never before achieved.

Under Stephanie Silverman's leadership, the organization launched a bold effort to do just that. With support from the board and community stakeholders, the Belcourt initiated a $5 million capital campaign to fund a comprehensive renovation of its historic space. The campaign's goals were clear: modernize the facility, expand audience capacity, improve accessibility, and enhance both the visitor experience and operational efficiency.

As fundraising progressed, the staff and board emphasized the theater's growing role not just as a place to see films, but as a civic anchor for film education, community discourse, and cultural engagement. This positioning proved persuasive. Contributions came from a broad coalition of foundations, city officials, longtime patrons, and national film partners, each recognizing the Belcourt's unique blend of historical preservation and forward-looking programming.

FIGURE 10.4. Facade of the Belcourt Theatre during renovation, 2016. Visible are the gutted second theater, the 1966 Hall, and the lobby. Belcourt Theatre Collection. Courtesy of Vanderbilt University Special Collections.

FIGURE 10.5. Contributors to the 2016 Capital Campaign seated for a banquet in the newly renovated lobby during the Donor Dinner honoring them, July 21, 2016. Photograph by Michael Bunch. Belcourt Theatre Collection. Courtesy of Vanderbilt University Special Collections.

The theater closed temporarily in 2015 to begin construction. During the renovation, programming continued off-site and at partner venues throughout Nashville, maintaining a presence in the community while building anticipation for the theater's return.[24] The project itself honored the Belcourt's century-old roots while introducing major updates: two fully upgraded screening rooms, improved projection and sound systems, new classroom and event space, enhanced lobby and concession areas, and fully ADA-compliant design. For longtime board leaders such as H. G. Webb, the renovation represented the logical culmination of years spent keeping the institution afloat long enough to imagine a more permanent future.

FIGURE 10.6. Ribbon-cutting ceremony at the Belcourt Theatre's reopening, July 22, 2016. Photograph by Michael Bunch. Staff, donors, and local civic leaders pictured (left to right): Jessica Griffith, Van G. Pond Jr., Susannah Berry, H. G. Webb, Nan Flynn, Chase Cole, Thelma M. Harper, Megan Barry, Stephanie Silverman, Toby Leonard, Terrance Hurd, Jeff Yarbro, and Dillon Watson. Belcourt Theatre Collection. Courtesy of Vanderbilt University Special Collections.

When the Belcourt reopened in 2016, it wasn't just a revitalized venue, it was a redefined institution. The newly renovated space offered a seamless blend of history and innovation, allowing the Belcourt to operate with the capacity, flexibility, and technological sophistication expected of a modern film center.

With improved facilities and an expanded footprint, the Belcourt could now offer a more ambitious year-round calendar of screenings, retrospectives, premieres, and public programs. It had also deepened its commitment to education, creating dedicated spaces for workshops, seminars, and school visits.

The transformation wasn't purely physical. With its renovation, the Belcourt clarified its institutional identity and mission: it was now unambiguously Nashville's nonprofit home for film, and one of the few remaining independent cinemas of its kind in the United States.

CULTURAL IMPACT AND NATIONAL RECOGNITION (2016–2025)

THE YEARS FOLLOWING THE RENOVATION marked a period of unprecedented influence and visibility for the Belcourt Theatre. Its enhanced space allowed for increased attendance, broader programming, and a stronger emphasis on

FIGURE 10.7. Exterior of the newly renovated Belcourt Theatre, 2016. Photograph by Tom Gatlin. Visible are the major additions completed that year, including a marquee, an annexed wing of second-floor administrative offices and classroom, and the first-floor lobby. Belcourt Theatre Collection. Courtesy of Vanderbilt University Special Collections.

both local partnerships and global cinema. At a time when many independent theaters were closing or struggling to remain solvent, the Belcourt thrived by staying true to its mission, and by continuing to evolve.

Programming under Toby Leonard deepened in scope and ambition. With an eye toward discovery, Leonard championed films that might otherwise not reach Nashville screens. His selections ranged from underseen international gems and restored classics to challenging experimental works and landmark retrospectives. These choices attracted not only dedicated cinephiles, but also curious newcomers, building an inclusive community of filmgoers that reflected the city's changing demographics.

That programming reached audiences not only through selection, but through the strong public voice of one of the theater's most recognizable and enduring figures. Jason Shawhan's relationship with the Belcourt began long before he worked there. He had attended films there as a child, returned to Nashville after college and criticism work, and joined the reopened theater around 2000 during its most chaotic nonprofit years. What he became was not easy to reduce to a single title. Part front-of-house presence, part introducer, part critic, part ambassador, Shawhan helped give the Belcourt a human face distinct from corporate multiplex culture. He became especially important in shaping the theater's more adventurous public identity

FIGURE 10.8. Interior of the newly renovated, restored, and preserved 1925 Hall at the Belcourt Theatre, 2016. Photograph by Tom Gatlin. Belcourt Theatre Collection. Courtesy of Vanderbilt University Special Collections.

through introductions, repertory screenings, and series built around cult, underground, and queer cinema. His work on Nashville Cinema Underground and, later, Queer Qlassics helped create recurring space for films and audiences that might otherwise have remained marginal in Tennessee exhibition culture. Just as importantly, he brought showmanship to the task, treating introductions and events not as formal obligations but as ways of making difficult or unconventional programming feel alive, contextualized, and communal. Through figures like Shawhan, the Belcourt's programming did more than broaden in range; it developed a personality that audiences could recognize and trust.

Leonard also continued to build national partnerships, further solidifying the Belcourt's standing within the independent film ecosystem. Distributors, filmmakers, and peer institutions recognized the theater's curatorial excellence and reliable audience. It became common for the Belcourt to be included among the top-performing venues in national specialty releases, often alongside theaters in much larger markets.

The Belcourt's leadership also maintained a clear vision of its civic role. Public programming tackled contemporary social issues, pairing screenings with community panels, guest speakers, and post-film discussions. Collaborations with schools and nonprofits expanded the theater's educational impact, and its location in Nashville, home to multiple universities, arts organizations, and cultural festivals, made it a vital partner in citywide initiatives.

By the time the 2016 renovation was completed, the Belcourt had fully integrated education and engagement into its institutional identity. New physical spaces, such as dedicated classrooms and multipurpose areas, allowed the team to expand their offerings year-round. From school visits and film seminars to public symposia and issue-driven programming, education had become a central part of how the Belcourt served Nashville.

By the start of the theater's third decade as an arthouse cinema, the Belcourt had become not only a fixture in Nashville's cultural life, but also a recognized model within a larger network of regional and national independent arthouse, neighborhood, and nonprofit cinemas. The Belcourt helped shape a national conversation about what independent cinemas could be: not just screening venues, but community institutions that preserve film heritage, nurture conversation, and foster connection.

EPILOGUE

ON MAY 18, 2025, the Belcourt Theatre celebrated its hundredth birthday. It did so not as a museum piece or a relic of the past, but as a living, breathing film center: vibrant, community-centered, and nationally recognized. In a city where change is constant and memory is often paved over, the Belcourt remains rooted. It is Nashville's longest-operating neighborhood theater and one of its most enduring cultural institutions.

Belcourt's story is one of adaptation. Over the course of a century, it has been a silent movie house, a vaudeville venue, a live theater stage, a Grand Ole Opry satellite, a foreign film haven, a concert hall, and a nonprofit cinema. Each reinvention was driven by people who saw not just what the Belcourt was, but what it could be.

That foresight and commitment saved the theater more than once. In the 1990s, when its future was uncertain and its marquee dark, a group of community members launched Belcourt YES! to preserve the space. Their grassroots campaign laid the foundation for a new chapter, one in which the Belcourt would no longer rely on commercial success alone, but instead thrive as a mission-driven organization.

What followed was nothing short of transformation. Under the leadership of figures like Tom Wills, who purchased the building in 2003 to give the nonprofit a path to ownership, and Stephanie Silverman, who professionalized its operations after becoming executive director in 2007, the Belcourt matured. With Toby Leonard as programming director, its film curation gained national attention. Retrospectives, repertory series, filmmaker visits, and educational programs all helped establish the Belcourt as a place where cinema was not just screened, but celebrated and studied.

Even crises could not dim its light. In 2020, the COVID-19 pandemic forced the Belcourt to close temporarily. Like so many other arts institutions, it faced the unknown. But through online screenings, parking lot drive-ins, and careful reopening strategies, the theater returned. It did not simply survive; it reaffirmed its place in Nashville's civic life.

As of its centennial in 2025, the Belcourt employs over two dozen full and part-time staff, offers year-round programming, and continues to grow its educational reach. Its original auditorium, now called the 1925 Hall, remains at the heart of its operations. But the building is more than its brick and plaster. It is layered with memory: the laughter and awe of those early vaudeville nights and community theater plays, the debates sparked by controversial narratives and documentaries, the music of artists on the verge of fame.

In 2016, on the eve of the theater's renovation, Jim Ridley, the late film critic for the *Nashville Scene*, said "What's going to happen over the next twenty-five years is [the Belcourt] is going to become the center of a lot of other people's lives, and it's going to transform itself in a way that I think will transform the city. People can make this place whatever they want it to be. They can make it as big and brilliant and beautiful as they're willing [if] they're willing to pitch in."[1] His name is now etched in the theater's lobby. His words and his name are more than tribute—they are a challenge to preserve what makes the Belcourt matter.

That work continues. Though the Belcourt is thriving, it is not immune to the pressures that shuttered so many of its peers. Rising costs, evolving media habits, and ongoing development in Nashville all pose challenges. But the Belcourt's longevity offers lessons worth remembering.

First: Historic preservation and innovation can coexist. The Belcourt succeeded not by freezing itself in time, but by adapting. It honored its past without being bound by it.

Second: Film and music, so central to Nashville's identity, are natural allies. The theater's years as a music venue during the early 2000s helped sustain it. Those concerts brought new audiences and revenue, but more importantly, they demonstrated the flexibility and cultural power of the space.

Third: Grassroots efforts matter. The Belcourt would not exist without the determination of volunteers, organizers, and everyday moviegoers. Its survival is a case study in what community stewardship can achieve.

The Belcourt's significance is also intellectual. It is a place where film is contextualized and interrogated, not just consumed. Its programming often bridges past and present: silent films accompanied by live scores, historic documentaries followed by panels, anniversary screenings enriched by educational material. This curatorial model ties the Belcourt to a lineage of exhibitors like Tony Sudekum and M. A. Lightman, friendly competitors who once shaped how Nashville saw the world through cinema.

To walk into the Belcourt in 2025 is to enter a space still very much alive. The theater continues to premiere independent films, host local festivals, and bring international cinema to Tennessee audiences. But layered within its walls are echoes of the past: the reel changes heard in the projection booth, the posters from decades of film runs, the memory of Minnie Pearl and Sam Tarpley on its stage or Gillian Welch and Dave Rawlings in concert.

The Belcourt is not only a Nashville story. It is an American one. It reflects a century of cinema-going habits, the rise and fall of downtowns, and the resilience of independent culture. It reminds us what happens when a city chooses to gather in the dark, to watch, to reflect, and to be changed.

As the theater stands, one hundred years old, one thing is clear: The Belcourt's future is not guaranteed, but its value is undeniable. In a time when entertainment is increasingly private, algorithmic, and fragmented, the Belcourt offers something radical—shared experience, curated meaning, and cultural continuity.

For the next hundred years, may it continue to be that place.

Where Nashville gathers, together.

APPENDIX 1

BELCOURT THEATRE ERAS

1925–1927	Hillsboro Theatre
1926–1932	Nashville Little Theatre Guild
1931–1958	Nashville Children's Theatre
1934	Nashville Experimental Theatre and Avon Players
1935–1936	Grand Ole' Opry
1935–1958	Nashville Community Playhouse
1958–1965	[New] Theatre Nashville
1964–1997	Belcourt Cinema
1997–1999	Watkins Belcourt
1999–current	Belcourt Theatre

APPENDIX 2

NASHVILLE THEATERS AND CINEMAS (1880s–2020s)

THIS LIST IS INCOMPLETE; there are almost certainly many more theaters than the ones listed here. Many opening and closing dates are uncertain or missing completely due to the difficulty of tracking down the information.

Ace Theatre	?–1955
Adult World Theater	?–1996
Alhambra Theatre	1910–1927?
Alpine Theatre	1915–?
AMC Bellevue 12	2017–present
AMC Classic Bellevue 8	1980–1994
Avante-Garde Film Club	
Avante-Garde West	
Bel-Air Drive-In	1953–?
Belle Meade Theatre	1905–1991?
Bellevue Cinema 12	1995–2010?
Belmont Theatre	1925–1961
Bijou Theatre	1904–1913; 1916-1957
Bordeaux Drive-In	1951–?
Capitol Theatre	1926–?

Capri Twin Theatre	1969–1989
Center Theatre	1905–1950
Cinema South 4	?–1998
Circle 3	
Colonial Auto Theatre	1950s–?
Colonial Theatre	1905–?
Crescent Drive-In	1948–?
Crescent Theatre	1905–1905
Crystal Theatre	1905–1918
Dixie Theatre	1907–?
Donelson Theatre	1940s–?
Elite Theatre	1905–1930
Elite Theatre	1950–1970
Ellwest Stereo Theatre	
Fantasy Cinema	?–1978
Fifth Avenue Theatre	1909–1960?
Fountain Square 14	1987–1999
Fred Douglass Skydome	1910–?
Gem Theatre	?–1907
Gem Theatre	1940? –1955?
Grand Theatre	?–1926
Green Hills Stadium 16	1998–present
Green Hills Theatre	1951–1978
Harding Place 6	1990–2003
Hillsboro Theatre	1925–present
Inglewood Theater	1950–1977?
Jolar Adult Cinema	?–1978
Knickerbocker Theatre	1916–1957?

Leroy Theatre	1912?–1913?
Liberty Theatre	1905–1928
Lincoln Theatre	1905–1955?
Lions Head 5 Cinema	1980–1998
Loew's Crescent Theatre	1905–1982
Loew's Vendome Theatre	1926–1967
Madison Theatre	1969–1993
Majestic Theatre	1905–1905
Martin Theatre	1966–?
Melrose Theatre	1942–?
Midtown Theatre	
Mini-Adult Theater	
Montague Drive-In	1950s–?
New South Theatre	1905–1912?
Nippers Corner 10 Cinema	1992–2001
Old Hickory Theatre	
Orpheum Theatre	1910–1937
Paramount Theatre	1930–?
Parthenon Theatre	1915–1916
Peafowl Theatre	1918–1926
Playhouse Cinema	
Plaza Cinema	1971–1997?
Princess Theatre	1894–1912
Private Screenings	
Rainbow Theatre	1920s–?
Regal Hollywood 27-Nashville	1998–present
Regal Opry Mills 20 & IMAX	2000–present
Rex Theatre	1912–1905

Rialto Theatre	1918–1926
Ritz Theater	?–1969
Roxy Theatre	?–1960
Royal Amusement Parlor	1905–?
Royal Palace Theodome	1905–?
Ryman Auditorium	1892–present
Sarratt Cinema	?–present
Sixth Avenue Cinema	?–1974?
Skyway Drive-In	1950–?
Star Theater at Coney Island Park	1905–1905
Star Theatre	1905–?
Strand Theatre	1915–?
State Theatre	
Swinger's World	1970? –1989?
Tennessee Theatre	1952–?
12th Avenue Theatre	1905–1915?
Vendome Theatre	1887–1905
Victoria Theatre	
Warner Park Drive-In	1956–?
Welede Theatre	?–1917
The Wheel	
Woodbine Theatre	1939–?
Woodland Theatre	1924–1955

APPENDIX 3

BELCOURT YES! FOUNDERS COMMITTEE AND BOARD OF DIRECTORS

Thomas C. Strohm
Frank Garrison
Cindy Steine
Jane Cleveland
Ann Reynolds Roberts
Randy Rayburn
Chase Cole
Jean Wilson
Ron Samuels
Will T. Cheek
Scott Manzler
Mimi Manzler
Tom Wills
Daniel Brabson
Kathy Conkwright
Twinkle Haslam
Shan Overton
Mary Reaves
Julia Sutherland
Doug Taylor
F. Clark Williams
Michael Uhle

APPENDIX 4

BELCOURT BUILDING PURCHASE CAMPAIGN

LEADERSHIP GIFTS

Pat and George Bullard
LifeWorks Foundation
Mimi and Scott Manzler
Joan and Will T. Cheek

GOLD GIFTS

Amy P. and Frank M. Garrison Jr.
Chase Cole
Lillias and Will Johnston
Nina and H. G. Webb
Wills Family Foundation

SILVER GIFTS

Laurie and Steve Eskind
Will Cheek and Kathryn Barnett
Frist Foundation
Freeman Webb
Betsy Vinson McInnes
Ronnie Steine
Metro Nashville City Council

BRONZE GIFTS

Brooks and Bert Matthews
Mark McDonald
Sandy Orr
Village Realty Foundation
Jennifer and Mark Chalos
Jane Eskind
Joel Gordon
Jan Riven

APPENDIX 5

THE BELCOURT CAMPAIGN

The Belcourt Theatre was renovated, preserved, and strengthened in 2016 thanks to these generous leadership gifts:

Amy P. and Frank M. Garrison Jr.

Annette S. Eskind

Babs and Bill Freeman

Belmont-Hillsboro Neighbors Inc.

Betsy Bahn and David Maddox

Bob Webb and Gail Plucker

Bruce, Megan, and Max Barry

Cal Turner Family Foundation

Chase Cole

Danielle and Cindy Mezera

David, Gail, Samantha, and Nicholas Williams

Donna M. Drehmann

Donna and Jeffrey Eskind

Edward D. Lanquist Jr.

Hillsboro-West End Neighbors

Iris Buhl

Jackson National Life Insurance Company

Jan and Steve Riven

Jennifer Fay and Scott Juengel

Joan Cheek

John M. Sloop and Bonnie J. Dow

John R. Wallace and Eldon S. Yuille

John and Natasha Deane

Josephine and John Darwin

Kates and Matt Potempa and The Philip Snyder Foundation

Keith Merrill in Honor of Stella, Lucy, Oski, and Emmy

Laurie and Steve Eskind

Lee Lee and Wally Dietz

Leigh Walton

Lillians and Will Johnston

Marlene and Spencer Hays

Mimi and Scott Manzler

Nate Martin

Neil De Crescenzo and Brenda Reilly, MD

Nina and H. G. Webb

Pam and Tom Wylly

Paul Kuhn

Reggie Hill

Robin and Bill King

Rosemary Ramsey

Rosetta Miller Perry Family and *Tennessee Tribune*

Ryman Hospitality Properties Foundation

Sandy Orr

Sissy and Ed Stevinson

The Danner Foundation

The Fugitive Foundation

The HCA Foundation

The Røros Foundation

The Sandra Schattan Foundation

Whole Foods Market

Will Cheek III and Kathryn Barnett

NOTES

Chapter 1

1. Cynthia Cumfer, *Separate Peoples, One Land : The Minds of Cherokees, Blacks, and Whites on the Tennessee Frontier* (University of North Carolina Press, 2007), 132.
2. Joseph Coleman, "An Act," *Tennessee Gazette*, November 15, 1806, 3, https://www.newspapers.com/image/585811615. Newspapers.com is a subscription database that provides access to historical newspapers; the links in these citations may not work if you don't have access to the database. Many local libraries provide access to historical newspapers through this and other databases.
3. William Nichol, "A Bill," *Republican Banner*, July 3, 1837, 3, https://www.newspapers.com/image/585811615.
4. Rachel Stephens, "Curious Men and Their Curiosities: Ralph E. W. Earl's Nashville Museum and the Precedent of Charles Willson Peale," *Early American Studies* 16, no. 3 (2018): 545; James C. Kelly, "[Catalogue]," *Tennessee Historical Quarterly* 46, no. 4 (1987): 208.
5. "Tennessee Museum," *Nashville Republican*, January 29, 1820, 1, https://www.newspapers.com/image/585594998.
6. According to the item description accompanying a sketch of the Nashville Theatre in *William A. Eichbaum's Sketchbook*, housed in the Special Collections Division of the Nashville Public Library, the Nashville Theatre was also known as the Adelphi Theatre, Grand Opera House, Gaiety Theatre, Nashville Opera House, and Bijou Theatre. William A. Eichbaum, "The Nashville Theatre, circa 1859," still image, 5.75 × 9 in., Eich - 10 - The Nashville Theatre, Special Collections Division of the Nashville Public Library, Nashville, Tennessee, https://digital.library.nashville.org/digital/collection/nr/id/280.
7. Martha Rivers Ingram and D. B. Kellogg, *Apollo's Struggle: A Performing Arts Odyssey in the Athens of the South, Nashville, Tennessee*, Tennessee Heritage Library (Hillsboro Press, 2004): 7–9.
8. Advertised as "12,000 feet of canvas," the panorama was likely either 12 feet or 1,200 feet (about a quarter-mile): "Great Moving Picture of the Hudson River," *Nashville Daily Union*, December 4, 1847, 2, https://www.newspapers.com/image/603775004; Wade William, *Wade & Croome's Panorama of the Hudson River from New York to Albany*, J. Disturnell, 1846, engraved copper

plate, 396 × 16 cm, Lionel Pincus and Princess Firyal Map Division, New York Public Library Digital Collections, https://digitalcollections.nypl.org/items/510d47da-4d21-a3d9-e040-e00a18064a99.

9. "Novel and Interesting Exhibition and Concert, or Musical Entertainment," *Republican Banner*, May 20, 1841, 2, https://www.newspapers.com/image/118824696.
10. *Nashville: The Occupied City. A Walking Tour of Civil War Nashville* (Metro Nashville Historical Commission, June 2012), 7, https://www.nashville.gov/sites/default/files/2025-10/Occupied-City-Walking-Tour.pdf.
11. "Aerial Navigation," *Republican Banner*, September 13, 1866, 3, https://www.newspapers.com/image/604876249.
12. "A Brilliant Street Pageant," *The Tennessean*, June 1, 1867, 2, https://www.newspapers.com/image/83327325.
13. "A Night in Pekin," *The Tennessean*, September 13, 1891, 5, https://www.newspapers.com/image/603977142.
14. "The Biggest Exhibition," *Nashville Banner*, May 30, 1891, 4, https://www.newspapers.com/image/603611438.
15. "Wanted," *The Tennessean*, February 19, 1895, 6, https://www.newspapers.com/image/604236910.
16. "The Vitascope," *Nashville Banner*, June 11, 1896, 5, https://www.newspapers.com/image/604572772; "The Vitascope," *Nashville Banner*, June 13, 1896, 2, https://www.newspapers.com/image/604572824.
17. John Lark Taylor, Typescript Autobiography, 1944, box 1, folders 1–10 (mixed materials), John Lark Taylor Papers, Vanderbilt University Special Collections and University Archives.
18. *Six Days of Delight . . . A Week at the Tennessee Centennial* (Marshall & Bruce, 1897), 87, Smithsonian Libraries and Archives, archived July 24, 2018, at Internet Archive, https://archive.org/download/officialguideteootenn/officialguideteootenn.pdf.
19. *Nashville Banner*, May 1, 1897, 14.
20. "The Edison Mirage Ground Plan," *The Tennessean*, February 27, 1897, 5, https://www.newspapers.com/image/119130553; "Vanity Fair," *Nashville Banner*, June 3, 1897, 7, https://www.newspapers.com/image/604539879; "Vanity Fair Is a Gay Place," *Nashville Banner*, May 1, 1897, 14, https://www.newspapers.com/image/604547511.
21. T. A. Waters, *The Encyclopedia of Magic and Magicians* (Facts on File, 1988), 285–86, http://archive.org/details/encyclopediaofmaoowate.
22. "Out on Vanity Fair," *The Tennessean*, June 13, 1897, 6, https://www.newspapers.com/image/119140222; "Corbett-Fitzsimmons Fight," *Nashville Banner*, June 26, 1897, 2, https://www.newspapers.com/image/604540662; "The Movies of 1897 in 'Apple Pie' Order," *The Reel Journal*, July 25, 1925, 25, http://archive.org/details/reeljournal1925reelrich.
23. Frederick Tilberg, *Gettysburg National Military Park Handbook* (Historic Print & Map, 2012), 92, http://archive.org/details/gettysburgnationoooOtilb.
24. According to the United States Bureau of Labor Statistics, a purchase of $80,000 in 1897 has a "real price" of $3,040,896.39 in 2025, as measured by inflating the amount by the Consumer Price Index at an average rate of 2.88 percent per year.

25. Biographs were produced and distributed by the American Mutoscope and Biograph Company, a pioneering enterprise established in New Jersey in 1895 by William Kennedy Laurie Dickson, a former inventor for Thomas Edison. As the United States' first comprehensive film production and distribution company, Biograph quickly emerged as a leading force in the silent film era. They produced and distributed thousands of films for groundbreaking filmmakers like director D. W. Griffith and actors Mary Pickford, Lionel Barrymore, and sisters Dorothy and Lillian Gish.

    Originally constructed in 1850 as the Adelphi Theatre, the building was renamed the Nashville Theatre c. 1859, then renamed the Grand Opera House in the 1870s. "At the Play-Houses," *The Tennessean*, December 27, 1898, 5, https://www.newspapers.com/image/604225056.
26. J. Stuart Blackton and Albert E. Smith founded Vitagraph Studios in 1897 in Brooklyn, New York, as part of the American Vitagraph Company. By 1907, it was producing the most films of any production company in the United States. It was bought by Warner Bros. in 1925. "Coming Week at the Local Play-Houses," *The Tennessean*, October 15, 1899, 14, https://www.newspapers.com/image/604223536.
27. "Crescent Amusement Co. Saga Follows Industry Closely," *The Tennessean*, February 24, 1952, 64, https://www.newspapers.com/image/109409598.
28. "Crescent Amusement," 64.
29. Arthur J. Lamb and John W. Bratton, "The Town at the End of the Line" (Shapiro Music Publisher, 1906), box 059, item 101, Lester S. Levy Sheet Music Collection, Johns Hopkins Sheridan Libraries & University Museums, https://levysheetmusic.mse.jhu.edu/collection/059/101.
30. "Closing Exercises. A Good Programme Rendered at the Tennessee Academy of Music," *Nashville Banner*, May 28, 1897, 4, https://www.newspapers.com/image/604539708; Professor Franz J. Strahm, Nashville, Tennessee, circa 1908, photo, John Lawrence Connelly Collection, Nashville Public Library; Arthur Jr. White, "UA94/6/1 Professor Franz Joseph Strahm" (1982), Western Kentucky University Digital Commons, Student/Alumni Personal Papers, Paper 42, 5. https://digitalcommons.wku.edu/stu_alum_papers/42/.
31. "Crecent Amusement," 64.

Chapter 2

1. Walter Stokes, "Hillsboro Pike and Something Personal," *Tennessee Historical Quarterly* 24, no. 1 (Spring 1965), 70–71.
2. Stokes, "Hillsboro Pike," 71.
3. Stokes, "Hillsboro Pike," 70–72.
4. Eugene TeSelle, *The Belmont Area and Hillsboro Village* (Belmont-Hillsboro Neighbors, 2009), 6–7, Reading Room, Tennessee State Library and Archives, Nashville, Tennessee.
5. Alan Lightman, *Screening Room: Family Pictures* (Pantheon Books, 2015), 8.
6. June Granatir Alexander, *Daily Life in Immigrant America, 1870–1920: How the Second Great Wave of Immigrants Made Their Way in America*, rev. ed. (Ivan R. Dee, 2009), 11.

7. Leslie Konnyu, *Hungarians in the United States: An Immigration Study* (American Hungarian Review, 1967), 22; "Here a Little, There a Little," *The Tennessean*, March 5, 1887, 4, https://www.newspapers.com/image/603973880.
8. US Department of State, "U.S. Passport Applications, 1795–1925," digital image, s.v. "Joseph Lightman" (born Dec. 25, 1864), archived at Ancestry, Library Edition.
9. Lee Dorman, *Nashville's Jewish Community* (Arcadia Publishing, 2010), 51; "Fruits, Foreign and Domestic," *The Tennessean*, Dec. 19, 1886, 4, https://www.newspapers.com/image/603555593; "Grand Steamboat Excursion," *The Tennessean*, June 22, 1887, 4, https://www.newspapers.com/image/604001047.
10. "Nashvillian Dies," *The Tennessean*, June 27, 1928, 1, 5, https://www.newspapers.com/image/181172008.
11. "Competent Men Is World Demand," *Nashville Banner*, September 8, 1917, 5, https://www.newspapers.com/image/604642867.
12. *Norman Kerr Company, et al. v. Mattie L. Spencer*, 1921, Tennessee Supreme Court Cases, Tennessee State Library and Archives, Nashville, TN, https://supreme-court-cases.tennsos.org/; May T. Drummond, "Federal Office Building, Customs House," National Register of Historic Places Nomination Form (US Department of the Interior, National Park Service, 1972).
13. "Excavations for Big Vanderbilt Hospital Are to Be Begun Today," *The Tennessean*, October 22, 1923, 1, https://www.newspapers.com/image/178361715; "Sterling Court," *The Tennessean*, June 21, 1925, 20, https://www.newspapers.com/image/178417254.
14. Dorman, *Nashville's Jewish*, 51.
15. Lightman, *Screening Room*, 9, 34–35.
16. Lightman, 8.
17. Lightman, 13.
18. By 1942, Carlton Avenue had been renamed Belcourt Avenue. "Movie Planned for Hillsboro," *Nashville Banner*, April 9, 1924, 7, https://www.newspapers.com/image/604846987.
19. "More Than Quarter of Century of Dependable Service by Restaurant," *The Tennessean*, November 15, 1925, 32, https://www.newspapers.com/image/178978532.
20. According to the United States Bureau of Labor Statistics, adjusted for inflation, $50,000 in 1925 is equal to $900,000 in 2024; "Movie Planned," 7.
21. "Standard Country Club Plans to Open New Years," *Nashville Banner*, November 30, 1924, 14, https://www.newspapers.com/image/604877204.
22. "Hillsboro Theater Will Open May 4," *The Tennessean*, March 8, 1925, 5, https://www.newspapers.com/image/178410354.
23. "New Hillsboro Theater Opens on May 18," *Nashville Banner*, May 10, 1925, 47, https://www.newspapers.com/image/604804005.
24. "Griffith's 'America' to Be Shown at New Hillsboro Which Opens Monday," *The Tennessean*, May 17, 1925, 42, https://www.newspapers.com/image/178411147.
25. "Hillsboro Opens with 'America,'" *The Tennessean*, May 19, 1925, 11, https://www.newspapers.com/image/178411211.

26. "The Greatest Story of All," *Moving Picture World*, December 29, 1923, 762, Media History Digital Library, Wisconsin Center for Film and Theater Research at the University of Wisconsin-Madison, Internet Archive (hereafter MHDL), https://archive.org/details/movpicwor65movi/page/n611/mode/2up.
27. "New Organization in Southern Territory," *The Moving Picture World*, Nov 9, 1918, 678, MHDL, https://archive.org/details/movpicwor38movi/page/678/mode/2up; "W. H. Productions Announces Big Sales," *Motion Picture News*, Dec 14, 1918, 3,534, MHDL, https://archive.org/details/motionpicturenew18moti_7/page/3534/mode/2up.
28. David Pearce, *The Survival of American Silent Feature Films: 1912–1929* (Council on Library and Information Resources and Library of Congress, 2013), 1, https://www.loc.gov/static/programs/national-film-preservation-board/documents/pub158.final_version_sept_2013.pdf.
29. Dr. John W. Landon, "Biographical Dictionary of Theatre Organists," *Theatre Organ* 27, no. 5 (1985): 39–40, SHAREOK Repository, https://journals.shareok.org/theatreorgan/issue/archive; Harold J. Lyon, "The Organ in Motion Picture Theatre," *Musical Observer* 25, no. 10 (1926): 40; Eddie Zollman, "Eddie Zollman (1903–1999)," interview by Bill Bunch and Russ Evans, *Puget Sound Pipeline* (newsletter), Puget Sound Theatre Organ Society, https://www.pstos.org/organists/wa/zollman.htm.
30. "Kurtzmann the Piano That Endures," *Nashville Banner*, February 22, 1925, 29, https://www.newspapers.com/image/604966266.
31. "W. A. Sheetz 'Old Vendome Manager,' Friend of Stage's Immortals, Dead." *The Tennessean*, August 25, 1931, 12, https://www.newspapers.com/image/169925215.
32. "WSM Arranges to Broadcast Programs from Loew's Theater," *Nashville Banner*, January 29, 1928, 30, https://www.newspapers.com/image/604924754.
33. "Skyscrapers Under Construction to Cost Over $2,000,000," *The Tennessean*, May 24, 1925, 41, https://www.newspapers.com/image/178411424; "The Beautiful New Belmont Theater," *The Tennessean*, August 30, 1925, 34-34, https://www.newspapers.com/image/604855695.
34. Louise Davis, "Silently, Tom Marr Brought New Look to City's Skyline," *The Tennessean*, May 8, 1988, 54, 62, https://www.newspapers.com/image/112460909.
35. "Little Theater Guild Plans for Active and Brilliant Season," *The Tennessean*, October 09, 1927, 26, https://www.newspapers.com/image/178970710.
36. "Nashvillian Dies," *The Tennessean*, June 27, 1928, 1, 5.

Chapter 3

1. United States Census Bureau. 1920 Fourteenth Census of the United States, Nashville, Davidson County, Tennessee, digital image, s.v. "William G Hynes" (born 1864), archived at Ancestry, Library Edition.
2. William Gertrude Hynes, *Negroes Looking Up!: Saw the Past, Sees the Present and Looks for the Future in Well Selected Moving Race Pictures* (Clarion Printing Company, 1905), 17, available through HathiTrust, https://hdl.handle.net/2027/emu.010001066820.

3. "Announcement," *The Nashville Globe*, November 15, 1912, 8, https://www.newspapers.com/image/174164577; "Royal Palace Theodome," *Nashville Banner*, April 17, 1914, 12, https://www.newspapers.com/image/604548072.
4. "Prof. Hynes at Houston, Tex.," *The Nashville Globe*, Sep 27, 1912, 7, https://www.newspapers.com/image/174160858.
5. "Theatrical News," *The Nashville Globe*, February 9, 1917, 8, https://www.newspapers.com/image/174200240; "Bijou Theatre," *The Nashville Globe*, September 14, 1917, 8; "Noble M. Johnson," *The Nashville Globe*, May 18, 1917, 8, https://www.newspapers.com/image/174214199.
6. "A Remarkable New Departure in the Business Life of Nashville," *The Nashville Globe*, September 13, 1907, 2, https://www.newspapers.com/image/143765751.
7. "African Methodist Ministers Protest Against 'Birth of a Nation,'" *The Nashville Globe*, May 3, 1918, 1, https://www.newspapers.com/image/174646170.
8. T. Clay Moore, "Property Owners of Nashville," *The Nashville Globe*, September 4, 1908, 18, https://chroniclingamerica.loc.gov/lccn/sn86064259/1908-09-04/ed-1/seq-18.
9. Griffith Morgan Hopkins, "Atlas of the City of Nashville 1908 [Plate 27A]," in *Atlas of the City of Nashville: From Official Records, Private Plans and Actual Surveys* (G. M. Hopkins, 1908), NPM 1908 - Plate 27A, Special Collections Division of the Nashville Public Library, https://digital.library.nashville.org/digital/collection/nr/id/1016/rec/55.
10. Eugene TeSelle, "The Nashville Institute and Roger Williams University: Benevolence, Paternalism, and Black Consciousness, 1867–1910," *Tennessee Historical Quarterly* 41, no. 4 (1982): 360; Jalen Blue, "A Blaze of History: A Prominent Black University That Endured Two Fires Once Was Located on the Peabody Campus," *Vanderbilt News* (blog), November 7, 2019, https://news.vanderbilt.edu/2019/11/07/a-blaze-of-history-a-prominent-black-university-that-endured-two-fires-once-was-located-on-the-peabody-campus.
11. August Meier and Elliott Rudwick. "Negro Boycotts of Jim Crow Streetcars in Tennessee." *American Quarterly* 21, no. 4 (1969): 756, https://doi.org/10.2307/2711607.
12. "'Showboat' Rehearsals Set," *The Tennessean*, August 2, 1964, 206, https://www.newspapers.com/image/112076796.
13. Louis Nicholas, "'Showboat' Tightened, Improved," *The Tennessean*, September 3, 1964, 28, https://www.newspapers.com/image/111894480.
14. The term "silenced" is borrowed from Michel-Rolph Trouillot, *Silencing the Past: Power and the Production of History*, 20th anniv. ed. (Beacon Press, 2015), and refers to Trouillot's definition of the active and transitive process by which power structures intentionally or unintentionally omit, distort, or marginalize certain voices, perspectives, and events from historical narratives and the collective memory.

Chapter 4

1. Van West, "Theater."
2. John Lark Taylor, Typescript Autobiography, 1944, box 1, folders 1–10 (mixed materials), John Lark Taylor Papers, Vanderbilt University Special Collections and University Archives.

3. "Little Theatre." *Encyclopedia Britannica*, January 3, 2018, https://www.britannica.com/art/little-theatre-American-theatrical-movement.
4. Ingram and Kellogg, *Apollo's Struggle*, 134.
5. Andrea Anderson, "Nashville Community Theatre: From The Little Theatre Guild to the Nashville Community Playhouse" (master's thesis, University of Missouri, Kansas City, 2012), 7.
6. Van West, "Theater"; Albert McCleery and Carl Glick, *Curtains Going Up* (Pitman Publishing: 1939), 111–48, https://archive.org/details/curtainsgoingup007877mbp/mode/2up.
7. According to Andrea Anderson, "Nashville Community," the Drama League of America emerged in 1910 from the broader national movement of women's clubs dedicated to civic and cultural improvement. By 1921, Tennessee had established its own chapter, organized by the Centennial Club, a Nashville-based women's society originally formed in 1894 to support the Tennessee Centennial Exposition. Though its initial mission was fundraising, the Centennial Club evolved into a lasting civic institution, promoting the arts and supporting cultural initiatives in the state well into the 1970s.
8. Anderson, "Nashville Community," 5.
9. Raymond Johnson, "The Theatre Movement in Nashville," in *Publication, "2nd Decade of the Playhouse," Nashville, Tennessee, 1945*, October 8, 1945, Wilhelmina Webb Collection, Metropolitan Nashville/Davidson County Archives, Nashville Public Library, Nashville, TN, https://digital.library.nashville.org/digital/collection/nr/id/9209.
10. Anderson, "Nashville Community," 8.
11. Anderson, "Nashville Community," 46.
12. "The Little Theatre Guild ad," *Nashville Banner*, April 26, 1926, 11.
13. "Stagecrafters to Present 'Sun-Up' Here April 22-25," *The Tennessean*, April 21, 1929, 39, https://www.newspapers.com/image/167733554.
14. Phillip Langsdon, *Tennessee: A Political History* (Hillsboro Press, 2000), 232–37.
15. "Mrs. L. McMillin, Federal Ex-Aide," *New York Times*, February 26, 1949, 15, https://www.nytimes.com/1949/02/26/archives/rmrs-l-mmillıh-i-federal-ex-aidei-civil-service-commissioner-in.html; Adelaide Handy, "Women Gain Government Posts Through Civil Service Tests," *New York Times*, February 23, 1941, D, 4, https://www.nytimes.com/1941/02/23/archives/women-gain-government-posts-through-civil-service-tests-mrs-lf.html; Anderson, "Nashville Community," 124.
16. "Little Theater's 'Star Sapphire' to Open Monday," *Nashville Banner*, December 26, 1926, 25, https://www.newspapers.com/image/604982072.
17. "'Great Flood' Created 60-Block Lake Downtown," *The Tennessean*, September 25, 2002, 24, https://www.newspapers.com/image/111760167.
18. "Artists in Charity Play Raise $250," *Nashville Banner*, January 6, 1927, 17, https://www.newspapers.com/image/604984665.
19. "Presenting," *The Tennessean*, April 17, 1949, 32, https://www.newspapers.com/image/108999576.
20. "Guild Will Give Backstage Party," *Nashville Banner*," December 31, 1926, 10, https://www.newspapers.com/image/604983121.

21. Anderson, "Nashville Community," 47-49.
22. "Lark Taylor Dies; Services Set Sunday," *Nashville Banner*, March 27, 1946, 1, 5, https://www.newspapers.com/image/602922687.
23. "Experimental Group Will Present Comedy," *Nashville Banner*, February 18, 1934, 15, https://www.newspapers.com/image/605251216.
24. "Mrs. Roosevelt to Speak for Orchestra over WLAC Today," *The Tennessean*, February 25, 1934, 18, https://www.newspapers.com/image/168022235.
25. "Director and Cast Confer," *Nashville Banner*, March 13, 1934, 5, https://www.newspapers.com/image/605251075.
26. "About Chickie's Daughter," *Nashville Banner*, April 3, 1934, 16, https://www.newspapers.com/image/605253938.
27. "Midnight Show at The Hillsboro Tonight," *The Tennessean*, December 02, 1934, 11, https://www.newspapers.com/image/172751600; "Shakespeare to Barnum," *The Tennessean*, December 02, 1934, 4, https://www.newspapers.com/image/172750428; "Nashville Home of the Avon Players," *Nashville Banner*, November 13, 1934, 7, https://www.newspapers.com/image/605231823.
28. Robert Roberts, "A History of Nashville Children's Theatre: 1977–2019" (master's thesis, Belmont University, 2020), 1, https://repository.belmont.edu/education_theses.
29. "Large Audience Sees 'Aladdin' at Little Theater," *Nashville Banner*, December 12, 1931, 7, https://www.newspapers.com/image/605245843.
30. Roberts, "A History," 7.
31. "'The First Mrs. Frazier' Is Players' Offering for the Week," *The Tennessean*, September 10, 1933, 38, https://www.newspapers.com/image/168045902; "Broadway Players to Open in August at Hillsboro Theater," *The Tennessean*, July 9, 1933, 30, https://www.newspapers.com/image/167848619.
32. "Broadway Players Score as They Open in 'Private Lives,'" *The Tennessean*, September 5, 1933, 10, https://www.newspapers.com/image/168038159.
33. "Broadway Players Not to Be Open This Week," *The Tennessean*, September 11, 1933, 2, https://www.newspapers.com/image/168046860; "Director and Cast Confer," *The Tennessean*, September 11, 1933, 5, https://www.newspapers.com/image/605251075.
34. Before 1936, NCT was named the Junior League Children's Theatre, and sometimes referred to in press as Nashville's Children and Art Theater, and Children's Theater of Nashville, indicating that the branding had yet to be solidified.
35. Roberts, "A History," 9.
36. Roberts, 10.
37. Roberts, 10–11.
38. Roberts, 12.
39. Roberts, 15.
40. Roberts, 17.
41. "Among Stars in '3-Cornered Moon,'" *Nashville Banner*, November 17, 1935, 30, https://www.newspapers.com/image/605251083.

42. William Rich Beyer, "Playgoer's Holiday," *The Tennessean*, May 17, 1936, 40, https://www.newspapers.com/image/159073289.
43. McCleery and Glick, *Curtains*, 181.
44. "Curtain's Rise Delayed," *The Tennessean*, November 21, 1936, 2, https://www.newspapers.com/image/159083332.
45. Valentine B. Windt, "Directing Amateurs." *Theatre Arts Monthly*, July 1937, 564, http://archive.org/details/sim_theatre-arts_1937-07_21_7.
46. "Playhouse Begins Workshop Plans," *The Tennessean*, November 8, 1936, 24, https://www.newspapers.com/image/159081898/.
47. *Annual Catalog and Announcement*, (The Ward-Belmont School, October 1943), 61, Ward-Belmont School (1913–1951), Harpeth Hall Archives, digital collections archived at the Internet Archive (hereafter Ward-Belmont), http://archive.org/details/annualcatalogoct1943ward.
48. "Remodeling," *The Tennessean*, October 3, 1937, 7, https://www.newspapers.com/image/161075920.
49. "Movies (Continued from Page One)," *Nashville Banner*, October 14, 1938, 11, https://www.newspapers.com/image/605280947.
50. "What Nots," *Nashville Banner*, October 19, 1938, 14, https://www.newspapers.com/image/605215110.
51. "Powerful Social Dramas," *Chattanooga Daily Times*, October 25, 1936, 42; "Nashville Community Theater Praised by *Stage Magazine*," *Nashville Banner*, May 23, 1937, 31. The *Chattanooga Daily Times* described *Country Sunday* as a prize-winning "social drama" sponsored by the Association of Southern Women for the Prevention of Lynching, while the *Nashville Banner* reported that members of the Nashville Community Playhouse Workshop performed the play before the Association's Atlanta convention.
52. Jon Krampner, *The Man in the Shadows: Fred Coe and The Golden Age of Television* (Rutgers University Press, 1997), 3-15; Delbert Mann, *Looking Back . . . at Live Television and Other Matters*, ed. Ira Skutch (Directors Guild of America, 1998), 1–5.
53. "'Margin of Error' Opening Will Mark Fifth Year of Director Kleibacker with Community Playhouse," *The Tennessean*, October 13, 1940, 5, https://www.newspapers.com/image/166300062/.
54. Installment Deed of Sale from M. A. Lightman, et al. to Nashville Community Playhouse, Inc., October 28, 1939, deed book number 794, page 110, Davidson County Register of Deeds Office, Nashville, Tennessee.
55. "Play Tickets On Sale Here," *Ward-Belmont Hyphen* (Nashville, TN), October 7, 1944, 86, Ward-Belmont, http://archive.org/details/WardBH_1944_Vol_32-33.
56. "Boothe's Play Is Playhouse Hit," *The Tennessean*, Wednesday, October 16, 1940, 8, https://www.newspapers.com/image/166321926.
57. "Irwin to Direct Production of 'Pinafore,'" *Nashville Banner*, April 17, 1941, 24, https://www.newspapers.com/image/603264537; "Playhouse Holds 'Pinafore' Over," *The Tennessean*, April 27, 1941, 19, https://www.newspapers.com/image/143498570.
58. "Kleibacker, Playhouse Director, Gets Commission in U.S. Army," *The Tennessean*, October 03, 1942, 3, https://www.newspapers.com/image/148003035.

59. Johnson, "The Theatre Movement," 4.
60. "Classification Center Official Indorses Playhouse," *Nashville Banner*, October 1, 1942.
61. Raymond Johnson, 4.
62. "'The Women' Will Play Two More Nights," *The Tennessean*, February 1, 1942, 4, https://www.newspapers.com/image/148628136.
63. "News and Notes." *Theatre Arts* 26, no. 7 (July 1942): 482, http://archive.org/details/sim_theatre-arts_1942-07_26_7.
64. "'Hamlet' Ticket Sales Begin Today," *The Tennessean*, April 15, 1946,12, https://www.newspapers.com/image/143547855; "Community Playhouse Starts Membership Drive," *The Tennessean*, September 15, 1946, 24, https://www.newspapers.com/image/143347132; Nashville Community Playhouse, "Something New Has Been Added," in "Program, The Nashville Community Playhouse, Presentation of 'Tonight At Eight-Thirty,' 1946–1947 Season," November 20, 1946, Wilhelmina Webb Collection, Metropolitan Nashville/Davidson County Archives, Nashville Public Library, Nashville, TN, 22, https://digital.library.nashville.org/digital/collection/nr/id/9199/rec/7.
65. "Playhouse Officials Inspect Building," *The Tennessean*, September 8, 1949, 9, https://www.newspapers.com/image/112041678.
66. Raymond Johnson, "Report from the South." *Theatre Arts* 33, no. 8 (September 1949): 56, http://archive.org/details/sim_theatre-arts_1949-09_33_8.
67. Virginia Bivin, "Gilbert Dickey, Jr. Takes Reins of Combine Theaters," *Nashville Banner*, June 23, 1958, 15, https://www.newspapers.com/image/603325514.
68. Bruce Weber, "New England Director Gets Theatre Nashville Post," *Nashville Banner*, August 18, 1958, 1, https://www.newspapers.com/image/603551260; "Gene Feist, Founder of Roundabout Theater Company, Dies at 91," *New York Times*, March 22, 2014, https://www.nytimes.com/2014/03/23/nyregion/gene-feist-founder-of-the-roundabout-theater-company-is-dead-at-91.html; Robert Simonson, "Gene Feist, Founder of Roundabout Theatre Company, Dies at 91." *Playbill*, March 19, 2014, https://playbill.com/article/gene-feist-founder-of-roundabout-theatre-company-dies-at-91-com-216350.
69. Clara Hieronymous, "New Life at the Playhouse," *The Tennessean*, Oct 5, 1958, 79, https://www.newspapers.com/image/111639989; Virginia Bivin. "Curtain Time," *Nashville Banner*, Oct 01, 1958, 21, https://www.newspapers.com/image/603570909.
70. "Theater Nashville Schedule Listed," *Nashville Banner*, Aug 25, 1958, 15, https://www.newspapers.com/image/603555691.
71. "The New Theatre Nashville," *The Tennessean*, September 13, 1959, 78, https://www.newspapers.com/image/111622629.
72. General Notes for Mr. Ewing by Gene Feist, personal correspondence, series I, box 18, folders 10-14, Gene Feist Papers, Billy Rose Theatre Division, New York Public Library, New York, New York (hereafter, Gene Feist Papers).
73. Clara Hieronymous, "Storm, Stress, Success," *The Tennessean*, April 26, 1959, 83, https://www.newspapers.com/image/111750492; Clara Hieronymous, "Artists Air Plans For New Theater," *The Tennessean*, May 4, 1959, 10, https://www.newspapers.com/image/111598036.

74. "New Face for Theater Nashville," *The Tennessean*, September 13, 1959, 78, https://www.newspapers.com/image/111625366; New Theatre Nashville School of Performing Arts, brochure, December 28, 1959, Gene Feist Papers.
75. Gene Feist, personal correspondence to "Dear Friend," December 28, 1959, Gene Feist Papers; "Theater Plans Apprenticeships," *The Tennessean*, April 24, 1960, 43, https://www.newspapers.com/image/112106323.
76. Gene Feist to Dear Friend, Gene Feist Papers.
77. Robert Cowan to Mr. Fred Harvey, personal correspondence, February 9, 1960, Gene Feist Papers; Robert Cowan to Mr. Guilford Dudley, President Life & Casualty Insurance Company, personal correspondence, February 9, 1960, Gene Feist Papers.
78. Kathe Feist to Mr. H. G. Hill, personal correspondence, May 10, 1960, Gene Feist Papers.
79. Newspaper story, Tuesday, August 2, by Gene Feist, Gene Feist Papers.
80. John L. Chambers to Mr. Gene Feist, personal correspondence, March 11, 1964, Gene Feist Papers; Bailey, Ewing, Davies & Bailey to The Nashville Community Playhouse, ℅ Robert H. Cowan, personal correspondence, August 2, 1960, series II, box 1, Theatre Nashville Scrapbooks (1964–1965), Special Collections Division of the Nashville Public Library.
81. Virginia Bivin, "Curtain Time," *Nashville Banner*, June 29, 1960, 27, https://www.newspapers.com/image/603216487.

Chapter 5

1. Gene TeSelle, "Hillsboro Theatre Historical Marker Nomination," August 3, 1993, Tennessee Historical Commission, Nashville, Tennessee.
2. Chet Hagan, *Grand Ole Opry* (H. Holt, 1989), 30.
3. "WSM," *Radio Wave*, Nov. 7, 1935, 7, https://www.newspapers.com/image/630921482.
4. "Program Notes," *Broadcasting*, November 1, 1935, 1,188, MHDL, http://archive.org/details/broadcasting89unse.
5. Grand Ole Opry Ticket, with WSM et al., June 6, 1936, 6 in. × 4 in., Tennessee State Museum, Nashville, Tennessee.
6. "Church of God Will Open Convention Here Tonight," *The Tennessean*, June 4, 1936, 5, https://www.newspapers.com/image/161050247.
7. Alcyone Bate Beasley Interview - 1970-03-05 - Oral History, 44.1/16, March 5, 1970, 5th Floor Archives, Country Music Hall of Fame, Nashville, Tennessee.
8. "Dr. Humphrey Bate (Continued from First Page)," *The Tennessean*, June 13, 1936, 2, https://www.newspapers.com/image/161062629.
9. Grand Ole Opry Ticket, Tennessee State Museum.
10. Charles K. Wolfe, *A Good-Natured Riot: The Birth of the Grand Ole Opry* (Country Music Foundation Press and Vanderbilt University Press, 1999), 23.
11. "Hillsboro Theater Will Open on May 4: 1,100 to Be Capacity of the New Motion Picture House," *The Tennessean*, March 8, 1925. Though advertised as opening May 4,

1925, the Hillsboro Theatre *actually* opened May 18, 1925. Just as one is instructed to do in woodworking, "measure twice, cut once," the same rule can be applied to sources. People make mistakes; triangulate.

12. "'Broadcasting' At Ward-Belmont," *Ward-Belmont Hyphen* (Nashville, TN), April 21, 1922, 1, Ward-Belmont, http://archive.org/details/WardBH_1922_Vol_11-12.
13. Craig Havighurst, *Air Castle of the South: WSM and the Making of Music City* (University of Illinois Press, 2007), 1-2.
14. "Bradley Recording Studio Hillsboro Village," Historical marker, erected 2020. Nashville, Tennessee. Location: 36° 8.168" N, 86° 48.065.
15. "Bully of the Town," by Harkins and Moran, recorded May 1927, Broadway 4590-1, Shellac, 10", 78 RPM.

Chapter 6

1. "Art Theater Opens Doors to Public," *Nashville Banner*, November 1, 1962, 14, https://www.newspapers.com/image/603534735.
2. Clara Hieronymous, "'Poet' Rehearsals Marred—Theater Nashville Homeless, but Keeps Working," *The Tennessean*, November 25, 1962, 81, https://www.newspapers.com/image/112929327; "Face Lift," *The Tennessean*, September 2, 1962, 47, https://www.newspapers.com/image/112922079; "New Role for Theater," *The Tennessean*, August 12, 1962, 60, https://www.newspapers.com/image/112914762.
3. Clara Hieronymous, "Belcourt Playhouse Makes Debut" *The Tennessean*, November 1, 1962, 15, https://www.newspapers.com/image/113002008; "Luxury Seating in Remodeled House," *Boxoffice*, July 8, 1963, 29, MHDL, http://archive.org/details/boxofficejulsep183boxo.
4. "The Belcourt Playhouse ad," *Nashville Banner*, Oct 31, 1962, 15, https://www.newspapers.com/image/603336588; "The Massey's Host Theater Party," *The Tennessean*, November 2, 1962, 28, https://www.newspapers.com/image/113002141.
5. "Theater Plan," *The Tennessean*, July 12, 1964, 178, https://www.newspapers.com/image/112113544.
6. "Home for Theater," *The Tennessean*, October 4, 1964, 25, https://www.newspapers.com/image/112928862/.
7. "*Showboat* Rehearsals Set," *The Tennessean*, August 2, 1964, 206, https://www.newspapers.com/image/112076796.
8. Virginia Bivin, "Curtain Time," July 29, 1964, newspaper clipping, series 2, box 1, Theatre Nashville Scrapbooks (1964–1965), Special Collections Division of the Nashville Public Library.
9. Bailey, Ewing, Dale & Bailey to Mr. Gene Feist 351 West 24th Street New York, New York 10011, personal correspondence, May 19, 1965, Gene Feist Papers.
10. *Showboat* playbill by Theatre Nashville, August 26–September 5, 1964, series 2, box 1, Theatre Nashville Scrapbooks, Special Collections Division of the Nashville Public Library.
11. "Home for Theater," 25.
12. Tom Gillem, "Theater Nashville Eyes Site After Fire," *The Tennessean*, August 6, 1966, 6, https://www.newspapers.com/image/116597910.

13. "Tax Prompts Theater Nashville Sale," *The Tennessean*, October 30, 1966, 8, https://www.newspapers.com/image/113232839.
14. Bailey, Ewing, Dale & Bailey to Mr. Gene Feist, May 19, 1965, Gene Feist Papers.
15. "Belmont Theater Closes Down," *Nashville Banner*, March 9, 1961, 44, https://www.newspapers.com/image/603494223.
16. "Belmont Theater Closes," 44.
17. Albert Cason, "Belmont Theater to Be Converted," *The Tennessean*, January 22, 1961, 62, https://www.newspapers.com/image/112154884.
18. "Obituary, Fred Henley Massey," *The Tennessean*, May 23, 1974, 42, https://www.newspapers.com/image/110396622.
19. Ralph Dawson, "Officer Cobb Clubs Big, Bad Film *Who's Afraid of Virginia Woolf?*" *The Tennessean*, July 18, 1966, 1, https://www.newspapers.com/image/111937020.
20. "Youth Against Censorship," *The Tennessean*, July 30, 1966, 5, https://www.newspapers.com/image/111946353/.
21. "Hillsboro's Belcourt Announces 'Twins,'" *The Tennessean*, December 15, 1966, 154, https://www.newspapers.com/image/113275014; "Hillsboro's Belcourt Gives Birth to 'Twins,'" *The Tennessean*, Aug 30, 1968, 60, https://www.newspapers.com/image/112215724.
22. "Hillsboro's Belcourt Announces," 154; "Hillsboro's Belcourt Gives," 60.
23. "Hillsboro's Belcourt Announces," 154; "Hillsboro's Belcourt Gives," 60.
24. Canadian exhibitor Nat Taylor is often credited with inventing the multi-screen theater on December 31, 1957, when he twinned the Elgin Theatre in Ottawa—a concept that led to the rise of multiplex cinemas and his co-founding of the company Cineplex Odeon. "Nathan A. (Nat) Taylor (1906–2004)," Heritage Toronto, September 5, 2001, historical marker, Toronto, Ontario, Canada. https://web.archive.org/web/20080516202028/http:/www.torontohistory.org/Pages_MNO/Nathan_Taylor.html.
25. Harry Haun, "Film Alphabet Soup That Says Something," *The Tennessean*, November 1, 1968, 26, https://www.newspapers.com/image/113244547.
26. Marc K. Stengel, in-person interview by T. Minton. March 30, 2023, The Belcourt Theatre Collection, Special Collections and University Archives, Heard Libraries, Vanderbilt University, Nashville, TN (hereafter, Belcourt Collection).
27. Randall Brady, remote interview by T. Minton, September 13, 2023, Belcourt Collection.
28. Belmont-Hillsboro Neighbors. *Hillsboro Village: Yesterday, Today, and Tomorrow* (Belmont-Hillsboro Neighbors and Vanderbilt University, 1993), 4.
29. Marshall Chapman, remote interview by T. Minton, November 2, 2023, Belcourt Collection.
30. "'Dinah' Is Camp-Chronicle," *Los Angeles Times*, February 26, 1971, 77, https://www.newspapers.com/image/384790006/.
31. "Stuck in Fun City," *The Tennessean*, January 6, 1974, 132, https://www.newspapers.com/image/111522705; "10:30 a.m.—WPLN-FM," *The Tennessean*, Apr 16, 1974, 18, https://www.newspapers.com/image/111646552.

32. "More Hendrix," *The Tennessean*, July 15, 1973, 190, https://www.newspapers.com/image/111627943.
33. "Ask Showcase—Re-Baiting," *The Tennessean*, April 28, 1974, 214, https://www.newspapers.com/image/111696140.
34. "'Tango' a Sellout Even Without DA," *The Tennessean*, July 28, 1973, 13, https://www.newspapers.com/image/111500641.
35. "'Tango' to Run 8 Weeks . . . Uncut," *The Tennessean*, July 25, 1973, 20, https://www.newspapers.com/image/111495587.
36. "Porno Ruling Confuses Film Exhibitors," *The Tennessean*, July 15, 1973, 2, https://www.newspapers.com/image/111621161.
37. "'Tango' a Sellout," 13.
38. "Obituary, Fred Henley Massey," 42.

Chapter 7

1. Michael Dougan, "Opie Read (1852–1939)," in *Encyclopedia of Arkansas*, July 28, 2023, https://encyclopediaofarkansas.net/entries/opie-pope-read-2254/.
2. Stephen Lawton, *Santa Barbara's Flying A Studio* (Fithian Press, 1997), 130.
3. "Ad for 'The Starbucks,'" *Chattanooga Daily Times*, November 12, 1912, 2, https://www.newspapers.com/image/605505278.
4. "Noted Novel by Opie Read Filmed," *Nashville Banner*, April 10, 1921, 43, https://www.newspapers.com/image/604610113.
5. "Take Industrial Motion Picture," *Nashville Banner*, January 23, 1914, 4, https://www.newspapers.com/image/604677645/.
6. "1,500 Children in Moving Pictures," *Nashville Banner*, September 05, 1914, 5, https://www.newspapers.com/image/604569203.
7. "Exhibitor News—Tennessee," *Moving Picture World*, October 3, 1914, 81, MHDL, https://archive.org/details/movingpicturewor22newy/page/80/mode/2up.
8. "View from Capitol to Be Taken Today," *The Tennessean*, August 26, 1914, 5, https://www.newspapers.com/image/119534038.
9. "Motion Picture to Be Made Today," *The Tennessean*, January 30, 1914, 11, https://www.newspapers.com/image/119389380.
10. "Moving Pictures of Suffrage Parade," *Nashville Banner*, May 08, 1914, 3, https://www.newspapers.com/image/604552499.
11. "Sam Davis Film Work to Start," *Nashville Banner*, May 05, 1915, 6, https://www.newspapers.com/image/604565847.
12. "Mrs. Lucille Sudekum to Be Buried Today," *Nashville Banner*, February 20, 1954, 9, https://www.newspapers.com/image/603165660.
13. "Girl Novelist Made Star by Jesse Lasky," *Screen Mirror*, March 1931, MHDL, https://archive.org/details/screenmirror193000plus/page/n10/mode/2up.
14. Richard Carlin, *Country Music: A Biographical Dictionary* (Routledge, 2003), 68.
15. J. W. West Jr. "Many Stars at Birthday Party of Nashville Girl in Hollywood," *Nashville Banner*, January 26, 1933, 13, https://www.newspapers.com/image/605219387.

16. According to the Bureau of Labor Statistics' Consumer Price Index, $400,000 in 1929 is equivalent in purchasing power to about $7,480,678 in 2024.
17. "Got His Start by the Seat of His Pants," *The Tennessean*, October 28, 1955, 24, https://www.newspapers.com/image/112056938.
18. "Nashville Boy May Be Picked for Leading Role in 'Yearling,'" *Nashville Banner*, February 26, 1945, 6, https://www.newspapers.com/image/602804512.
19. Steve Libby, "Cinderella Tale," *The Tennessean*, October 4, 1953, 101, https://www.newspapers.com/image/111999016.
20. Thomas W. Bohn and Richard L. Stromgren, *Light and Shadows: A History of Motion Pictures*, 3rd ed. (Mayfield Publishing, 1987). Industry figures from this era are based on reported averages during the time by the US Census Bureau and Theatre Owners of America. See "The American Film Industry in the Early 1950s," Encyclopedia.com, https://www.encyclopedia.com/arts/culture-magazines/american-film-industry-early-1950s.
21. Bohn and Stromgren, *Light and Shadows*, 236; *United States v. Paramount Pictures, Inc.*, 334 U.S. 131 (Supreme Court of the United States May 3, 1948), https://tile.loc.gov/storage-services/service/ll/usrep/usrep334/usrep334131/usrep334131.pdf.
22. Kathryn Cramer Brownell, "'Movietime U.S.A.': The Motion Picture Industry Council and the Politicization of Hollywood in Postwar America," *Journal of Policy History* 24, no. 3 (July 2012): 518.
23. Movietime U.S.A. collection, Margaret Herrick Library, Academy of Motion Picture Arts and Sciences, Beverly Hills, California.
24. "Movie Celebration Spotlights Grandstaff Film Plans," *The Tennessean*, October 9, 1951, 7, https://www.newspapers.com/image/111941570.
25. Brownell, "'Movietime U.S.A.,'" 519.
26. The colloquial term "hick flick" was adopted for the title of Scott Von Doviak's book *Hick Flicks: The Rise and Fall of Redneck Cinema* (McFarland, 2005). This comprehensive study of the films gave them credibility as an official filmmaking genre.
27. Harry Haun, "In Spring Cameras Turn Lightly," *The Tennessean*, April 10, 1969, 35, https://www.newspapers.com/image/113307646.
28. "'Dear Dead Delilah' to Premiere Here," *The Tennessean*, April 16, 1972, 96, https://www.newspapers.com/image/112621439.
29. Harry Haun, "'Dear Dead Delilah' Debuts," *The Tennessean*, May 5, 1972, 26, https://www.newspapers.com/image/112104797.
30. Kevin Nance, "Jeremy Childs Has a Big Problem," *The Tennessean*, January 27, 2002, 49–50, https://www.newspapers.com/image/113584945; Evans Donnell, "Steve Earle's 'Karla': Souls in Limbo, Seeking Forgiveness," *The Tennessean*, October 29, 2002, 14, https://www.newspapers.com/image/112570690.
31. Sharon Theimer, "New Media Ownership Rules Inspire Protest Tour," *The Tennessean*, November 12, 2003, 43, 5E, https://www.newspapers.com/image/112706851.
32. Eugene Wyatt, "What I Consider America Is Today," *The Tennessean*, June 6, 1975, 57, https://www.newspapers.com/image/112076234.

33. Burt Reynolds, on *Ask Me What I Am*, recorded 1973, Mercury – SRM-1-693, vinyl, LP, album.
34. "'Driving Miss Daisy' Headed to the GJCC's Shalom Theater" *The Tennessean*, March 16, 2005, M1, https://www.newspapers.com/image/275915186; "Pairs Piano Performances Faithfully Pack Pews," *The Tennessean*, May 08, 2011, W8, https://www.newspapers.com/image/283317971.
35. Sandy Smith, "Bright Lights, Music City," *The Tennessean*, March 20, 1994, 58, 63, https://www.newspapers.com/image/112560095; Louise Davis, "Tennessee Was Music to Williams' Ears," *The Tennessean*, March 27, 1983, 91, 95, https://www.newspapers.com/image/112311612.
36. Tennessee Williams's works *The Glass Menagerie* (1944); *Cat on a Hot Tin Roof* (1955), and *Orpheus Descending* (1957) have all been staged at Belcourt by the Community Playhouse and New Theatre Nashville; Brad Schmitt, "Next DeNiro Flick Has Some Twang to It," *The Tennessean*, July 17, 1997, 3, https://www.newspapers.com/image/113411592.
37. Gina Jurlando, "The Kids Are Not Alright: A Study of Harmony Korine and New Punk Cinema," Master's thesis, State University of New York Purchase College, 2015.
38. Lars von Trier and Thomas Vinterberg, "Dogme 95: The Vow of Chastity," in *Technology and Culture: The Film Reader*, ed. Andrew Utterson (Routledge, 2005).

Chapter 8

1. Chapman, interview.
2. Chapman, interview.
3. Second-run theaters showed films after they had left first-run theaters; tickets were significantly cheaper, and many times the quality of the film print was lower as second-run theaters were literally using the same prints the first-run theaters had already used.
4. "Columbus, Ga. Firm Buys Martin Theatres," *The Tennessean*, February 27, 1982, 11, https://www.newspapers.com/image/112249520; "Theaters Reportedly Sold," *Park City Daily News*, February 28, 1982, 2, https://www.newspapers.com/image/661957131.
5. "Martin Buying Theaters Here," *The Tennessean*, October 1, 1974, https://www.newspapers.com/image/111498559; "Belmont Theater Closes Down," *Nashville Banner*, March 9, 1961, 44, https://www.newspapers.com/image/603494223.
6. Jim Ridley, "Attack of the Megaplexes: It's the Future, and 30-Screen Theaters Rule the Earth!," *Nashville Scene*, May 7, 1998, https://www.nashvillescene.com/news/attack-of-the-megaplexes/article_d4b978f4-13a1-5c38-a67a-bbc89bdccd69.html.
7. Ridley, "Attack."
8. Ridley, "Attack."
9. Mimi Manzler and Scott Manzler, in-person interview by T. Minton, November 13, 2023, Belcourt Collection.

10. Bill Carey, "Belcourt Gets Go-Ahead," *The Tennessean*, July 16, 1996, 30, https://www.newspapers.com/image/113373462; "Now Showing at Belcourt: A Fall from Grace," *The Tennessean*, July 13, 1996, 37, https://www.newspapers.com/image/113382420.
11. Carey, "Belcourt Gets," 30.
12. "Watkins Takes Over Belcourt Next Weekend," *The Tennessean*, October 17, 1997, 19, https://www.newspapers.com/image/113435269.

Chapter 9

1. National Weather Service, "Tennessee Tornado Stats," https://www.weather.gov/ohx/tntornadostats.
2. Kevin Nance, "A 'Community Jewel' Stages a Comeback," *The Tennessean*, May 28, 2000, 69–70, https://www.newspapers.com/image/109010988.
3. Nance, "A 'Community Jewel.'"
4. Ridley, "Attack."
5. Mike Kilen, "Belcourt Group Signs Lease on Theater," *The Tennessean*, November 19, 1999, 16, https://www.newspapers.com/image/113560730.
6. Carrington Nelson, "Projections Drop Curtain on Belcourt," *The Tennessean*, December 17, 1998, 54, https://www.newspapers.com/image/113449281.
7. Jim Ridley, "Fade To Black: Can the Watkins Belcourt Be Saved?," *Nashville Scene*, January 21, 1999, https://www.nashvillescene.com/news/fade-to-black/article_7940db9e-1811-5841-966a-7746e34e60b7.html.
8. Jim Ridley, "Fade To Black."
9. F. Clark Williams, in-person interview by T. Minton, May 23, 2023, Belcourt Collection.
10. Julia Sutherland, in-person interview by Jessica Griffith, 2015, Belcourt Collection.
11. Manzler and Manzler, interview.
12. Manzler and Manzler, interview.
13. Kilen, "Belcourt Group Signs," 16.
14. Jim Ridley, "A Semi-Charmed Life: After Almost 18 Months, the Belcourt Is Back in Business," *Nashville Scene*, June 1, 2000, https://www.nashvillescene.com/arts_culture/a-semi-charmed-life/article_388ed8e3-bc48-5f9f-aaa6-9e8025f1e976.html.
15. As of 2024, all contributed income—grants, memberships, donations, and income from events—accounted for approximately 30 percent of the theater's annual budget.
16. Jane Stumpf, in-person interview by T. Minton, March 20, 2024, Belcourt Collection.
17. Tom Wills, in-person interview by T. Minton, May 25, 2023, Belcourt Collection.
18. Williams, interview.
19. Manzler and Manzler, interview.
20. Wills, interview.
21. Wills, interview.

22. Ridley, "A Semi-Charmed Life."
23. Stephanie Silverman, in-person interview by Jessica Griffith. 2015.Belcourt Collection.
24. Kevin Nance, "Belcourt Play Has the Right 'Stuff,'" *The Tennessean*, Mar 25, 1999, 20, https://www.newspapers.com/image/113505643.
25. Jim Reyland, in-person interview by T. Minton, June 26, 2024, Belcourt Collection.
26. Reyland, interview.
27. Bobby Boucher, in-person interview by T. Minton, September 8, 2023, Belcourt Collection.
28. Richard Stein, remote interview by T. Minton, June 28, 2023, Belcourt Collection.
29. Stein, interview.
30. Stein, interview.
31. Boucher, interview.
32. Boucher, interview.
33. Stein, interview.
34. "Belcourt Bargains," *The Tennessean*, June 03, 2000, 34, https://www.newspapers.com/image/112010276.
35. Mary Gauthier, in-person interview by T. Minton, August 28, 2023, Belcourt Collection.
36. Tim O'Brien, in-person interview by T. Minton, October 5, 2023, Belcourt Collection.
37. Jim Pitt, in-person interview by T. Minton, July 24, 2023, Belcourt Collection.
38. Pitt, interview.
39. Questlove and Oz Rodriguez, dirs. *Ladies & Gentlemen . . . 50 Years of SNL Music* (NBC/Peacock, 2025).
40. Rick Whetsel, remote interview by T. Minton, December 13, 2023, Belcourt Collection.
41. Whetsel, interview.
42. Whetsel, interview.

Chapter 10

1. "Theater Groups Rallying to Save Belcourt," *The Tennessean*, March 13, 1999, 19, https://www.newspapers.com/image/113487823.
2. "Belcourt Bargains," *The Tennessean*, June 03, 2000, 34, https://www.newspapers.com/image/112010276.
3. Steve Small, in-person interview by T. Minton, May 19, 2025, Belcourt Collection.
4. H. G. Webb, in-person interview by T. Minton, August 24, 2023, Belcourt Collection.
5. Toby Leonard, in-person interview by T. Minton, April 25, 2025, Belcourt Collection.
6. Stephanie Silverman, in-person interview by T. Minton, April 09, 2025, Belcourt Collection; *Belcourt YES! Inc. 2006 Annual Report* (Belcourt Theatre, 2006), 8, Belcourt Collection.

7. Silverman, interview.
8. Leonard, interview.
9. Matt Polman, in-person interview by T. Minton, May 08, 2025, Belcourt Collection.
10. Silverman, interview.
11. Silverman, interview.
12. Silverman, interview.
13. Silverman, interview.
14. Context for this section comes from Toby Leonard's film synopsis and repertory series "Milestones of the Last Quarter Century," which ran May 15 to June 2, 2026, as an endcap to a year's worth of film programming, seminars, and special events dedicated to celebrating the theater's centennial year. https://www.belcourt.org/events/milestones.
15. MoviePass launched in 2011 as a subscription movie-ticket service, later gaining millions of users after its 2017 acquisition and $9.95 monthly plan. Rapid growth led to financial collapse, and the company shut down in 2019 before its parent company filed for Chapter 7 bankruptcy in 2020. Caitlin Kelly, "A Timeline of MoviePass' Many Ridiculous Business Plans," *Wired*, March 20, 2019, https://www.wired.com/story/timeline-of-moviepass-ridiculous-business-plans/; Todd Spangler, "MoviePass Parent Company Files for Bankruptcy," *Variety*, January 29, 2020, https://variety.com/2020/digital/news/moviepass-bankruptcy-parent-helios-and-matheson-1203485327/.
16. Allison Inman, in-person interview by T. Minton, April 17, 2025, Belcourt Collection.
17. Inman, interview.
18. Zack Hall, in-person interview by T. Minton, April 29, 2025, Belcourt Collection.
19. Hall, interview.
20. Hall, interview.
21. Brooke Bernard, in-person interview by T. Minton, April 08, 2025, Belcourt Collection.
22. Bernard, interview.
23. Jim Ridley, "Brent Stewart, James Clauer, Michael Carter, Ryan Zacarias, Brooke Bernard - The Gang of Five," *Nashville Scene*, March 4, 2010, https://www.nashvillescene.com/news/brent-stewart-james-clauer-michael-carter-ryan-zacarias-brooke-bernard---the-gang-of/article_a0d3b2b0-3f6c-527a-a1dd-4a3cb50bbe63.html.
24. "Belcourt to Get Major Renovation," *The Tennessean*, December 23, 2015, A9, https://www.newspapers.com/image/142472939/.

Epilogue

1. Jim Ridley, in-person interview by Jessica Griffith, 2016, Belcourt Collection.

REFERENCES

Newspapers

Chattanooga Daily Time
Los Angeles Times
Nashville Banner
Nashville Daily Union
The Nashville Globe
Nashville Republican
Nashville Scene
New York Times
Park City Daily News
Playbill
Radio Wave
Republican Banner
Tennessee Gazette
The Tennessean
Ward-Belmont Hyphen

Archives

Country Music Hall of Fame and Museum, Nashville, TN
Gene Feist Papers. Billy Rose Theatre Division, New York Public Library, New York, New York
Lester S. Levy Sheet Music Collection, Johns Hopkins Sheridan Libraries & University Museums, Baltimore, MD
Media History Digital Library, Wisconsin Center for Film and Theater Research at the University of Wisconsin-Madison
Movietime U.S.A. Collection, Margaret Herrick Library, Academy of Motion Picture Arts and Sciences, Beverly Hills, California
Special Collections and University Archives, Heard Libraries, Vanderbilt University, Nashville, TN
The Belcourt Theatre Collection
John Lark Taylor Papers
Special Collections Division of the Nashville Public Library, Nashville, TN
John Lawrence Connelly Collection
Metropolitan Nashville/Davidson County Archives
Theatre Nashville Scrapbooks (1964–1965)
Tennessee State Library and Archives, Nashville, TN
Tennessee State Museum, Nashville, TN
Ward-Belmont School (1913–1951), Harpeth Hall Archives. Digital collections archived at the Internet Archive.

Secondary Sources

Alexander, June Granatir. *Daily Life in Immigrant America, 1870–1920: How the Second Great Wave of Immigrants Made Their Way in America*. Rev. ed. Ivan R. Dee, 2009.

Anderson, Andrea. "Nashville Community Theatre: From The Little Theatre Guild to the Nashville Community Playhouse." Master's thesis, University of Missouri, Kansas City, 2012.

Belmont-Hillsboro Neighbors. *Hillsboro Village: Yesterday, Today, and Tomorrow*. Belmont-Hillsboro Neighbors and Vanderbilt University, 1993.

Bohn, Thomas W., and Richard Stromgren. *Light and Shadows: A History of Motion Pictures*. 3rd ed. Mayfield Publishing, 1987.

Brownell, Kathryn Cramer. "'Movietime U.S.A': The Motion Picture Industry Council and the Politicization of Hollywood in Postwar America." *Journal of Policy History* 24, no. 3 (July 2012): 518–42.

"Bully of the Town." By Harkins and Moran. Recorded May 1927. Broadway 4590-1. Shellac, 10", 78 RPM.

Carlin, Richard. *Country Music: A Biographical Dictionary*. Routledge, 2003.

Cumfer, Cynthia. *Separate Peoples, One Land: The Minds of Cherokees, Blacks, and Whites on the Tennessee Frontier*. University of North Carolina Press, 2007.

Dorman, Lee. *Nashville's Jewish Community*. Arcadia Publishing, 2010.

Doviak, Scott Von. *Hick Flicks: The Rise and Fall of Redneck Cinema*. McFarland, 2005.

Drummond, May T. "Federal Office Building, Customs House." National Register of Historic Places Nomination Form. US Department of the Interior, National Park Service, 1972.

Hagan, Chet. *Grand Ole Opry*. H. Holt, 1989.

Havighurst, Craig. *Air Castle of the South: WSM and the Making of Music City*. University of Illinois Press, 2007.

Hynes, William Gertrude. *Negroes Looking Up!: Saw the Past, Sees the Present and Looks for the Future in Well Selected Moving Race Pictures*. Clarion Printing Company, 1905. Available through HathiTrust, https://hdl.handle.net/2027/emu.010001066820.

Ingram, Martha Rivers, and D. B. Kellogg. *Apollo's Struggle: A Performing Arts Odyssey in the Athens of the South, Nashville, Tennessee, Tennessee Heritage Library*. Hillsboro Press, 2004.

Johnson, Raymond. "Report from the South." *Theatre Arts* 33, no. 8 (September 1949): 56. http://archive.org/details/sim_theatre-arts_1949-09_33_8.

Jurlando, Gina. "The Kids Are Not Alright: A Study of Harmony Korine and New Punk Cinema." Master's thesis, State University of New York Purchase College, 2015.

Kelly, James C. "[Catalogue]." *Tennessee Historical Quarterly* 46, no. 4 (1987): 208. https://www.jstor.org/stable/42629707.

Konnyu, Leslie. *Hungarians in the United States: An Immigration Study*. American Hungarian Review, 1967.

Krampner, Jon. *The Man in the Shadows: Fred Coe and The Golden Age of Television*. Rutgers University Press, 1997.

Landon, John W. "Biographical Dictionary of Theatre Organists." *Theatre Organ* 27, no. 5 (1985): 39–40. SHAREOK Repository. https://journals.shareok.org/theatreorgan/issue/archive.

Langsdon, Phillip. *Tennessee: A Political History*. Hillsboro Press, 2000.

Lawton, Stephen. *Santa Barbara's Flying A Studio*. Fithian Press, 1997.

Lightman, Alan. *Screening Room: Family Pictures*. Pantheon Books, 2015.

Lyon, Harold J. "The Organ in Motion Picture Theatre." *Musical Observer* 25, no. 10 (1926): 40. https://hdl.handle.net/2027/nyp.33433085221830.

Mann, Delbert. *Looking Back . . . at Live Television and Other Matters*. Edited by Ira Skutch. Directors Guild of America, 1998.

McCleery, Albert, and Carl Glick. *Curtains Going Up*. Pitman Publishing, 1939. https://archive.org/details/curtainsgoingup007877mbp/mode/2up.

McPherson, James M. "Out of War, a New Nation." *Prologue Magazine* 42, no. 1 (Spring 2010). National Archives. https://www.archives.gov/publications/prologue/2010/spring/newnation.html.

Meier, August, and Elliott Rudwick. "Negro Boycotts of Jim Crow Streetcars in Tennessee." *American Quarterly* 21, no. 4 (1969): 756, https://doi.org/10.2307/2711607.

Nashville: The Occupied City. A Walking Tour of Civil War Nashville. Metro Nashville Historical Commission, June 2012. https://www.nashville.gov/sites/default/files/2025-10/Occupied-City-Walking-Tour.pdf.

"The Movies of 1897 in 'Apple Pie' Order." *The Reel Journal*, July 25, 1925. http://archive.org/details/reeljournal1925reelrich.

"News and Notes." *Theatre Arts* 26, no. 7 (July 1942): 482. http://archive.org/details/sim_theatre-arts_1942-07_26_7.

Pearce, David. *The Survival of American Silent Feature Films: 1912–1929*. Council on Library and Information Resources and Library of Congress, 2013. https://www.loc.gov/static/programs/national-film-preservation-board/documents/pub158.final_version_sept_2013.pdf.

Questlove and Oz Rodriguez, dirs. *Ladies & Gentlemen . . . 50 Years of SNL Music*. 2025. United States: NBC/Peacock. TV broadcast/streaming.

Reynolds, Burt. *Ask Me What I Am*. Recorded 1973. Mercury – SRM-1-693. Vinyl, LP, album.

Ridley, Jim. "Attack of the Megaplexes: It's the Future, and 30-Screen Theaters Rule the Earth!" *Nashville Scene*, May 7, 1998. https://www.nashvillescene.com/news/attack-of-the-megaplexes/article_d4b978f4-13a1-5c38-a67a-bbc89bdccd69.html.

Ridley, Jim. "Brent Stewart, James Clauer, Michael Carter, Ryan Zacarias, Brooke Bernard – The Gang of Five." *Nashville Scene*, March 4, 2010. https://www.nashvillescene.com/news/brent-stewart-james-clauer-michael-carter-ryan-zacarias-brooke-bernard---the-gang-of/article_a0d3b2b0-3f6c-527a-a1dd-4a3cb50bbe63.html.

Ridley, Jim. "Fade To Black: Can the Watkins Belcourt Be Saved?" *Nashville Scene*, January 21, 1999. https://www.nashvillescene.com/news/fade-to-black/article_7940db9e-1811-5841-966a-7746e34e60b7.html.

Ridley, Jim. "A Semi-Charmed Life: After Almost 18 Months, the Belcourt Is Back in Business." *Nashville Scene*, June 1, 2000. https://www.nashvillescene.com/arts_culture/a-semi-charmed-life/article_388ed8e3-bc48-5f9f-aaa6-9e8025f1e976.html.

Roberts, Robert. "A History of Nashville Children's Theatre: 1977–2019." Master's thesis, Belmont University, 2020. https://repository.belmont.edu/cgi/viewcontent.cgi?article=1001&context=education_theses.

Six Days of Delight . . . A Week at the Tennessee Centennial. Marshall & Bruce Co., 1897. Smithsonian Libraries and Archives. Archived July 24, 2018, at Internet Archive, https://archive.org/download/officialguideteootenn/officialguideteootenn.pdf.

Stephens, Rachel. "Curious Men and Their Curiosities: Ralph E. W. Earl's Nashville Museum and the Precedent of Charles Willson Peale." *Early American Studies* 16, no. 3 (2018): 545. https://www.jstor.org/stable/10.2307/90024205.

Stokes, Walter. "Hillsboro Pike and Something Personal." *Tennessee Historical Quarterly* 24, no. 1 (Spring 1965): 70–72. https://www.jstor.org/stable/42622798.

TeSelle, Eugene. *The Belmont Area and Hillsboro Village.* Belmont-Hillsboro Neighbors, 2009.

TeSelle, Eugene. "Hillsboro Theatre Historical Marker Nomination." August 3, 1993. Tennessee Historical Commission, Nashville, Tennessee.

TeSelle, Eugene. "The Nashville Institute and Roger Williams University: Benevolence, Paternalism, and Black Consciousness, 1867–1910." *Tennessee Historical Quarterly* 41, no. 4 (1982): 360. https://www.jstor.org/stable/42626319.

Tilberg, Frederick. *Gettysburg National Military Park Handbook.* Historic Print & Map Co., 2012. http://archive.org/details/gettysburgnationooootilb.

Trouillot, Michel-Rolph. *Silencing the Past: Power and the Production of History.* 20th anniv. ed. Beacon Press, 2015.

United States Census Bureau. Fourteenth Census of the United States: 1920 Population Schedule. Nashville, Davidson County, Tennessee. Digital image. Entry for William G. Hynes (born 1864). Archived at Ancestry.com.

United States v. Paramount Pictures, Inc., 334 U.S. 131. Supreme Court of the United States. May 3, 1948. https://tile.loc.gov/storage-services/service/ll/usrep/usrep334/usrep334131/usrep334131.pdf.

US Department of State. "U.S. Passport Applications, 1795–1925." Digital image. Entry for Joseph Lightman (born Dec. 25, 1864). Archived at Ancestry.com.

von Trier, Lars, and Thomas Vinterberg. "Dogme 95: The Vow of Chastity." In *Technology and Culture: The Film Reader*, edited by Andrew Utterson. Routledge, 2005.

Waters, T. A. *The Encyclopedia of Magic and Magicians.* Facts on File, 1988. http://archive.org/details/encyclopediaofmaoowate.

White, Arthur Jr. "UA94/6/1 Professor Franz Joseph Strahm." 1982. Western Kentucky University, Student/Alumni Personal Papers, Paper 42. https://digitalcommons.wku.edu/stu_alum_papers/42.

William, Wade. *Wade & Croome's Panorama of the Hudson River from New York to Albany.* Engraving. J. Disturnell, 1846. Engraved copper plate, 396 × 16 cm. Lionel Pincus and Princess Firyal Map Division, New York Public Library Digital Collections. https://digitalcollections.nypl.org/items/539e5c10-c5aa-012f-1684-58d385a7bc34.

Windt, Valentine B. "Directing Amateurs." *Theatre Arts Monthly*, July 1937. http://archive.org/details/sim_theatre-arts_1937-07_21_7.

Wolfe, Charles K. *A Good-Natured Riot: The Birth of the Grand Ole Opry*. Country Music Foundation Press and Vanderbilt University Press, 1999.
Zollman, Eddie. Eddie Zollman (1903–1999)." Interview by Bill Bunch and Russ Evans. *Puget Sound Pipeline* (newsletter), Puget Sound Theatre Organ Society. https://www.pstos.org/organists/wa/zollman.htm.

INDEX

Page numbers in italic refer to photographs.